Imagine being a twenty-year-old middle class land owner in the morning, and after lunch, the first King of ancient Israel? Difficult to even imagine, but that is what the Bible tells us happened to Saul.

We are not told how Saul coped, only that he was haunted by 'evil spirits.' But what if the 'evil spirits' were not 'evil spirits' but the first king's all-too-human struggle to manage the responsibilities thrust upon him? The second book in *The Covenant and Scrolls* series: *Saul: The First King*, explores that possibility.

It's a fresh new perspective on the classic biblical tale of a normal man's struggle to find meaning and a workable relationship with God in order to cope with an extraordinary challenge.

Meet all the famous characters: Samuel, the prophet, David, slayer of Goliath, Saul's children – Jonathan and the warrior Princess Michal, both David's lovers and the Witch of Endor. Experience this classic thrilling tale of spiritual questing, black magic, kinky sex, massive horrible slaughter of human beings, mortal combat, courage and great love.

As Devorah did, Saul must find ways to unite the Twelve Tribes, maintain the Hebrews' belief in the One God and overcome Philistine military might while walking a tightrope between his personal view of the One God as a present, loving force—the Covenant, and the prevailing view of God as a distant, punishing power—the Scrolls.

# Saul:
# The First King

*The Covenant and the Scrolls*
*Book Two*

Steven Liebowitz, Ed.D.

Published By

**Harmony-Quest Publications**
7825 SW 103 Pl
Miami, FL
www.HarmonyQuestPublications.com     sliebowitz@aol.com
305-595-2338

Copyright © 2013 Steven Liebowitz, Ed.D. All rights reserved.

No part of this book may be reproduced, stored in a retrieval system, or transmitted by any means, electronic, mechanical, photocopying, recording, or otherwise, without written permission from the author.

This book is printed on acid free paper.

Printed in the USA

# Dedication

*To my wonderful wife, Tanya, without whose support this book would never have been written and Myra Brown without whom this book would never have been published.*

# A Note from the Author

This is a work of historical fiction, based on biblical, scholarly and archeological data. Some characters as well as names for places and things are made up to support the story and are not intended to be correct, accurate or factual. The relevant Old Testament portions are Judges, First Samuel and Second Samuel.

The book's inspiration came from a trip to Israel six years ago. My wife and I visited the tel at Meggiddo. A tel is an archeological term for a site that has numerous civilizations one on top of the other. The one at Megiddo had 35 civilizations going back perhaps 5,000 years! Struck by the multitude of civilizations represented there about which I knew nothing, I resolved to learn more at least about my own Jewish heritage. This book represents some of what I have learned.

One of my favorite references was given to me by my brother, Sandy-Joe Liebowitz: Chronicles News of the Past Volume 1 in the Days of the Bible (From Abraham to Ezra, 1726-444 BCE), (Reubeni Foundation, 1968). The book is actually printed on newsprint broad sheets to add authenticity, and describes biblical events as a modern contemporary newspaper would.

# Characters, Places and Terms in Order of Appearance

**Joel the Danite** – Saul's life-long friend (chaver) from the tribe of Dan

**The Shephelah** - heartland of ancient Israel, a strategic place west of the Judean mountains and foothills that controlled access to both. Most of it occupied by the Philistines, almost cutting the country that Barak and Devorah had united in half.

**Barak** - famous general in the time of Devorah, 150 years before Saul's time.

**Devorah** - strong spiritual leader, prophetess and the one and only woman to be a Judge (semi-judicial leadership role) over ancient Israel.

**Gibeah** - small strategic hamlet three miles west of Jerusalem

**Benjamin** - Saul's tribe

**Ephod** – a household idol

**Samuel** - Renowned prophet and Judge at the time of Saul's anointing

**Necromancers** – magicians able to raise the dead to ask them questions about the future. Banned since the time of Moses, but still very popular in Saul's time.

**Kish** – Saul's father an elder in the Tribe of Benjamin

**Janina** – Saul's mother

**Abadantha** (Dantha) – Saul's sister

**God of the Scrolls** (Scrolls – written laws, Ten Commandments) (Yahweh) – Traditional view of God as Zeus, as score keeper, punisher and rewarder

**God of the Covenant** (the original promise or covenant of mutual love between God and humanity) – Non-traditional view of God in which God is a not chief score-keeper and punisher, and is instead a loving power available to all.

**Simcha and Abija** – Samuel's wicked sons

**Ahinoam** – Saul's wife

**Saul's sons**: Jonathan, Ish-Boshet, Abindab, and Malchishua

**Saul's daughters:** Michal, and Merab

**Zulph** – Samuel's hometown

**Captain Hafiz** – Philistine soldier

**King Nahash of Ammon** – Saul's first war challenge

**Jabesh** - town besieged by King Nahash and rescued by Saul

**Abner** – Saul's cousin and General-in-Chief

**Dathan** - Ammonite warrior captured at Jabesh but recruited by Abner to serve in the Army

**Shasheesha** – Ammonite priestess captured at Jabesh, wife of Dathan, who uses her feminine wiles and skills as a priestess of Astarte to enslave Jonathan.

**Michmash** – Battle between Saul and Philistines that Saul almost losses, but is saved by Michal and Jonathan

**Amalekites** – Perennial enemies of the Hebrews going back to Moses' time

**David** – shepherd boy anointed by Samuel as King on Yahweh's order while Saul is still King

**Goliath** – giant Philistine warrior, a distant cousin of David's

**Valley of Elah** – place where David and Goliath meet

**Rizpah** – Saul's Egyptian concubine

**Nob** - site of Yahweh's temple

**Abimelech** – High Priest at Nob

**Doeg** - the Edomite, observes David and Abimelech at Nob

**Gareth** – one of David's lieutenants

**Keilah** – a small city that welcomed David at first, then turned against him

**Gath** – a large and powerful Philistine City-Sate

**King Achish** – ruler of Gath

**Uriah the Hittite** – one of David's lieutenants

**Nabal** – rich farmer and land owner

**Abigail** – Nabal's wife who eventually marries David

**En-gedi** - oasis on western shore of the Dead Sea where David and Saul meet in a cave

**Endor** – the place Saul meets the necromancer witch

**Mt Gilboa** – location of Saul's final battle

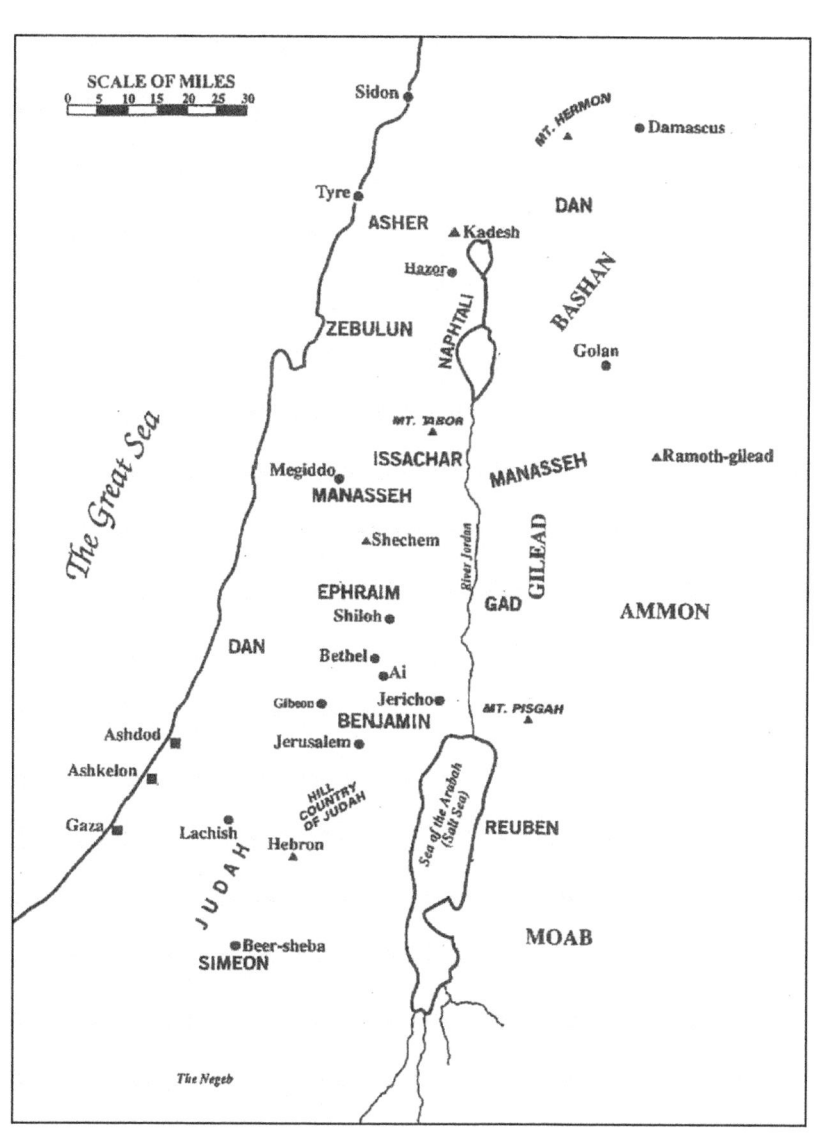

# Prologue

Saul stood mute and emotionless as the dry desert air surrounding him. "Can this be correct, Prophet? It does not feel right to me."

Samuel stepped forward and gripped the young man's shoulders with both hands. "It is natural to have doubt, Saul. But, it is true. The Lord God Yahweh himself has commanded that you become King of Israel." He stared into Saul's face and saw the stirring of realization there. "Fear not. You will not remain as you are. The power of the Lord God Yahweh will transform you."

Saul pulled in a long breath. "I am not sure, Prophet."

"Have you no faith?" Samuel's voice was deep and hoarse with anger. "It is not for you to decide; it has been decided. You shall be King! Yahweh, the Lord your God, the God of the Scrolls, shall transform you, make you capable, give all you need."

But Yahweh, the God of the Scrolls, did not make Saul either capable nor give him all he needed, and unable to surrender to the God within him, the God of the Covenant, Saul was conflicted, twisted and struggled to the end of his days.

# Chapter One

Joel the Danite ran rapidly across the stretch of open desert towards the spear shaft. "Perhaps there's still an iron head on it, Saul," he shouted. Saul was ten cubits behind his friend, panting hard. Joel was a much better runner and spearman, and Saul was bothered by his friend's skill. He didn't like being second best.

They were in the Shephelah, the heartland of Israel, a strategic place west of the Judean mountains and foothills that controlled access to both. Now the Philistines occupied most of it, almost cutting the country that Barak and Devorah had united in half. Almost. For reasons only known to them, the Philistines were content to establish a stronghold in Gibeah, three miles from Jerusalem, in easy striking distance of it and the western and southern slopes on northern Judah and Benjamin.

Saul wondered about the strategic folly of this. The Philistines with their hollow square were the military masters. "If I was in their place," Saul thought, "I'd have taken Jerusalem and linked up with the Moabites in the east." This state of affairs was embarrassing and painful, actually physically painful for Saul, sometimes filling his skull near to bursting when he thought of it. Once again, Israel was weak and without self esteem.

Joel pulled the spear from the sand as Saul trotted up to him. It did indeed have an iron tip. That was another thing; as in the time of Barak and Devorah, Israel's enemies again had a monopoly on iron ore and smithing. The Philistines with their strangle hold on the ports, prevented the importation of ore, and with their lock on smithing, made it rare for an Israelite to learn the skill.

"We Danites will make good use of this," Joel said, hefting the weapon. "It has a fine balance."

Saul held out his hand. Joel handed him the spear. Saul hefted it then threw it a distance of fifty cubits.

"Good throw, Saul!"

"Thank you," Saul said, looking bashfully at his friend as they walked to retrieve the spear. "You could have done better."

"Perhaps, but that takes nothing from your throw; it was a good one. Nothing to be ashamed of; look there," Joel pointed.

"Looks like a sword," Saul said as they walked toward a long object lying on the ground. It was a sword, but a bronze one, unlikely to withstand more than two or three blows of an iron sword. Saul dropped it, looking around, his eyes wide. "This field is littered with ancient weapons," he said voice filled with wonder.

"Indeed," Joel agreed. "It is said that Samson deposited the Gates of Gaza around here and Rehoboam and Jehoash fought here with their armies."

"The Philistines knew well what they were doing to fortify Gibeah," Saul said. "Someday, we too will fight here."

"You forget, we Danites are already fighting the Philistines here," Joel scowled. "While you and the other heroes of Benjamin do nothing, and the sons of Judah," Joel spat in contempt.

"Benjamin is the smallest of the tribes," Saul said, defensively.

Joel patted his shoulder, "But the fiercest. That is why you are here with me now, chaver."

"Thank you, my good friend. But you are right," Saul said. "We must have a king; the tribes must be united! We will never beat the Philistines disunited as we are."

"I agree, Saul. I do believe that most of the elders of the tribes wish to have a king for the very reasons you speak of, but it is Samuel who resists the idea."

"Samuel," Saul spat the name out. "Who is he to resist the will of the people? All in the name of his god; a god no one has seen and who has done nothing for his so-called chosen people. Chosen for what, I ask you? Misery? Rape? Powerlessness?"

"Be careful, Saul, you blaspheme."

Saul had worked himself up. "Blaspheme? Blaspheme? May this god strike me down if I blaspheme!" He stretched his arms out wide and looked up to heaven, his big 6'5" frame bent back like a bow. When nothing happened, he turned to Joel. "See, this so-called god has done nothing against me."

Joel smiled at him. "That does not mean that God does not exist or is powerless. It may simply mean he has other uses for you."

Saul looked startled, almost stunned. That is what his mother and sister kept telling him! Strange to hear it from a warrior like Joel, a friend he respected so.

"Maybe you should be still and listen for Its small voice within you," Joel said, patting Saul's shoulder. "Come; let us go to the stream in the grove and sit quietly."

Though Saul was normally too agitated to sit quietly, when he was able to still the raging inside of him, he felt not only felt refreshed, but clearer and stronger, too. "I did not truly mean to blaspheme; you know that, don't you Joel?" Saul looked intensely at his friend as they crossed the last of the dunes to the shade of the grove. Joel dipped his head in agreement and tousled Saul's reddish hair playfully. Saul pushed him away, gently. "Samuel might also be a force for unification, might he not? After all, he could just as easily change his mind and hear God encouraging unity."

"You are right," Joel said, dropping down next to Saul. "It's difficult to know what the future will bring, isn't it chaver?"

"Yes. At times I am desperate to know, *must* know." Saul took a deep breath and exhaled expansively. "But in moments like these, when I feel the Covenant, I am content to let be what will be."

Joel touched Saul's broad shoulder. "Indeed, I love you when you're like this, but it is very rare. So rare, that I would say it is not the real you. In fact, wasn't it just last month that we went to Kenin, the necromancer, in search of a husband for your sister?"

Saul frowned. He had a healthy respect for necromancers and their familiars in the land of the dead, but felt that they were somehow unclean. Still, necromancers were everywhere and very popular, every town and village had at least one and everyone consulted them about everything. His own father, Kish, kept two on his estates. Still, his mother, Janina, and sister, Abadantha, would have nothing to do with them, saying that whatever it was that spoke through the necromancers, it was not God. God needed no intermediary to connect with his people. On this subject as with most issues Saul was torn between two points of view. When things were under control, as they were now, he tended to favor the inner knowing advocated by his mother and sister. When things were difficult and beyond his control, he was ready to grasp at anything that promised concrete, rapid results.

Now he smiled, thinking of how upset Dantha would be if she knew he'd consulted a necromancer in search of a husband for her. Their mother would be upset, too. Although not Kish's first wife, Janina was the favorite of his five, and knew she did not have to worry about a good bride price, or finding a suitable husband for Abadantha. Similarly, though Saul was not the first-born, his size, skill with weapons and honest humility made him Kish's favorite, also.

As Saul looked with soft eyes into the face of his friend, his mind overlaid Joel's face with Dantha's. His sister meant as much to him as his friend, maybe more. Both had a positive influence on him; both made him feel accepted and loved and both gave him good counsel. And although the tingle of forbidden lust floated just below the surface of both relationships, Saul felt it most strongly in Dantha's presence.

Joel slapped him gently on the cheek. "Where are you, chaver, my friend? You're looking right through me."

Saul tapped him right back and looked off to the wind-blown sand and rough rocks on the horizon. He sighed, gratefully. "Indeed," he reflected, "I need do nothing but remain quietly on my father's estates, work my portion, and live a gentle prosperous life, honoring both the Covenant and the God of the Scrolls." Ah, there was another choice. But really, did one have to choose? Couldn't one do as he did, as so many seemingly did, honoring each in its place?

Not according to Dantha and indeed, not according to his own heart. Honoring the God of the Scrolls was easier in many physical and habitual ways; one didn't have to think too deeply, just do the rituals. But the god of the Covenant, who was with him now, ah, that was a true experience of God! To have that experience, though, he had to let go of his needs, drives and ambitions, to be empty, and as the ancient wisdom said, come naked unto your god and with empty hands. One needed a great deal of trust and faith for that. More than Saul thought he had.

Saul was not the only one who wrestled with the two aspects of the one living God. Ever since Devorah's time, people had struggled to make use of the two contradictory aspects of the one God. The traditional and most familiar aspect was Yahweh, God of the Scrolls, the fierce, demanding and punishing God. The God who intervened in human affairs, parted the Red Sea and killed the first born of Egypt.

The newer less traditional aspect was the God of the Covenant. Actively promulgated by Devorah, the God of the Covenant did not intervene in human affairs, was not fierce, nor punishing. The God of the Covenant was neither male nor female, though from force of habit most people thought of It as male. It demanded no sacrifices nor worship rituals, and was always present and guiding in the hearts of its people. Because It was all internal and informal without the external trappings of worship such as temples, priests, Sabbaths and ritual, most people found the God of the Covenant not only too difficult to worship, but too difficult to even comprehend.

"My, you're deep in thought, Saul," Joel said softly, almost tenderly.

"I was thinking about our going to the necromancer for Dantha, and how I dislike consulting them, but can't seem to help myself."

Joel snickered. "Good of you to think about your sister. Oh, so generous, but what about a mate of your own?"

"Maybe that's a way of avoiding my situation," Saul observed with uncharacteristic insight.

Joel clapped his hands. "Yes! You *are* deep today, chaver."

Saul smiled wryly. "Kish has asked me again. He wants

grandchildren from me. He says I am getting older, as if twenty-five is too, old. Besides, I have many children already."

"Yes," Joel slapped his shoulder. "That you do! You are a wonder with women, Saul, tender and dominant all at once. They adore that. But none of those children are officially Kish's grandchildren."

"Do I detect a note of jealousy?" Saul wondered. There was no need; there was no one like Joel in Saul's life. "Officially? What does that matter? These rules and rituals," Saul sputtered. "They are all Kish's grandchildren, aren't they? In the sight of God?"

"True; but they can inherit nothing from Kish," Joel soothed, "and you can give them nothing, legally. You favor Ahinoam, the daughter of Ahimaag, don't you? We've spent enough time with them."

Saul dipped his head in agreement. "I do. She is lovely and no doubt I will marry her." He stood, looked about him and raised his arms. "But also, deep inside, Joel, I feel the call for something more than a peaceful life on my father's estates with Ahinoam."

Joel stared at him skeptically.

"No. This is more than simple restlessness. I am called though I don't want to be." Saul put his hands to his head. "Ah, it does pain me, chaver. My head aches so; my heart does, too. How shall it all end?"

Joel gently lowered Saul's hands and hugged him tightly. "I do not know." He stepped back and looked deeply into Saul's tortured eyes. His friend's face had become almost as red as his hair and the normally tight fair skin across his features was as taught as a mask. "A moment ago, when you were not concerned about choosing, you were at peace. Let the God of the Covenant decide for you, chaver. Give it over. He loves you; allow Him to show you. Stop struggling; you are in His way!"

"Yes," Saul said, filling his lungs with the dry desert air. The throbbing in his temples dissipated and he looked around. "Look there, chaver!" He pointed at an object glinting in the sun. "Let's go see what it is!"

It was a well-preserved, large Philistine iron battle shield with a coiled serpent emblazoned on its face. "Look at all this iron, Saul!" Joel marveled.

Saul shook his head in disbelief. "This is the first time I've seen one of these up close, or touched one. Imagine the wealth that can produce such weapons!"

"Indeed," Joel said, "and enough for thirty or forty thousand soldiers! Plus, their double-edged, curved swords, knives, spear tips and arrowheads. Wealth indeed! Is it any wonder my people here in Dan are so demoralized?"

"I understand, chaver. But must they be servants in the Philistine army?"

Joel blushed. "They are conscripted, chaver," he said, looking down. "They have no choice. They nearly took me."

Saul hugged his friend. "Agreed. I am grateful they did not take you. But must those taken also adopt the pagan worship and bow down before idols?"

Joel smiled a salacious, sensual smile. "Those pagan rituals are most exciting and sensual. Much more moving than ours. Have you been to one?"

Saul had, with Dantha, but said nothing.

"They are hard to resist, chaver, and oh, so readily available. It's a wonder more of our people have not converted."

Saul nodded; it was true. The pagan worship *was* very enticing, even hypnotic.

"Of course," Joel continued, "you know the story of how Yael, Devorah's lieutenant, was seduced by a priestess of Astarte?" Before Saul could say anything, Joel rushed on. "Certainly you remember the story. I think I first heard it when you told it to me after Janina told it to you on your Bar Mitzvah day. Did your mother tell it to Dantha too, on her Bat Mitzvah day?"

Saul nodded, eyes growing distant. "No doubt she did," he thought. "But I told her first." He could still see his eight-year-old sister's eyes widening in shock and embarrassment, and how she'd touched herself, there. "Poor Janina," Saul thought. "If she'd only known what an inspiration those stories would be, perhaps she wouldn't have told them." It had been only a few months later, shortly after Dantha's eleventh birthday, that Saul and his sister had snuck into Astarte's temple in Gibeah.

They had come to town innocently enough, with one of Kish's caravan's, bringing grain, dates, and fowl to sell. He and his sister managed to slip away from the busy caravan master un-detected. They knew exactly where the temple was, having passed it numerous times on previous visits to Gibeah. But this day, they approached its trellised courtyards with thudding hearts and a mixture of fear and excitement.

It was three o'clock and the afternoon worship was commencing. People were streaming into the outer court. Saul and Dantha fell in with the crowd. The music of lyres, flutes, and tambourines drifted sensually, rhythmically, on the soft dry air. Strong, arousing incense entwined the music and drifted around them filling their lungs. It became darker as they moved into the heavily curtained inner court, and as they entered the walled-in sanctuary through the biggest doors they'd ever seen, the light came from rows of crackling high-mounted torches. At the far end of the huge room, on a raised dais, high above the prostate worshippers, surrounded by smoldering braziers, sat the Goddess.

The press of people coming in behind Saul and Dantha pushed them forward. As they neared the Goddess's idol, they were forced to bow down and prostrate themselves, as everyone else was doing, or else draw attention to themselves. They hesitated, feeling thrills of fear and guilt run through them then sank to their knees and prostrated themselves. The act of obeisance, of submitting to this powerful, foreign deity, combined with the sensual music and incense was erotic and sexy. As they joined in the chanting, praising the great Goddess, and swayed and bent themselves in rhythmic kow-tows, they grew more aroused.

They felt their hearts and minds open. Their fear and resistance fell away. For the next hour, as priests and priestesses performed rituals and their bodies joined the hundreds of others writhing in sensual devotion, Saul and Dantha felt something inside them shift. They would always be Hebrews, but they had been changed. A new place within had been opened and revealed to them; a place that could not be denied, one that they would have to nurture from time to time with rituals similar to Astarte's.

It was one thing to be in a temple among a multitude bowing down and worshipping in naked sensual abandon and quite another for just the two of them to worship that way. Without the erotic music, incense and gauze-shrouded idol it was awkward. But stirred by the powerful memories and their desire to return to the place that had been opened and revealed to them, they persisted. As was their habit with these rites, Abadantha led the way.

In a small grassy clearing at the center of a dark grove of eucalyptus trees in a far corner of Kish's estate, shielded by the thick trunks and foliage, Abadantha began to sway hypnotically as she removed her robe. The flesh of her body shone alabaster in the shafts of sunlight. Saul watched and became entranced. She was so sensual; the way she caressed and thrust her pert breasts and hard nipples, ran her hands along the lascivious swell of her hips, pressed on the downy softness of her vagina; then twirling and leaning forward, offered him the voluptuous fleshiness of her buttocks and the dark, suggestive valley between them.

"You want to worship me, don't you?" she asked him.

"Oh, yes!" he whispered, his voice hoarse with desire.

"I am like the Goddess Astarte to you."

"Yes. You are the Goddess and I must worship you."

"Then kneel down, that you may worship *Me* properly."

Saul knelt before his sister. She swayed closer to him, put her fingers deep into her vagina, took them out dripping and smeared her sexual juices on his nose and mouth. He inhaled deeply, becoming more entranced. She held her sticky fingers to his mouth. He licked them off, savoring their taste and smell.

"This is the taste and smell of our sacred bond, our ritual of worship. As you taste and smell and bow down before *Me* you know yourself to be *My slave worshiper*. You are most fulfilled and at peace when you devote yourself to *Me* and *My worship.*" Abadantha stroked her brother's hair. "You know that I love you and honor you and it pleases *Me* when you return *My* affection and devote yourself to *Me* as *My slave* worshipper. Know that in return for your devotion I, as your Goddess, will only bless and nurture and sustain you. This ritual shall be our private, secret rite of adoration and devotion forever. It will always only bring you peace, clarity and strength."

She touched his engorged penis beneath his robe. "Get naked and spill your seed on *My* bare feet, slave." Moaning and writhing, Saul obeyed. "Lick your seed from my precious feet." Saul obeyed. "When you have finished and licked *My* feet clean, you will be consecrated to *My* worship forever, even beyond death."

Saul blinked, returned to the present and hefted the shield. It was heavy. He handed it to Joel. "It takes a strong, fit, and well-trained man to use this."

Joel nodded.

"But the Philistines I have seen do not seem so fit."

Joel looked at him.

"I think the Philistines, especially their nobles, are losing their stomach for fighting."

Joel smiled, slowly, Saul's insight dawning on him. "It is so, chaver. The conscripts I have talked with say there are fewer and fewer Philistines in the ranks, while more Danites, Moabites, and Amalekites are being allowed to bear arms. The Philistines are becoming dependent on mercenaries."

"Still," Saul said, looking around, searching for more iron, "their battle formations, tactics, armament, and chariots are unsurpassed." Saul kicked a rock. "That square formation, with men in heavy armor and shields carrying two spears who become the outer wall, with lightly armed archers on the inside, is a rock in battle." He looked up at a windblown sky of effortless azure, with high wisps of cirrus, totally removed from human beings and their talk of war. "My cousin Abner told me of a recent battle with three hollow squares," Saul looked at his friend. "The Benjaminites hurled themselves at the squares, wave after wave and didn't bend them. Most of Abner's troops never even got to use their swords, but were cut down by spears and arrows ten cubits from the outer wall of soldiers."

Joel shook his head sadly, knowingly. "We cannot fight them on their terms." Saul nodded. "But we have our own ways and our own strengths."

# Chapter Two

Samuel was arguing with God again. Not arguing exactly, for he knew there was but one God, the God of the Covenant, the One God of Israel, and he was one with It. Yet was his head dominated by the arrogant demands of the God of the Scrolls, the God of judgment and retribution. Samuel feared this God and His vicious wrath and fierce implacable destructiveness more than he loved the reality of the mother-father God of the Covenant. Samuel sought to entwine both aspects of the One God in his own beingness, by living his life one day at a time. But, he found that Yahweh, the God of the Scrolls always had the last word. As was the situation now, and Samuel had not the strength to resist Him.

Hair snow white, old, tired, and persnickety, Samuel's life force and enthusiasm were as wrinkled and shriveled as his skin. In order to rest and enjoy what time was left him on his small farm in Zulph, he had set up his two sons, Joel and Abija, as judges in Beth Shan to rule in his place. They were incompetent. Samuel knew it, and was ashamed. Now the Yahweh was telling him to replace them with a king. "No, no Lord," Samuel pleaded. "You, *Yourself* said a king could fall into evil ways."

"The people want a king, Samuel. It is time. Do you recall the words I put in Moses' mouth, the prophecy I gave him to say, foretelling a king over Israel?"

"No, Lord."

*When you come into the land which the Lord your God is giving you and inherit it and live in it, and you say, 'Let us appoint over me a king like all the nations around me,' [then] you will appoint over yourself a king whom the Lord your God shall choose. From among your brothers are you to appoint over yourself a king. You may not appoint over yourself a foreigner who is not your bother.*

"Yes, Lord." There He was, getting the last word again. "But, although it is Your will we proceed, and we shall proceed, are You not concerned about the manner of the people's asking?"

*I am, Samuel. Still, I charge you to listen to the voice of the people according to all that they say to you for they have not rejected you but they have rejected Me from reigning over them.*

"Yes, Lord that is so, and they say, '... now set up for us a king to judge us like all the nations... ' is it not so that a king over Your Chosen is not supposed to be a king 'like all the nations' had; that a king over Israel was supposed to be a model of what an ideal Hebrew is all about—a model for the rest of the nations to emulate.

"Their manner of asking, 'give us a king *like all the nations'* suggests the people want a strong man as the other nations have, an all-powerful leader who would make all the decisions. Then the people could sit back and throw off the heavy burden of ethics and self-responsibility. You have given them, and asked them to accept, and focus more upon, in addition to their every day affairs. After all, Lord, is it not much easier to have someone decide for you, even to be a slave? A slave who is well treated will give up his freedom to know that he is taken care of and decisions are made for him."

The wind rustled the leaves and high above, in the cloudless blue sky, a hawk wheeled. *You are My most wise and thoughtful servant, Samuel. There is much merit in what you say and much of it will be made manifest. Nonetheless, you are to anoint the first King of Israel. His name is Saul, son of Kish, the Benjamite.*

Samuel was still, his face impassive, but he burned with a slow anger. After all his years of service and dedication, this was his thanks? And a Benjaminite? Is this what their shame got them? A king from among the Benjaminites?

Although the difficulty with the Benjaminites was nearly a hundred and fifty years in the past, the memory of it burned bright in Samuel's memory... On a journey from Bethlehem to the hill-county of Ephraim, the weather forced a Levite and his concubine to take shelter at an inn in the territory of Benjamin. A drunken crowd of Benjaminite men surrounded the inn and demanded that the Levite's concubine be given to them for their sexual pleasure.

To spare himself, the frightened Levite pushed the woman out the door. All night long, the frightened Levite and his host cowered inside, as the woman, howling and crying pitifully, was raped to death. In the morning, demanding retribution to cover his cowardice and shame, the Levite, hacked what was left of the woman's body into eleven pieces, one for each of the other tribes, as a call to war against the Benjaminites. All of Israel rallied and the Benjaminites were nearly exterminated. Six hundred men and no women or children were left alive. Realizing their crime, the tribes sent the six hundred to Shiloh and in another crime, allowed them to seize the virgins of the town and use them to repopulate the tribe.

Samuel's stomach churned and his heart thudded at even these bare-bones recollections of his people's past. Where had the God of the Covenant been? Would It ever counter-balance the God of the Scrolls power in men's hearts? Now, those who wanted a king like other nations used this horrible tale to justify their demands. See what happens, they said, when men are left on their own, without a king to rule over them? Samuel leaned back against the tree and sighed. Were we aware of the God of the Covenant's presence in our hearts, no king would be necessary. But such awareness was rare, even for him and the God of the Scrolls had the last word.

*You will use afarsimon oil to anoint Saul King,* Yahweh said.

Even worse, Samuel thought. This was the special oil used by Moses himself to anoint and consecrate the Tabernacle and its vessels, and by Aaron and his sons as the Priests. The use of this anointing oil designated a person or object as chosen by God for a special purpose.

*Saul will come to you in search of his father's lost livestock, at this very time of day. You will know him immediately. He is tall, handsome, courageous, head and shoulders above other men. Bring him here, to your home, and anoint him then.*

Interesting how Yahweh sounded like a proud lover, praising His beloved's virtues. Still, Samuel had to reason with Him one final time. "I know You returned the Ark of the Covenant to us, Lord, after its loss to the Philistines at the battle of Ebenezer. It was You who visited the plague upon them that made them give it back. But the people, Lord, the people are forgetful and do not remember what You did for them. The loss of the Ark provoked their cries for a King. Now You have returned the Ark and the need for a King is passed." Silence greeted Samuel's words, but the prophet smiled nonetheless as he recalled what Yahweh had done to the Philistines...

Following their great victory at Ebenezer, the Philistines had taken the Ark to Ashdod, into the temple of their fertility god, Dagon, and placed it at the idol's feet. The next morning, Dagon, had fallen, face downward, before the Ark. The people raised their god, but the next morning, not only had it fallen on its face again, but its head was chopped off and left on the threshold of the temple. The next day, the people of Ashdod, and those in its territories were stricken with tumors, buboes.

The elders of Ashdod wanted no more of the Lord's Ark and sent it to Ekron. But the people of Ekron, would not take it and a great council of the five Philistine city-states was called. The greatest magicians, sorcerers, and necromancers were consulted and it was decided to send the Ark back to the Hebrews with an offering of five golden tumors and five golden rats, the source of the plague, to appease Yahweh.

Samuel remembered himself at the forefront of the jubilant crowd at Beth Shemesh, watching as the Ark and golden offerings, carried on a driverless cart pulled by two milk white cows, followed by the lords of Philistia, came straight down the road. After the Philistines departed, the Ark was placed on a great flat rock, the cart itself was broken up for firewood, and the cows made into a burnt offering.

But the jubilation turned to horror, and Samuel's face blanched as he recalled it. Five people drunk on their joy looked inside the Ark and seventy men were struck down as lightening fell repeatedly from a cloudless sky, a sky like this one, so seemingly benign. "Enough," the old prophet thought, shivering, "enough. Your will be done, Oh Yahweh, Lord God of Israel."

Even as he accepted God's plan for a King that would relieve his sons, Joel and Abija, of their judgeships and return them to the status of everyday farmers, albeit wealthy ones, Samuel was worried about them. Even now, he knew they were meeting with the leaders of the two largest, most powerful tribes, Ephriam and Judah, as well as with the elders of Asher and Dan. Richly robed and reclining on divans in the garden of the brothers' seat, they drank un-watered wine and spoke of threats and opportunities.

Simcha, the younger, more athletic, and Abija, heavier and dissolute, listened, nodding to one another, as the elder of Judah, spoke. "We want a king, must have a king." He looked at the other elders and they dipped their heads in agreement. "Yet, he cannot be too strong." Again, the others nodded their agreement. "You," the elder gestured to the two brothers, "must use whatever influence you have with your father to bring this about."

"But," Simcha protested, standing, "a king would mean the end of our role as judges!"

"Sit down, my brother," Abija said with an indolent gesture of his hand. "The fact is, we are poor judges and would be well advised to return to Zulph and our father's estates."

"Our people are ambivalent about kings," the elder of Dan said, looking each of the others in the face. "One ruler to preside over all the tribes, like a Pharaoh—we tried that many years ago, with Gideon, but he would not do it. Then, later, it was tried on a smaller scale, with Abimelech in the Shephelah, one ruler over a city, like the Canaanites, and that was a disaster. Why now?"

"Because," the elder of Judah, said, "clearly we cannot go on as we have!" He stood and paced. "And also because, the people are finally ready for a king. But he must be a weak king."

"Yes," the elder of Ephriam said, nodding emphatically, the tip of his beard bouncing off his chest. "A weak king. The power of the tribal elders is essential."

"Agreed," said the elder of Asher and the other elders, parroted, "a weak king."

"Except in war," Abija said, a sly smile creasing his thick features. "Let us not forget Ammon, Philistia, the Amalekites, and Moabites."

"Yes. Yes, of course," the elder of Asher hastened to say. "We all agree on that."

Joel seated himself. "How do you propose to keep a king strong in wartime and weak at other times?"

The elder of Judah sighed. "Ah, that is the trick."

"Indeed," said the elder of Dan. "But that is the work we must be about. The people want a king and we need a king to wage war. We, and I, speak for all of us," he made an inclusive gesture. "And the other tribal elders not present as well, must take whatever actions we can, short of treason, to keep the king, whoever he is, weak and off balance."

"Won't that spill over into wartime?" Simcha asked. "Won't that endanger our security and make us vulnerable? Wouldn't that be treason?"

The others looked at him. Finally, Abija spoke. "It can be viewed that way. Yet we can only do what we must and hope for the best." The other elders looked at one another and dipped their heads in agreement.

"But isn't it against the Covenant to have a king?" the elder of Dan observed.

This was Simcha's area of expertise. He puffed himself up and responded emphatically. "No. *The Torah* lists seven conditions that must be met if a monarch is ever established in Israel."

Abija nodded.

"They are," Simcha continued. "The king must be chosen by God. He must come from among the people. He cannot accumulate an inordinate amount of horses or lead the people back to Egypt. He must not have many wives, and he must not store up large amounts of silver and gold. Also, he must make a copy of the Law and be well versed in its provisions."

Abija nodded. "Those provisions will tend to keep whomever becomes king weak, won't they?" The others smiled and dipped their heads in agreement. "And from which tribe should our new king come?" Abija asked, looking first at the Ephramite, then at the Judean. At the moment, Ephraim was the most powerful tribe, but Judah was gaining rapidly. A king from either tribe would mean civil war.

"Perhaps," the elder of Asher said, looking pointedly at the Danite. "The king should come from a smaller tribe, one not too closely aligned with either Judah or Ephraim. What do you think, Dan?"

The Danite dipped his head in agreement. "Perhaps even Benjamin," he said.

Joel jumped to his feet and clapped. "Brilliant. Positively brilliant! The smallest and most despised of the tribes. A Benjaminite king would be constantly off balance and weak, not having a power base of his own."

"But during war," Abija said, "he could rally all the tribes."

The others were nodding and smiling.

"Such a king would need a Council of Elders to govern effectively," the Judean said. "Those of us here," he gestured expansively to include all those present, "would naturally serve on such a Council; would we not?"

"Indeed," the Ephramite said enthusiastically. "But," he looked down a moment, then into the faces of his colleagues. "How do we know a Benjamite will be selected?"

Silence settled over them. "We do not know," Simcha said, finally.

"All we can do is pray," Abija said.

"You can use your influence with your father," the Judean said.

The Ephramite smirked. "You are new to our deliberations. If you had been with us longer, you would know Samuel is displeased with Joel and Abija. They have no influence with him."

Simcha and Abija's faces reddened, but they did not dispute the Ephramite's comments.

"The Lord works in mysterious ways," Abija said. "Our prayers are as good as Samuel's, if we pray believing the Lord will hear us. The final decision is God's. All we can do is ask for what we want. If it pleases the Lord and serves His purposes to give us a Benjaminite for a king, He will do so."

"What if the Lord is ambivalent?" the Judean asked.

"I don't understand you," the Ephramite said.

The Judean looked long and hard into the Ephramite's eyes, "What if the Lord does not know what He wants; one moment a king, the next, no king at all; one moment a strong king, the next, a weak one?"

The Ephramite looked back smiling. "Yes," he said, nodding and appreciating the Judean's wisdom, "that is the most likely state of affairs." The others nodded. "I feel sorry for the man who will bear such a burden."

# Chapter Three

"Kish asked me again this morning when you would marry," Janina said, smiling into the sparkling green eyes of her rapidly ripening fourteen-year-old daughter.

Abadantha scowled, annoyed by the veiled hint, even though she knew her mother did not take such traditional notions as seriously as others. They were baking; two of Kish's other wives and a few household women bustled around them. Janina threw up her hands in mock despair. "Don't blame me, Dantha. I did not bring up the subject."

Dantha brushed drops of sweat from her forehead and left a white streak of flour. "No," she said, looking into her mother's face. "I know you didn't. But I also know you wonder about it yourself."

"I do and I don't, Daughter," Janina said. "You know how proud I am of you, your spirit, intelligence and beauty. I want only the best for you. I feel no need to force you for appearances sake. Spirit is strong in you and I trust in your ability to decide for yourself."

"Thank you, Mother!" Dantha leaned forward and kissed her mother's cheek, careful not to touch her flour-covered hands to Janina's blue striped robes. "As I have grown older, I realize how unusual your attitude is. Many of my friends are being forced to wed. I know there is pressure on you to have me wed."

Janina nodded and smiled with wry amusement. "'Pressure' is a kind word for it. But, if Saul, who is much older than you, is still unwed, I see no reason that you should be. Besides, you are a good companion to him. I think without your influence, he would be in greater pain than he is." Tears started in the corner of Janina's eyes.

"Please, Mother, don't. Saul is his own person; his pain is no fault of yours. In fact," Dantha wiped her hands on her apron and hugged Janina then went on. "In fact, without your teaching of the Covenant to us and my conversations with him, he would be worse."

Janina hugged Dantha back. "Thank you, Daughter. But you too, are a person unto yourself." She held Dantha at arm's length. "Look at you! You are blossoming. You are all but a woman. Surely you are beginning to have a woman's needs and urges?"

Dantha blushed.

"You are, aren't you?" Janina asked.

Dantha's blush deepened.

"Your blood came last year. What do you do when desire comes? Do you touch yourself?"

"I, I, yes; I touch myself." Dantha stared into her mother's eyes, wishing she could tell her what she really did, how she went to the sacred grove with her brother.

"And wouldn't you like a man to touch you there?"

"I would. But, I don't want to marry only for that. I must have companionship, as I have with Saul, the ability to talk of the Covenant and the important subjects in life. Saul even talks to me about Samuel, the tribal elders and the need for us to have a king."

"Ah, yes," Janina said, a wistful look in her eyes, "the important things. What are those? Kish never speaks of them to me, yet I have you and Saul. And, Saul will marry, probably soon. What will you do then?"

Abadantha drew herself up. "I will still be his sister. He will still talk to me. I will have a new sister, a sister in law. That is all. And we will continue our rituals," she said, shaking out her hair and thrusting her breasts forward with pride.

As if reading Abadantha's mind, Janina looked at her sharply. "Saul is not for you." Her voice was low and guttural. "Not for you."

Abadantha glared back at her mother. "You yourself said I was a positive influence on him, and so I shall remain!" she said, certainty flaming from her eyes.

"Let us pray that it be so, daughter, for both your sakes."

And so it is, Abadantha thought, wishing again that she could tell her mother of the joy and power of her rituals with Saul. After all, what they did was consistent with the Covenant. But Janina probably wouldn't understand. Even though they never had intercourse, the sex and domination would repel her. Abadantha sighed. The look of adoration in Saul's eyes as he knelt humbly before her, the sense of power it gave her, the sense that he would do whatever she asked, these were almost enough, and at times, more than enough. Dantha stepped back, took a deep breath and changed the subject.

"Kish may not speak to you of affairs of state, Mother, but you are aware and have opinions. What do you think of Samuel? Will he anoint a king to rule over us?"

Janina smiled gratefully, because Dantha was correct, she *was* aware, had a mind, and did have an opinion. Dantha was one of the few people she could talk with about this sort of thing. "Samuel is an old style Judge, of a style that predates Devorah. He's more like Devorah's nemesis the old High Priest Malachizer, a servant of the God of the Scrolls. He would rather have things stay as they are."

"I agree," Dantha said, "and so do Saul and his friend, Joel." Dantha smiled at the sound of Joel's name on her lips.

Janina noticed and smiled a small smile. "But I think he will anoint a king if his sense of God demands it."

Janina dipped her head in agreement. "It will go hard with whomever is selected. The old prophet will not just give over his power. The new king will have to be deeply rooted in the Covenant, his sense of himself and his connection to the One power. If he relies on Samuel for support and guidance, his rule will be difficult; he may even be betrayed."

"Yes," Dantha said, "woe unto him who is chosen. Saul thinks it will be someone from Judah."

Janina disagreed. "No. Judah already has too much power. Remember Devorah's concerns about them? I think those concerns still fit. No, I think it will be someone from one of the smaller tribes, Dan or Reuben, or perhaps from our own tribe."

Dantha looked thoughtfully into her mother's eyes, and then nodded. "That would keep the balance of power, wouldn't it?"

Janina nodded. "Maybe even shift the power to the new king."

"Janina!" Elba, Janina's sister wife shouted. "Mind the oven! Smoke is coming from your bread."

Janina turned to the oven. "Thank you, Elba." Then to Dantha, "Let's mind what we're doing, daughter."

"Yes, Mother."

Saul and Joel were on the road to Kish's estates. They passed numerous smaller farms, shepherds with their flocks, blossoming olive groves, and here and there, an artisan's workshop. Saul was well known in the area. The contradiction of his size (he was a head taller than most men) and his non-aggressive and his self-effacing manner made him a memorable character. People waved and called out to him. Sometimes Saul waved back; mostly, he did not.

"You don't like people noticing you, do you, Saul." Joel said. It was a statement, not a question.

Saul scowled at his friend. "You've known that forever, Joel, since we've been children." He took a deep breath, looked away, and then waved to a coppersmith standing in the doorway of his workshop. "There," he said. "Satisfied? I prefer they mind their business, and I mind mine." Saul sighed. "I have a hard enough time understanding myself, much less them." Saul stopped walking to massage his temples.

"Is the headache very painful, chaver, my friend?" Joel asked.

"Not so bad." Saul sighed, taking a deep breath, he started walking again. "If I could just get more clearer about what God wants from me, I think I'd be better off."

Joel reached an arm up around Saul's shoulders and pulled the big man to him. "For such an imposing, active, and athletic man," he said, smiling, as they kept walking, "you often sound like a young girl."

Saul bumped Joel's side, knocking his arm away.

Joel continued, "You worry too much, even though you have much to be grateful for."

"I do," Saul said, smiling boyishly into his friend's handsome face, "don't I?"

Joel nodded. "You are big, strong, and healthy."

"But I have these terrible headaches," Saul answered.

Joel ignored Saul's complaint. "Everybody knows you."

"But I am shy and don't want to know them in return."

"Once you start something," Joel said, "you don't quit until it is finished. You have stamina and persistence."

"I am full of doubt that I do not reveal."

"You set a good example," Joel said. "People gravitate to you and follow you. You are a natural leader."

"But I am going nowhere anyone else should go."

"You are scrupulous in the rituals of our religion."

"Out of fear. They bring me no real comfort." Saul stopped walking and turned to face Joel. "You do not honor the rituals, Joel, and still you feel at peace with God, isn't that so?"

Joel dipped his head in agreement.

"Yet," Saul went on, "I, who scrupulously honor the rituals, feel tormented." Saul raised his hands to his head and shuddered. "It is as if I have a demon in my head and heart where God ought to be. I have accepted these rules and rituals, the demands and commandments of a God who does not love or nurture me, to placate Him, to keep Him from harming me, rather than from a love of Him and a desire to join with Him."

Joel looked deeply into Saul's eyes and saw the truth and power of his words shining there, and for the first time, he understood what it all meant to his childhood friend.

"But," Joel said, "you have often talked about another god who loves you better. Not this fierce and punishing God of the Scrolls, but a compassionate peace-loving God of the Covenant. Can you not dwell with this God?"

Saul looked gratefully at his friend. "I can and I do, Joel. But the God of the Scrolls is my first God, the God of our people. The God of the Covenant is new, and," Saul blushed, "the God of women.

Devorah was his first open advocate and my mother and sister speak of him to me. Men, warriors, judges and priests know him not."

Joel hugged Saul to him. "I might not speak of the God of the Covenant as Janina and Abadantha do, but when I think of God, that is the god I think of." Saul looked at him wide-eyed. Joel nodded, smiling. "The God of the Scrolls is a force to be reckoned with, do not mistake my meaning. To me, he is as the rocks and trees, real, palpable but something I just accept, deal with and work around. I feel no deep connection or allegiance to Him." Joel winked. "And besides, I enjoy talking with Abadantha about him."

"You do more than enjoy talking with her, Joel. I've seen the way you look at her."

"She is lovely, is she not?" Joel observed, running his tongue across his lips.

Saul nodded. "She grows more beautiful and powerful with each passing day." He placed his hands on Joel's shoulders. "Why not talk with Kish about marrying her? For the last few years, you have told me of your love for her."

"When you marry Ahinoam, I will speak to Kish about your sister."

Saul's face darkened. Ahinoam. She was well bred and lovely, a perfectly conventional woman, with none of the fire and charm of Abadantha. He shook his head. Why would a loving God create a situation like this—place *both* the love in his heart *and* the rules that made the love impossible? To be torn so, not just about marriage, but almost everything, was not only making him ill, it was shortening his life, killing him. He would have to choose between these competing Gods. He could not go on as he was— loving the one, fearing the other, nurtured and blessed by one, driven and shamed by the other.

The contest was uneven, the conclusion, foregone. He identified too deeply with his inner tyrant, Yahweh, God of the Scrolls. He *aspired* to the God of the Covenant, was even able to identify with it on rare occasions, espousing Its love and compassion. For himself, in his own life, he was nothing but a cowering slave, a whipped dog cringing at the feet of its master begging for a crumb of favor and forgiveness for his terrible sins, one of which was aspiring to be connected to the God of the Covenant.

This might be otherwise. He need not live and feel this way, if he realized the power he feared and attributed to Yahweh was his own. Were he to allow the dim flickering tiny candle of illumination in that infinitesimal portion of his mind to burn a bit brighter, he could choose to feel differently, as Joel, Janina and Abadantha did,

# Chapter Four

The contest had indeed been uneven, but Saul had managed to keep his inner tyrant at bay, tamp down its persistent demands for more and better, great deeds and challenges, and eke out a modicum of satisfaction in the lands of Kish. In fact, after twenty years, he was so successful 'tamping down' the inner demands for greatness, that he came to distrust them when they arose, which was less and less now, taking them to be threats to his identity.

He had a family. He'd married Ahinoam and had four sons and two daughters by her: Jonathan, Ish-Boshet, Abindab, and Malchishua, Michal, and Merab. What did the clamor for involving himself in politics and fighting the Philistines have to do with him? He was a father, a husband, a landowner. Yet, true peace of mind, the peace of the Teaching of the Covenant that came from knowing he was one with God, His beloved and sinless child, eluded him.

Joel remained Saul's closest friend, and as promised, had married Abadantha. They also had six children. The special relationship between Saul and his sister persisted and grew stronger. Marriage had given them insights and a new awareness of intimacy along with the skills to enhance it. Marriage, child rearing, and the friendship between the two couples, had also given them more socially acceptable reasons to be often in one another's company.

Their mother, the beautiful Janina, was still well and vigorous and in addition to her duties as matriarch and grandmother, found time to advance the Teaching of the Covenant. Kish had set aside a fine small plot of land, upon which she erected a room to hold classes. People came from all parts of the land and from all the tribes to study with her. Other than her concern for Saul's headaches, Janina was grateful and felt her life was blessed.

Now, as the early morning sun rose higher in the sky, Janina watched her son and daughter walk hand in hand from the well to Abadantha's house. She knew that none of the people bustling around the large compound of Kish remarked or even noticed their behavior. Handholding between friends and relatives was considered normal. Yet Janina knew there was a power in their handholding that was remarkable; and about which she was ambivalent. It was a power that had grown between them from the time Abadantha was twelve. For Saul and Abadantha, common, everyday handholding contained sexual arousal, dominance, and submission, and deep, soothing peace. Janina frowned, and then waved. They waved back and she went into her house.

"Michal is so much like you," Saul said, "she might as well be your sister."

Dantha squeezed his hand. "She is my niece, Saul; we share the same blood."

"Still, it is remarkable. Are you and Janina spending much time with her? Is she mastering the Teaching?"

"We are," Dantha said, "and with Jonathan, too." She smiled up into her brother's eyes. "You don't mind, do you?"

He shook his head no.

"I think Jonathan senses the love and compassion of It, more than you ever did, or do even now. But like you, the deep and full loving experience of Oneness is beyond his grasp."

Saul smiled back and looked down. She was nearly eighteen inches shorter, so if he didn't look down when they talked, he'd be talking to her full, luxurious black hair. Ah, the way it framed the oval of her face and gave her delicate features an angelic look. 'Angelic look' indeed. He coughed at the occasional irony of that. "Good," he said. "I do not mind. I wish I *could* feel It more. Jonathan is a fine athlete and warrior. That combined with the Teaching's compassion will serve him well." He squinted and rubbed his temple.

*Saul* 30

Dantha reached up and touched his cheek. How hot it was and how taut the flesh. "Is it bad, brother?"

He sighed, putting his hand over hers. "Not so bad that your touch can't sooth it."

Joel came up to them through the fragrant pomegranate trees to their secret place in the garden, pecked Dantha on the lips and said, "Kish asks that we go immediately and look for the donkeys that have escaped."

Saul scowled. "He has had others looking but they failed. Since we are the best, he wants us to go."

"Very well," Saul said wearily.

They searched for a week without luck and were ready to return home.

"We are near Zulph," Saul said. "Samuel has his estate here. He is a great seer. Let us go and ask him about our donkeys."

"Is not that too petty a thing to ask of Samuel?" Joel asked.

Saul smiled. "Indeed it is, chaver." Let us leave it in God's hands. Let us go to the city for refreshment and if we encounter Samuel we will ask, and if not, we won't."

Joel agreed.

Zulph was a small town but the area around its gates was, like many similar towns, alive with activity, color and aromas. Beggars in rags called out for *tsdaka*. Merchants sold steaming, sweet-smelling cakes, colorful robes and all manner of clay pots. Modestly dressed women in striped robes, some veiled, some not, bargained earnestly. Donkeys and sheep under the watchful eyes of their owners moved in and out. Priests and well-dressed elders stood talking, and the ever-present well-fed and heavily armed Philistine troops of the occupation army based in Gibeah lounged about. Joel spat when he saw the soldiers, as did Saul.

"I can't wait for the day we have a king and drive these heathens from this land the Lord promised us," Saul said.

"Amen, Brother!" Joel affirmed.

As they entered Zulph's rudimentary gates, an old man dressed in clean white robes, accosted them. "Which of you is Saul, son of Kish of the Benjaminites?" the old man asked, looking them both up and down closely. Before either could answer, the old man pointed to Saul. "You are Saul, are you not?" The man's pointing finger trembled with age, his eyes were rheumy and his voice was hoarse and cracked. He did not seem to be pleased to see Saul.

"I am," Saul responded. "Who are you and why do you ask?"

"I am Samuel, Judge over Israel and prophet of the Lord."

Saul and Joel exchanged glances. "Do you know where my father's donkeys are?" Saul asked.

Samuel looked at him, then at Joel, wide-eyed and unbelieving. "What? What question are you asking? Are you not in your right mind?"

Saul was offended. "You're a seer, aren't you?" he said, hands on hips, chin jutting, eyes flashing.

"I do God's work, my good fellow, I know nothing of donkeys." Samuel too, was insulted and looked at Saul as if he were mentally incompetent. "Have you not heard of me?"

Joel stepped between them. "We have indeed heard of you, Samuel. And we are honored to make your acquaintance." Mollified, Samuel nodded.

Joel continued, "We have been looking for four missing donkeys for a week and thought they might be in this vicinity."

"I see," Samuel said, then turned to Saul, "The Lord our God has sent me to meet you. He has selected you for great work."

Saul looked down at his feet.

"As it happens," the Judge said, "my servants have found four donkeys recently. Come to my home and I will tell you what the Lord has in store for you, and you may see if the donkeys are yours."

Saul looked up smiling like a child who had been promised a sweet. "You have our donkeys?" he said eagerly.

Samuel looked annoyed. "That is what interests you most, the donkeys? Not what God would have you do?"

Saul looked like a hurt child.

"Of course, we are interested in God's word," Joel said, putting an arm around Saul's shoulders; "that and the donkeys."

The same look of annoyed, wide-eyed disbelief, now tinged with impatience crossed Samuel's face, and he spat. "Follow me, then; we will go to my home."

When they arrived, the prophet showed his two guests where to wash and waited a short distance behind to lead them to the verandah where the meal was laid. As they dried their hands and faces, Saul suddenly gripped his head and cried out. Before Samuel could speak or act, Joel gently took his friend in his arms and stroked his hair, humming softly to him.

Samuel was touched. The harsh aggravation he'd felt toward Saul and his friend softened, and compassion warmed his heart. "Would that I had a friend like that," he thought. It was so difficult and so lonely to be alone only with God, the chilly, persnickety Yahweh, God of the Scrolls, as one's only friend but there was that deeper, more accepting and ever-loving God of the Teaching, with whom he also had a covenant. Samuel shook his head, thinking, "Poor Saul. The man was already wounded, marked by God." The path ahead would not be easy for him. Yahweh was a harsh taskmaster. Who knew better than he? Perhaps the younger man was a kindred spirit, more like a son to him than his real sons.

"What ails you, Saul?" Samuel's voice was so changed and softened that both Saul and Joel looked at the prophet with startled expressions.

"I have fierce pains in my head, Prophet," Saul said, looking at him with hopeful, doggie eyes.

"I cannot help you, son," Samuel said, seeing his hope and his need. "Prayer and right living are all I can offer." He walked between the two young men leading them to the verandah.

"I understand, Prophet," Saul said. "It is better now. Thank you. The pain never lasts too long."

The board Samuel led them to, creaked beneath its heavy burden of feast foods, lamb, fish, fowl, fruits, vegetables, breads, and cakes, all laid out in and on shining ceramic dishes and bowls. There was wine, too, in many varieties.

"What is this?" Joel asked. "Who is to join us? This can't be all for only the three of us?"

Samuel turned to Saul and smiled into his face. "This is your coronation feast! The Lord has commanded me to anoint you the first King of Israel."

Saul stared back, his face expressionless.

"Is this a joke?" Joel asked.

"No," Samuel said. "God has commanded it."

Saul remained speechless and simply stood, staring into Samuel's face. Finally he said, "Why me?"

Samuel had no expectations about what Saul's reaction might be once he'd told him God's will. He felt this reaction, although obviously deeply honest, was inappropriate and did not bode well. "It is the Lord's will, Saul." His voice was frosty and formal, the compassion gone.

Joel stepped forward and hugged his friend. "Congratulations! You wanted us to have a king. You hoped Samuel would be in favor of a king, and now here he is saying you are to be that king!"

Still, Saul stood mute and emotionless. "Can this be correct, Prophet? It does not feel right to me."

Samuel stepped forward and gripped the young man's shoulders with both hands. "It is natural to have doubt, Saul. But, it is true. The Lord God Yahweh himself has commanded it." He stared into Saul's face and saw the stirring of realization there. "Fear not. You will not remain as you are. The power of the Lord will transform you."

Saul pulled in a long breath. "I am not sure, Prophet."

"Have you no faith?" Samuel's voice was deep and hoarse with anger. "It is not for you to decide; it has been decided. You shall be King! The Lord your God shall transform you, make you capable, give all you need."

Saul's face was tight, doubtful.

But the prophet was not annoyed. "Listen, my son, I know this is exceedingly strange and difficult for you to hear, much less understand."

Saul nodded, his face relaxing a bit.

"You are a man of faith," Samuel said. "Mark me then. Here is what will transpire before you return home. Let these events sanction me and the Lord to you. You will meet six holy men. They will be making a joyful noise unto the Lord. You will be drawn to them. Their music shall fill your soul and you shall dance in ecstasy before your God."

Saul's eyes widened and he smiled.

Joel put his arm around Saul's shoulders. "Let us feast, my King," he said, humbly.

As they ate, Saul continued to muse, "Could it really be so?" he wondered. "King? Oh, how we need a King! Could I do it? There is so much I lack and don't know." But with God's help, all would be possible, and wouldn't Samuel, the great prophet, be his ally? Still...

"Saul," Samuel called suddenly and reached his hand out across the table to slap him. With uncharacteristic speed, Saul's hand shot out and grabbed the prophet's wrist. He was amazed by his speed and Samuel smiled. "See," he said, "you are already being transformed. Search your heart now, soon-to-be-King. Who resides there as ruler, God of the Covenant or Yahweh, God of the Scrolls?"

Saul paused, shut his eyes, took a deep breath, and paid attention to his center. A hot, bubbling, urgent power pulsed there. He recognized it, and for the first time, smiled. It was Yahweh, mighty and irresistible, pure power, command, and seductive, sensual mindless obedience; the power he sometimes felt with Abadantha.

Samuel knew that expression well, had felt it on his own face. "Yahweh is your Master. You will be King in His holy name."

Saul's eyes flashed and Joel looked away, afraid. "Yes," Saul said, "in His holy name."

The prophet put a friendly hand on Saul's shoulder and drew him nearer. "He is my Master, too, Saul." He whispered into the young man's ear, "I am His slave, as you, too, will be. But, I warn you, His wrath is terrible to behold. You may only serve Him as a slave, totally obedient in all He asks. To disobey or openly serve another God, even to call on the God of the Covenant, whom I honor in my heart of hearts, will be to court disaster."

Saul dipped his head in agreement. "I have experienced the God of the Covenant and found peace with Him. Yet, am I drawn more to the power and glory of the God of the Scrolls. I shall gladly serve Him as His slave." He looked into the face of his new ally, seeking support and favor there. The curt nod and smile tinged with sadness and regret that Samuel gave him was not reassuring.

"When you are crowned, Saul, you must pass an ordinance banning necromancy and the worship of all other gods but Yahweh."

Saul looked deeply into the prophet's burning eyes and his throat constricted.

"I know you have used necromancy in the past, Saul, and you would like to be able to resort to it again, in the future. I also know that most of our people worship other gods along with Yahweh. Yahweh is first, but the people also worship Baal and speak of 'Yahweh's Astarte' and His consort Asherah. Shrines and idols reside in their own houses. The idols—teraphim, are everywhere, even in your house and your father's house. This must end! Among your first official acts will be to issue a proclamation ending the worship of all gods but Yahweh, stating that the punishments for such blasphemy shall be strict, even unto death!"

Saul looked away; this was too harsh. "But Samuel," Saul said. "Yahweh *is* God. No one questions that. The teraphim are merely traditional, a visible source of comfort because Yahweh is so strict and invisible. You're right. Even I have idols in my home, as do most of our people. Surely we cannot deny the people this tradition."

Samuel's stare was stony and unyielding. "Your Master, Yahweh, God of the Scrolls, commands us to have no gods before Him and demands that you, who will be His anointed slave, obey."

"Yes, Samuel," Saul said without enthusiasm. "I shall obey my Master." Deep in his heart, Saul knew the teraphim and necromancy were embedded in the Hebrew culture and would be beyond his ability and even beyond his desire, to eradicate.

And so they feasted, and afterwards, Samuel anointed him with the sacred oil of Moses. Yet, by the time they collected their donkeys and began the journey home, Saul again felt doubt. How could he abandon the God of the Covenant? He was his only refuge when the headaches became intolerable. How could he explain to Abadantha and Janina, who were Priestesses of the Covenant? Abadantha would understand more readily than his mother would. Dantha was able to give herself more fully to the formal power of the Scrolls. She was so self-possessed, she was even able to twist its rituals to her own, and his, fleshy desires.

What they did together was strangely comforting, and Saul relaxed a little, thinking of it. 'Strangely comforting' because it was a closely guarded guilty pleasure, very private, very disturbing. It had started innocently enough, years ago when they were children. They had wanted to mock the foolish pomposity of the formal rituals of worshipping the God of the Scrolls. Abadantha wanted to show Saul how the unconditioned love and forgiveness of the God of the Covenant accepted even blasphemies against Its brother God. As they matured, the mock rituals took on a more sensual, sexual quality, embracing some of the features they had seen or heard of in their pagan neighbors' worship. Now, they seldom performed their secret ceremonies, but when they did, the power in them was potent.

"I don't know, Joel," Saul said as they each rode a donkey and led a donkey. The countryside they passed on the way home was dotted with olive groves, tufts of scrub, flocks of sheep, and a few dwellings. The air was cool, and puffy white clouds drifted through a crisp blue sky. Saul suppressed visions of cheering crowds lining both sides of the road. "I feel the same; still just a rich farmer. No one knows I'm King but you, me and Samuel."

A heavily armed Philistine patrol of six troopers and a mounted officer, marched by, singing a campaign song at the top of their lungs. Joel spat, Saul looked down.

"And what about them?" Joel said, hesitating to say more, not knowing whether he preferred this angst-ridden Saul or the Saul inflamed by the God of the Scrolls. He was more used to this unfocused Saul, but that man was king now. Doubt and angst deserved no home in a king. If Saul didn't spit and curse at the sight of the Philistines, perhaps he ought not to be king.

Maybe, Joel thought, thinking of Dantha, it runs in the family. Not that she was angst ridden or wishy-washy. Far from it! In the nine years they'd been married, he'd rarely seen doubt cast its shadow upon her. No, the commonality was the terrifyingly inhuman passion for service to the God of the Scrolls, he sometimes saw in her, and had witnessed yesterday in Saul. It was like a demonic possession.

"You are King, Saul, whether anyone knows or not, *you* know it!" Joel said. "You are the first King of Israel! Remember how we talked, only two days ago, about how we needed a king to unite us, to get us iron and take on our enemies?"

Saul nodded, but did not look at his friend.

"You are that man, chosen by the Lord God Yahweh himself!"

Saul reined in his donkey and as Joel stopped also, the king turned to him, eyes blazing with anger and frustration. "Don't you think I *know* that, Joel?" his voice was ragged with passion. "But what am I to *do*? I have no palace, no army, or no followers, save you. I must return to my father's house and live as I did before. *Heneni*—I am here, ready for Yahweh's call. The next move is up to Him." Saul turned and dug his heels into his donkey's flanks, driving it forward.

Joel sighed. He knew that tone and demeanor, and knew Saul had made up his mind. He had shut down, making further discussion useless. "Will you at least tell your family?"

"Perhaps, Dantha," Saul responded. "But I abjure you to also remain silent." Saul's eyes flashed fire. "Do you agree?"

"I do, my lord King," Joel answered.

"Do not address me that way," Saul commanded. "At least, not yet."

"Yes, Saul."

"The difficulties will be great, Joel," the King said.

"True Sire, but you will not have to deal with them alone. You will be guided. Samuel said you will be transformed."

Saul harrumphed. "Yes, so he said. I'm not so sure. Will the God of my heart, the God of the Covenant guide me, or shall it be the god of my pride, the God of the Scrolls, who will lead?"

The desolate road unwound ahead of them, bleak and brown beneath the baking sun. How completely un-royal they were, Joel thought, each of them on a mule, leading a mule along this empty dusty road.

They rode on then Joel reined in and cocked his head. Saul heard it, too, music, coming from a hilltop half a mile ahead to their left. Their eyes met.

"Could that be what Samuel said you would hear?" Joel asked.

Saul, head cocked, nodded. He dismounted and handed the leads to Joel. "I will go ahead; wait here."

Heart beating rapidly with hope and anticipation, Saul walked around the hill, and as Samuel said, at its far side near the top, he saw the holy musicians. He clearly heard the clash of cymbals, the wail of flutes and the strumming of lyres and harps. The men were dancing as they played, whirling and jumping. Two of them were naked.

"Are you holy men of God?" Saul called out to them, but lost in their delirium, they heard nothing. As he watched and listened, Saul felt himself being taken, possessed. His eyes blinked, his body shook and he swayed softly. *Go up; go nearer*, something urged. He obeyed.

His step grew lighter, his body seemed to float and twist in the air. He raised his arms high above his head and swung around then dropped them to his side. Oh, how ebullient the music was, how ethereal and yet sensual! Now harp and lyre vibrations, next chimes, now wailing flutes, next a tambourine. Truly, the spirit of the Lord was upon him, moving him, whirling him. He tore at his robes. They were so heavy. He needed to be light, to float up to his God. "I must be naked before my Lord and Master. I *want* to be naked for Him, reveal myself to Him, surrender to Him and dance unashamed in our shared glory." *Shared* glory, surely this was the God of the Covenant! His robes fell away and he was dancing, fearlessly naked.

He knew not how long he danced. It must have been a long while, for dusk surrounded him and he was shaking with cold when Joel finally came in search of him and found him lying naked and disoriented on the dusty ground. "What became of the musicians?" Saul asked.

"I saw no musicians," Joel answered.

"Truly?" Saul's voice was dazed. "But you heard the music?"

"Aye, that I did," Joel said. He lifted Saul and helped him on with his robes.

As Joel helped him, Saul was looking down, studying the ground. As an experienced scout, he was stunned by what he saw. "I see the footprints of only one man," he said, unbelievingly.

Joel studied the ground. "Yes," he said. "The foot prints of only one man."

"But you heard the music. Who made it? Where did it come from?"

"Music without musicians," Joel said, eyes filled with wonder.

Saul was on his feet, dusting himself off.

"May your reign be filled with many such miracles, King Saul," he said.

"Thank you, chaver," Saul said, hugging his friend.

A little later, as they prepared their camp for the night, Saul's mind roamed around the seeming miracle, trying to understand and learn from it. There was a stillness within, he thought. At the height of his frenzy, he'd experienced a deep stillness, a fathomless quiet that was clearly the Peace of God, "the peace that passeth all understanding." He busied himself lighting the fire while Joel hobbled the mules. It had been a wondrous, renewing peace; the peace that was, really, as he thought about it, the point of everything, all he wanted or needed, the kind of feeling that came from being with his children, or hugging Joel, or talking with Abadantha. And, it came in the midst of the frenzy, the vigor and sensuality of dancing naked.

Did that mean, he wondered, watching the flames dance and glow blue, that the God of the Covenant was always there, waiting at the center of things, but until one went through the frenzy and sensuality of the world and worshipped the God of the Scrolls, It could not be reached? Did one have to surrender completely to the God of the Scrolls, become His slave, as Samuel said before, in order to partake of the Covenant and experience the peace at the center of all things?

When he reached home, Saul decided to tell his sister, but swore her to secrecy.

Abadantha was delighted. "I am a Princess, then," she said, full of joy and enthusiasm. "That means I am a *royal* Princess, doesn't it? If you are King and I am your sister, then I am a Princess." She strutted and preened, dancing around the bench in the arbor. "I am the *first* royal Princess of Israel!"

"Please, Dantha, please!" Saul begged. "Not so loud. I do not know what to do yet. Until I do, I want to keep this to ourselves. Besides, Samuel says it comes with a price. I must give up the God of the Covenant, and serve Yahweh as His slave."

Dantha danced up to him, pushed him to sit on the bench and

kissed his forehead. "The God of the Covenant cares not for outer show and ritual; those things matter to Yahweh, God of the Scrolls, and to us," she smiled lasciviously, exhaling her hot sweet breath across his face, "when we perform our secret rituals to Him."

She straightened, eyes smiling into his, seeing the beginnings of his arousal. "You will worship Yahweh as His most obedient servant, and I will assist you in His worship." She stroked his cheek, again letting her fragrant breath spill across his face, watching as he inhaled it. "And as for the God of the Covenant," her face grew less animated, calmer, as she experienced Its benevolent power, "It sees all, loves all and judges not, knowing it all to be Itself."

She sat down next to him, sobered. "You cannot stay here and be a farmer forever if you are anointed, Saul. The country cries out for its King."

"I know. But what am I to do?" he asked.

"Ask Samuel to conduct a coronation ceremony for you."

Saul's eyes lit up. "Excellent idea, Sister; excellent!"

Samuel agreed it was a good idea. "But," he said, "I want to do everything, including your selection, fresh and from the beginning. I believe if we do that, it will give you greater legitimacy in the eyes of the people." They were on the shady verandah of Samuel's estate, sitting at the same table in the very same seats they had occupied when they'd feasted a few days ago.

Saul had come alone. The trip had been uneventful, but he felt like he'd seen more Philistine soldiers than on his previous trip and wondered if there was a military reason for that or if he was just imagining it. Now he looked uneasily into Samuel's face, wondering why it was necessary to do 'everything fresh and from the beginning.' Was he not to be King?

As he stared back into Saul's face, Samuel realized the unease he saw there was also accompanied by a hint of trust as well. He considers me his ally," Samuel thought. He is depending on me, and my connection to Yahweh. And who could blame him? What a challenge he faces! But, Samuel sighed, if only he understood I can be no man's ally. I serve only the God. Should the God demand Saul's sacrifice, I would do it; not gladly perhaps, but I would do it.

But he *does* need allies! Look what I have asked him to do and the obstacles he faces! The first man to go from farmer to king, to take this divided, undisciplined group of primitive tribes to a state like the Philistines have. It took them decades, even centuries to evolve what they have. Saul's task is unimaginable. I could not do it; my sons could not do it. No one could do it, not in generations, much less in a single lifetime.

Samuel's heart went out to Saul. As long as he serves the God, I will do all in my power to aid and support him; I will be a good ally to him. Should Yahweh turn His face from him, I will have no choice but to do the same. But that is not the situation now. Yahweh has made him king and I must, not *want*, to be his ally.

"Saul," Samuel said, looking intently into the young man's face, "the path ahead is steep, difficult and littered with obstacles."

Saul's face tightened and he shuddered.

"What God has asked you to do, to be King over His chosen people, has never been accomplished by anyone. In fact, up until now, our people have been committed to the belief that having a King was wrong, that they should be ruled directly by God, without intermediaries. That is what it means to be 'chosen' and what the Covenant meant originally. Many people, I among them, still subscribe to that belief."

"I know, Samuel; I fear the task and my ability to accomplish it. But you will help me, will you not? Will you put aside your old belief and be my ally?"

"It will be difficult for me and for half our people, but yes, I will be your ally." Saul smiled gratefully into the old prophet's face. "And, as your ally, I want to recommend persistence."

"Persistence?" Saul repeated. "What do you mean?"

"You must go on, persist, no matter what. Yahweh is a fickle, jealous God. He supports you now and as His servant, I too, support you. But should things change, should He withdraw his support and cause me to withdraw mine, you must persist."

Saul looked concerned about that possibility.

"Good," Samuel said. "I see you appreciate the very real potential for change and shifts. That is why I encourage you to persist and persevere. There is a larger flow of life seemingly beyond the control of the God of the Scrolls."

Saul's face showed a glimmer of understanding. His shoulders relaxed and he noticed the fruit laden trees around them and the coolness of the dry air.

"You and I are part of that, too. It is, when we are able to embrace it fully and let go of our small personalities, our true Identity, our spiritual reality, what some call the God of the Covenant."

Saul nodded; this was what his mother and sister said.

"If you persist and persevere in your life and deeds as part of this larger flow of life, you will find peace, no matter what transpires."

Saul dipped his head in agreement.

Samuel gestured to the nearby stone bench and they sat down. "I believe this so strongly." Samuel looked deeply into Saul's eyes. "Words alone can barely express it." Samuel cast his gaze down and shook his head. "I have seen such dark and terrible things for our people in the future." The prophet looked up, into the sky, eyes hazy. "It is a distant future, perhaps thousands of years, but the pain and fear, the sheer horror of it surpasses anything we can conceive now."

He fixed his eyes on Saul's. "If I believed that anything I did now, today, could change that future, I'd be obligated to do it. But how can I know which things to do, and which not to do? I'd go out of my mind thinking about it. All I can do is trust in the belief that doingness itself—that sense of urgency and the need for certainty, a sense of absolute right and wrong, is the problem.

"Uncertainty is part of living, but we human beings are loath to accept it. We can't know, but *want* to know, *insist* on knowing. We rely too much on prophecy, Saul, and necromancy. 'Thou shalt not suffer a witch to live,' Yahweh decreed to Moses on Mount Sinai. All the black arts were flatly condemned as an 'abomination to the Lord.' Biblical law says, 'There shall not be found among you one that uses divination, a soothsayer, or an enchanter, or a sorcerer, or a charmer, or one that consults a ghost or a familiar spirit or necromancer. Make witchcraft, necromancy, magic and teraphim illegal when you assume your full powers.

"All of those ways of being certain and the need for certainty itself are blocks to the only certainty we can have, our identity as spiritual beings. I have to trust that when I relax into my identity as Spirit and allow It's joy and peace to guide me, that when I have to do something, I will do it from that place and whatever I do will be for the best." Samuel was silent a few minutes. "But I am torn, Saul. Always there is a sense of urgency; always the God commands me to act." He bowed his head and massaged his temples.

"My head aches with the doubt and the need to be sure, too, Samuel," Saul said, touching the old prophet's shoulder.

Samuel did not shake off Saul's hand, and they sat together in familiar silence. "It is the story of my own life," Samuel finally said, "and I offer it as an example to you. You know its broad outlines; how my mother was barren and how she bargained with God for my birth, then gave me to the Temple?"

"Of course." What an honor, Saul thought, to be sitting here talking with the prophet Samuel! "All Israel knows your story."

"What is not so well known, Saul," the prophet said, eyes gleaming, "is that Hannah, my mother was a Priestess of the Covenant and though she made pilgrimage to Shiloh to pray in the Temple, it was to the God of love and joy and peace she prayed, not Yahweh."

Saul's eyes widened with disbelief. "But her prayers were answered. Surely that was the God of the Scrolls?"

Samuel shook his head, no. "She prayed silently, by herself, without the priests, and, her prayers were so intense and focused that the priests, when they found her where she didn't belong in the sanctuary, thought she was drunk."

Saul nodded; those details were also widely known.

"That is not the way one is expected to pray to Yahweh, Saul; sacrifice is required and priestly benedictions, and much beseeching, weeping, and wailing."

"That is true!" Saul said, seeing it clearly for the first time. "My mother and sister are also Priestesses of the Covenant. Why have they never interpreted your story this way?"

"Perhaps they have, but have not told you." Samuel searched Saul's face then added for emphasis, "you know, of course, that our great matriarchs, Sarah, Rebecca, and Rachel were also barren, then were 'remembered' by God. Could it be they were praying to Yahweh in their bareness and when they let go of their need, fear, and pain, and allowed their experience of the Covenant, the truth of their spiritual identities to fill them they bore children?

"In fact, it was after each of these women, including my mother, conceived, having given up their teraphim to honor Yahweh, that they again took up their household idols, not to blaspheme the God of the Scrolls, not to worship the teraphim, but as symbols, reminders of their relationship to the God of the Covenant."

"So," Saul said, eyes wide with insight, "that is why women of the Covenant give teraphim to their daughters?"

The old prophet dipped his head in agreement.

"Yet you would have me eliminate that custom by banning teraphim." Samuel nodded. "And although you are the servant of Yahweh, you still speak of the God of the Covenant with such love and devotion. Do you not fear Yahweh's vengeance? Is he not a jealous God?"

"I do fear Him; but I love life itself, too. Old as I am, with all I have seen of the present and future, I could not exist without believing in the God of the Covenant. Of course, publicly, I serve and honor the God of the Scrolls, and obey Him in all his commandments. That is why I abjure you to ban necromancy and the teraphim. But in the absence of commandments, in the privacy of my heart, I honor the Covenant." Samuel put his hands on Saul's shoulders and looked deeply into his face, eyes shining. "The task before you is nearly impossible. I entreat you, as I would the sons who have so disappointed me, do not rely only on Yahweh, touch also the place of the Covenant deep within your heart.

"Now, here is what we will do about your coronation."

Saul listened, face skeptical and stony, but as the prophet explained his plan, the new King began to smile. Once again he felt the refreshing coolness of the arid air and enjoyed the symphony of scents it bore.

# Chapter Five

The huge crowd was in a holiday mood. Perhaps 300,000 people in a total population of 750, 000 responded to Samuel's call for convocation, engulfing the little town of Mizpah. Rumors abounded. What was to be discussed? How long would the convocation last? Was there enough food? Would sanitary conditions be frightful? The Philistines had reinforced their garrison, and smartly uniformed, heavily armed soldiers were visible everywhere. The soldiers left the Hebrews alone. However, their commanders were explicit about avoiding trouble, outnumbered as they were. One commander, a Captain Hafiz, asked his sergeants to listen carefully and bring him any information about why the Hebrews were there and what their intentions were.

Encampments were established by tribe and clan. Distinctive, multi-colored tents, flags and standards, even clothing and robes, marked the territories, and were a treat for the eye. The biggest tribes had the most space, but no one really had enough room. By the second day, Mizpah's facilities, fresh water for people and livestock, sanitary facilities, and even space itself, were strained and crumbling. No one in authority had expected so many people. The noise was a constant dull rumbling. The smell of unwashed bodies, human waste, smoke, and cooking food hovered in the air almost as a physical presence. The overcrowding, noise, and disorder weakened the holiday mood and made almost everyone testy and short tempered, everyone except Saul's family.

Ahinoam and their four sons and two daughters: Jonathan, Ish-

Boshet, Abindab, and Malchishua, Michal and Merab were enjoying themselves. They gloried in the break in routine and the opportunities for new experiences their first big trip as a family provided. Jonathan, nineteen, the oldest, lean, wiry and dark like Ahinoam, and Michal, sixteen, the second born daughter, sleek, fair complected and red of hair, like her father, rose to the challenge and helped their serene and patient mother supervise their younger siblings. Saul even managed to spend time alone with each of them and was surprised to find Jonathan more aware of the Teaching and better connected to the Covenant than Michal, who was closer to Yahweh. He'd thought it would be the other way round.

Michal bridled every time she saw a beefy, well-armed Philistine soldier. She hated them, called them oppressors and occupiers, and at one point, Saul had to keep her from throwing a stone at a mounted officer. Jonathan hated them, too, but spent his time when they were around, coolly observing them as if he was making tactical mental notes about their patterns of movement and command, their uniforms and weaponry.

Both were good company for their father, engaging Saul in meaningful conversations, although solicitous of his headaches. Michal and Jonathan were also favorites of Aunt Abadantha, and as they did at home, the four of them speculated about events of the day. Now they were seated cross-legged on the sandy soil outside their tent.

"Samuel is so old," Michal said. "Can he really see the future?"

"No!" Jonathan said. "Well in a way. Isn't that right, abba?" he asked Saul.

"You're correct, Jonathan," Saul responded. "He has a sense of what will come, but does not 'see' it as you see me now."

"Why has he gathered us?" Michal asked Dantha.

"I am not sure," she said, winking at her brother, "but the rumor is God has commanded him to select a king."

Both children jumped up. "A king!" they cried in unison.

"Now we can drive out the hated oppressors!" Michal declared.

Jonathan seemed subdued after his initial enthusiasm. "May God be with whoever becomes king. The work will be extremely difficult."

Saul felt his eyes water as he hugged his two children to him.

"Why is Samuel selecting the king?" Jonathan asked. "I thought he was against even the idea of a king, much less its reality."

"You're right, Jonathan," Saul said. "But he is Yahweh's servant, and if God commanded him to do it, he must obey, no matter what his own feelings."

"Samuel is very close to God," Jonathan said. "Isn't he, Father?" Saul nodded.

"I wonder what it would be like to experience God that way, as a real presence, as an actual almost tangible thing."

Saul mussed his son's hair. "I too, would like to feel that, my son."

"What would it be like to know It's oneness the way Samuel, Aunt Abadantha and Grandmother Janina know it? I long for the peace of it, Father, the certainty that would come from submission to God's almighty will."

A shofar, the ram's horn trumpet, sounded, then another and still another. Dantha looked up at the position of the sun in the sky. "It is time to gather round the bema, (the stage). Samuel will address us now."

Ahinoam and her other children emerged from the tent along with Joel and his children, and together they joined the multitude pressing forward. As Benjamites, they were furthest from the bema and could hear nothing Samuel said amidst the voices, shuffling and coughing of the crowd, and saw him only as a speck on the horizon. A continuous stream of chatter flowed from the front of the crowd to the back, carrying news of what transpired on the bema.

"What does Samuel have on the bema?" Michal wondered aloud.

The buzz soon brought her an answer. "He has an altar and a ram up there for a sacrifice commemorating the King's anointing," a man said. "The elders of all the tribes are there, too," another voice said. "They say he held up a circlet of burnished Phoenician gold with which to crown the king."

After thirty or forty minutes, the multitude parted and Samuel strode into the Benjaminite encampment. The tribal elders greeted him. "Did you hear what I have proclaimed?" Samuel asked them.

They had not. Looking annoyed, Samuel said he would say it again. Someone brought forth a tall, sturdy table and helped the fragile prophet onto it.

"Thus saith the Lord, the God of Israel: 'I brought up Israel out of Egypt, and I delivered you out of the hands of all the kingdoms that oppressed you.' But you have this day rejected your God, who Himself saves you out of all your calamities and your distresses, and you have said unto Him: 'Nay, but set a king over us.' " A more profound hush fell on the Benjaminites and the others within earshot.

The prophet looked directly at Saul, eyes burning into his. "I say unto you do not have a king! It is not too late. Repent! Choose again! You will not be pleased for this will be the manner of the king's reign over you." The prophet's voice boomed out. Saul looked away, feeling betrayed. "A king will take your sons to be his horsemen and to plow his ground and to reap his harvest, and to make his instruments of war, and they shall run before his chariots. And he will take your daughters to be perfumers, and to be his cooks and bakers. And he will take your fields, and your vineyards, and your olive yards, even the best of them. And he will take the tenth of your seed, and give to his officers. And he will take your men-servants, and your maidservants, and your goodliest young men, and your asses, and put them to his work. He will take a tenth of your flocks and you shall be his servants, under his yoke."

Samuel paused, a hint of hope in his eyes. "What say you, people of Israel?"

Shouts of: "Give us a king." "Let us be as other nations!" rang out.

Joel, standing beside Saul, spat. "Samuel is mad, truly mad, chaver. Has he not already anointed you? What is this insanity? His talk of a yoke only strengthens the peoples' determination for a king. The people need a yoke, for without it we turn and roam aimlessly, instead of achieving our purpose. Until now, we have been as a calf, playing and cavorting. The time has come to be an ox, tilling the soil, bringing forth substance. Just as the ox, our people need a guiding hand."

Saul felt better, but was still badly shaken. "Thank you, chaver, your words strengthen me."

Joel put his arm around Saul's shoulder. "And even if Samuel is right, and I think he is, isn't it better for our sons and daughters to be in service to a king of our own, rather than to a foreign ruler, as is the case now? Who would oppress us?"

"Yes," Saul said. "Of course; and I will endeavor to be a good king, even a great one."

Scowling, Samuel began speaking again. "Very well; you have chosen and shall have your way. The Lord God has declared I draw lots for the selection of king, since all men among His chosen people are equal and beloved by Him. I have drawn the first lot to select the tribe from which the king will come, and Benjamin has been selected."

An "Ohhh!" sounded from a thousand throats. Samuel drew again. "This lot falls to the clan of Matri." Another "Ohhh" released.

Saul felt dizzy; jagged bolts of pain tore through his skull. "I must go and lay down for a moment," he told Ahinoam.

"Shall I come with you?"

"No, stay. The prophet has many lots to draw. I will return before long."

An hour later, Saul was selected. His family was overjoyed. But he had not yet returned. "I will bring him to you, Samuel," Ahinoam declared.

When she led the new king forward, nearly blind, awkward and irritated by his still throbbing head, Samuel reached his hand down to help Saul up to the tabletop. "Do you see him whom Yahweh has chosen?" He held up Saul's hand. "See how he is head and shoulders above other men and that there is no one else like him among all the people?"

"Long live the King!" Someone shouted. Then others repeated the call, and in seconds a chorus of, "Long live the King!" swelled, roaring and echoing across the countryside like the tides crashing onto the shore. After ten minutes, Samuel stilled the multitude. "We go now to the bema for the anointing and the sacrifice."

As they walked to the bema, the crowd parted and made way for them. Those closest to Samuel and the King-to-be, gaped silently, while the others behind them cheered wildly. The bema was a high place, an island, surrounded by a sea of humanity. Constructed from strong acacia timbers, it stood six feet above the ground and was wide enough and long enough to accommodate an altar, a sacrificial lamb, and priests at one end, and the elders of all the twelve tribes at the other. Saul looked out from the top and saw nothing but human beings stretching away to the horizon in every direction. Scattered here and there among them, were mounted Philistine cavalry. The waiting priests and elders bowed deeply, the ram bleated.

Samuel held the vial of anointing oil aloft and the multitude fell silent. He gestured and a priest kindled the wood on the altar. Instantly, flames leapt up, their crackle clearly audible. Closing his tired grey eyes, the old prophet turned his head heavenward, uttering a barely audible prayer. Finished, he opened his eyes and looking straight at Saul, gestured for him to come. Saul stepped forward and knelt before the white-haired prophet.

Holding up the vial of oil, Samuel said, "This is the anointing oil of Moses himself. With this I will anoint Saul, son of Kish, clan of Matri, tribe of Benjamin, to be the first King of Israel!"

As the oil touched his head and ran down into his eyes and ears, Saul's pain diminished. He raised his head to look into the sea of faces surrounding him. The crowd roared out its approval. Samuel leaned forward and whispered into his ear, "You feel it now, don't you, the power of Yahweh, your Lord? Now, be ye transformed in His holy name, being His obedient servant, keeping the Covenant locked securely away in your heart; and say, 'Amen'."

"Amen!" The new King smiled as the hot power swelled his chest, and he waved to the multitude. "What do I do now?" he shouted to Samuel.

"I do not know, King," Samuel said, coldly. "You are the King, I am a prophet. I have done what Yahweh commanded me to do. I will return to Zulph."

"You will not advise me?" Saul's voice could barely contain his panic.

Samuel shook his head, a touch of sadness in his cold eyes. "My part is done. I am old and tired. I will go to my home in Zulph."

Gesturing for Saul to rise, Samuel lifted the glittering crown of Phoenician gold from the table and placed it on his head. "Behold your King," he said, the bitter taste of bile in his mouth. The crowd cheered exultantly. Taking the sacrificial knife, Samuel stepped behind King Saul, grabbed the ram by its shoulders and slit its throat. Blood gushed forth, covering his arms and white robes and staining his face. The priests lifted the animal and placed it on the altar. At first, the smell of roasting meat was pleasant, then, as it burned and was consumed, the smell was acrid.

"Please," the King begged. "Stay with me, Samuel."

Samuel again shook his head 'no,' the same cold sadness in his grey eyes. In a gesture of victory, the prophet lifted King Saul's hand, leaving sacrificial blood dripping from his wrist and robe. The crowd redoubled its cheering. Samuel released the new King's wrist, climbed off the bema and disappeared into the throng.

A deep sense of deprivation, loss and imminent disaster swept Saul. His heart ached and thudded; tears came to his eyes and his body trembled. The musicians gathered at the base of the bema, began to make a great, celebratory sound, taking the focus from Samuel's departure and the King's discomfort. Arranging themselves in a line, the musicians ascended the bema, snaking round and round the King and dignitaries, their joyful noise filling the air.

And Saul recalled the earlier music, that of his trip home with Joel, after his first anointing and willed himself to re-experience the ecstasy he'd felt then. He closed his eyes, inhaled deeply, tried to release all sad thoughts, let his body relax and along with it, his heart and mind, trying to become receptive, even expectant of experiencing Spirit. It didn't quite work; his mental, emotional and physical mumblings were not enough. He felt something, enough to realize he owed the people a show of enthusiasm, but truly, deeply, there was a hollow emptiness that Samuel could have helped fill.

He stood tall and big, head and shoulders above every other man on the bema. King Saul presented an imposing figure facing the cheering multitude acknowledging their joy with waves and bows. Their acclaim was deafening. At long last, they had a King to lead and protect them; and not just any man, but a man of stature. Saul was deeply moved and those nearest him saw tears running down his cheeks.

"Children of Israel!" King Saul shouted. "Children of Israel!" Gradually, seeing the King's lips moving and seeing him gesture, the multitude quieted. "My Master, Yahweh, the Lord God of Israel, has commanded that we honor the first and second commandments he gave Moses on Mount Sinai. 'You shall have no other gods before Me!' And 'You shall make no graven images.' Therefore, as my first official act as your King, I hereby proclaim that worship of any god but Yahweh or the creation of any graven images is forbidden upon severe penalty even unto death! Destroy your teraphim; keep no shrines or idols in your homes."

A moan rose from those who heard the King. "Yahweh also proclaims an end to necromancy. Uncertainty is part of being human. Accept that. Let go of your idols and need to know the future, and live in the faith that Yahweh will guide and protect you." Another moan. "Done," Saul thought. "But it shall not change in my lifetime, or in my children's lifetimes." King Saul gestured to the musicians and they began to play.

Lead by the musicians, the King and the dignitaries began to dance, and following their example, the multitude danced, too. Night came and the festivities continued by torchlight, with happy, exhausted Israelites sleeping where they fell, their fellows dancing around them. And from the mountains of Ephraim, Jerusalem and Hebron great bonfires blazed to tell the world Israel had a king.

Captain Hafiz had ridden the thousand cubits from his command tent in back of the Benjaminite encampment, to the edge of the human sea. Though he could not hear all the old prophet said, seated above the crowd on his horse, the bearded Captain was able to clearly see him anointing the big man standing next to him. Hafiz had been involved with the Hebrews for the last ten of his twenty years of military service. He knew their politics and rituals and knew what he was witnessing.

He thought, judging by the wild enthusiasm, that the Philistine Confederation would soon have a potent new adversary. For a moment,

Hafiz was shaken by the power of the raw energy and noise, and by the thought of the threat these implied. He backed his horse steadily away from the crowds that engulfed him. No point in presenting them with such an easy target. But then, as he attained the relative safety of open space, Hafiz realized that although his people occupied much of the so-called 'promised land,' the Hebrews had more immediate threats from Ammon, Moab, Edom, and their ancient foes, the Amalekites. The Philistines would have to be more alert and careful now, but they were, by no means, the main target. Not yet, at least.

# Chapter Six

At first, Saul was bereft without Samuel, but he kept his fear and concern private. In public, he was hale and hardy. A large number of complex decisions had to be made: how to raise revenue to pay for his official duties and court (taxation would be very difficult); where to locate his capital (probably Gibeah); whether to raise a standing army (good idea, but almost impossible without taxes); and how to transition from the Judges and tribal chiefs to a more centralized government. Only his immediate family and Joel's family were aware of his self-doubt and pain.

A few weeks after the Coronation, a small clique of men who did not recognize Saul as their King emerged. They had begun their dissent at the Coronation, with the question, "How can this man save us?" and that phrase became their rallying cry. Saul had no viable idea of how to deal with them. He had many violent, murderous ideas, but none that struck him as 'kingly' and would not make the situation worse.

Then, to damp down this rebelliousness, Samuel emerged from Zulph and presented King and people with a great innovation: a written constitution. He sent Saul a scroll explaining that centuries before God had foretold exactly these events, and had supplied Moses with regulations governing the King's actions. The scroll listed and explained these. Saul had it copied and sent to each of the twelve tribes with orders that it be re-copied and read aloud and proclaimed at worship services for the next ninety days. Although this helped quiet much of the clamor and doubt, Saul thought the scroll's restrictions on his kingly prerogatives might create difficulties for him later.

He was hurt and offended by the fact that Samuel *sent* the scroll and did not bring it himself. As Saul's public swagger and bravado grew, so did his private sorrow and self-doubt. He ruminated in endless circles, feeling sorry for himself. Being King wasn't my idea, he thought, wallowing in self-pity. It wasn't even Samuel's idea, or God's, for that matter. It was the people's idea. God had gone along with them and made Samuel anoint him. Samuel still favored the judges, the theocracy. Each time Saul followed this chain of logic, a nasty smile would twist his face. The people's idea, indeed, and here they were, some of them at least, not supporting the King they had clamored for. Actually, it was the idea itself that possessed the people, not the other way around. After all, there were kings in the nations around them; why shouldn't they have one, too?

"I just fell into this situation. It *happened* to me. I'm nothing special, just the biggest man with the broadest shoulders, and the most naïve, simplest mind. My becoming king is a tormented version of the common story of a willing, idealistic man who drifts into a trade and finds himself making a life of it, developing the calluses and muscles, the deformities of body and soul peculiar to it."

The deformities of soul indeed! Were these the transformation Samuel said he'd experience? To those nearest him, the deformities of his soul were quickly becoming a burden.

Abadantha complained that he spent less time with her than he had before and he laughed cruelly at her. "I am King now, not some gentleman farmer; of course, I have less time for you. You don't hear Ahinoam complaining do you? She understands me."

"She doesn't complain to you, for she knows it will get her nothing. But, she complains to me, and Joel."

"Joel," Saul sneered, "there's another disappointment! He counseled me not to bring Samuel's sons Joel and Abija to court, that they are low, unethical, incompetent men, not fit to be around me. As if I don't know that! I must transition from their rule to mine. I have no choice but to learn from them."

"I too, fear what you are learning from them, my brother," Dantha said, "and from the tribal elders Zeror, Aphiah, and Kenit. You seem to be playing them off against one another." Her mouth twisted in distaste. "Joel is right."

Saul put his hands on his hips and strutted around the room. "What would *you* have me do? I have no power of my own. These are the people with the power, I must work with them."

"To what end, Brother, if you lose your soul?"

"My soul belongs to Yahweh, the God of the Scrolls. It is His will I do. *He* decided there should be a King and that it should be me. My soul is in no danger. It is His. I but do His will and build His kingdom."

Dantha stepped closer to him. "You still have the Teaching of the Covenant in your heart, do you not?" Her voice was soft as she touched his cheek.

He paused in his pacing; put his hand over hers. She was so beautiful, pale and delicate; her face and figure so fetching. He longed to touch her hair. "I do," he said. "And it has been awhile since you and I worshipped It."

"I too, feel the longing to join in worship," Dantha said. "It *has* been a long time. But have you forgotten, Brother? Our worship now is of Yahweh, not the Teaching. The Teaching of the Covenant discourages fleshy, sensual worship, even as Yahweh discourages it. What we do, we do for the pleasure of it, not to please the Gods."

"Yes, yes," Saul said, distracted. "Of course, Yahweh." He leaned forward to touch his lips to hers.

Jonathan flung himself into the room; brother and sister backed apart. Had the boy seen anything? "The Ammonite King Nahash has surrounded Jabesh!" he declared.

Saul froze, stunned, and then smiled wickedly. "Good!" he said, putting a hand on Jonathan's shoulder. "Our first challenge. Go. Call the Council together. I shall meet you there." Jonathan used the new salute they had instituted, clenched fist, arm across chest touching shoulder, and left.

"He is quite thrilled," Dantha observed.

Saul paced a moment, and then crumpled to the floor. His sister rushed to him and knelt at his side. "What is it, Brother?" Her voice was full of concern.

"I know not what to do, Dantha! I have no one to turn to, no experience; my mind is a blank. How can I be King?"

Dantha stroked his head and kissed him gently on the lips. "There is that within you that knows, Saul." Her voice was full of soothing compassion. He looked at her with eyes wild as a crazed bull's. She again touched her lips to his. "Close your eyes; go within. You've done this many times before; you know how to do it, know that it works." He closed his eyes. Muffled sounds of alarm rippled through the tent walls.

"Sha, my brother; be still. Go within; peace and wisdom await. Another minute or two will not matter to those needing you, but will matter greatly to your ability to bring them success."

Saul's eyelids twitched, but his eyes remained closed. Seconds later, his eyelids ceased fluttering, and his breathing slowed and deepened.

"That's it my brother, my beloved," Dantha whispered, her mouth just grazing his ear. "Let the Teaching work, the God of the Covenant is within you; commune with It. Let It guide you. You feel Its power, do you not?"

Saul nodded.

"There is no real conflict between It and the God of the Scrolls; you feel that, don't you?"

Saul nodded.

"It is the One God, *your* God."

Saul sighed; "I see what I am to do," he said, starting to sit up.

"A bit longer, Brother," Dantha said, leaning her weight on his upper arms, gently holding him down. "Rest in It and awaken refreshed."

A moment later Dantha released him. He sat up and stared into her soft, glowing eyes. "Thank you, Sister," he said.

She leaned forward and gently kissed his mouth. "You needn't thank me, Brother. It is my duty as both your sister and your subject." They stood and embraced. The sounds of alarm grew louder and more intrusive. Dantha held him at arm's length and studied his face. "This, or something similar, will happen again, you know." He nodded. "Please, I beg you, remember that although the two Gods seem separate when you are away from the Teaching and locked in the embrace of the Scrolls, they are but two sides of the same coin and that the God of the Covenant is the coin itself. Remember what you did just now, it is what to do the next time the need arises; sit peacefully, close your eyes, breathe deeply, let your mind be empty, and allow Spirit to rule you completely."

Saul leaned forward and kissed her cheek. "I shall remember, Sister;" and left the tent. Jonathan and Michal both in armor were waiting for him. Saul had never before seen his seventeen-year-old daughter garbed for war. She looked adorable and quite fierce. Jonathan was calm and confident. A noisy crowd, swelling by the moment, milled around them. The King was a head taller than the tallest, and the frightened people looked up into his face. "You must do something, King!" a woman shouted. "Yes!" shouted many of the others. "Do something; save our brothers and sisters in Jabesh!"

King Saul gestured for them to be still. "I shall, my people," he said. "I shall. I am your King, Yahweh's servant, and with His help all things are possible." A cheer rose from the throng. "Tell me what has happened?"

"King Nahash of Ammon has surrounded the town of Jabesh," a man said. "Having no defenses, our people offered their surrender. But cruel Nahash would accept surrender only if every man in Jabesh allowed Nahash to gouge out his right eye."

A groan escaped the crowd. Joel stepped to Saul's side. "Nahash was leveraging his anticipated victory, reasoning that if the Jabeshites tolerated this, no other town would have the will to resist him," he said.

Saul nodded, his face stony.

"Wisely," Joel continued, "the people of Jabesh requested seven days to consider the Ammonite offer. Nahash agreed," Joel's face twisted, and he spat, "the taste of future effortless conquests must be rich in his mouth. The Jabeshites immediately dispatched messengers to us."

"Let us fight, Father!" Michal cried.

"Yes! Fight! Fight!" Cries rose from the multitude gathered round them.

The King raised his hands to still them. "We must do more than fight," he said when they were quieter. "We must win!" A cheer filled the air. "I want not only to win, but to so rally our tribes that we put the fear of the Lord God Yahweh into our enemies, all of them, everywhere, so they will think hard before attacking us."

The air erupted with cheers and shouts. "Victory!" "Long live King Saul!" "Death to Nahash!"

Saul gestured for them to let him pass and a path through the sea of humanity opened before him. "Like Moses at the Red Sea, so long ago," he thought, grinning as he made his way forward to the Council Tent.

"Long live King Saul!" "God bless King Saul!" They screamed, reaching out to touch and pat him. Michal, Jonathan, Joel and the rest of the Council were waiting for him. They stood as he entered and bowed deeply from the waist. The shouts and noise were still so loud that they couldn't hear one another. Saul went out to quiet them. Seeing him, the multitude redoubled its cheering, then, responding to their King's request for peace and quiet, they became still. Saul went inside, glowing from the adulation, and most of the crowd drifted away. A hundred or so remained milling around and muttering, waiting to hear the results of the Council meeting.

The twenty-five Counselors were seated on large cushions in a semi-circle facing a great wooden chair that served as the King's throne. Jonathan sat beside Ephriam, on the King's right and Michal, beside Judah, on his left. Michal was extremely proud of her father and thought he looked magnificent and totally regal, as he strode to the throne and seated himself. This was the fifth Council Meeting since Saul became king, and the third Michal had attended. She was the only woman present, and she and Jonathan, the only young people in attendance.

The Council consisted of elders from each of the twelve tribes, the former Judges, Samuel's sons Joel and Abija and twelve others selected by the King. Prominent among them were the King's twenty-eight-year-old cousin Abner ben Ner, well regarded for his military prowess, Zeror, elder of Judah, and Melchor, elder of Ephraim. Ephraim being of Devorah's tribe sat on the King's right, next to Jonathan, while Judah, a source of rapidly expanding power, sat on his left, next to Michal. In the five meetings preceding this one, only Abner had vigorously championed the King's agenda for a standing army and a unified nation. Michal and Jonathan were more observers than participants.

The King stood and the others rose with him. "Let us pray," he said. "Almighty Yahweh, ruler of the world, master of life, we, your humble and faithful servants, call upon you for guidance and support. Enemies have assailed your chosen people and we, the leaders You have appointed, would know Your will. Be with us in our deliberations and may what we decide find favor in Your holy sight." The King seated himself. The vision that had come to him moments earlier with Dantha, glowed in his mind's eye and was what he planned to execute, but he wanted the Council to believe it originated here and now with them. He smiled slightly; that was good kingship.

An hour later, when the meeting was over, King Saul left the Council Tent followed by his Council and the people who had waited outside, and strode to his home. Going inside, he returned a moment later carrying a large Philistine battle-ax with an 18-inch iron blade, one of the few iron weapons in the Hebrew arsenal.

With the Council and a growing crowd of curious onlookers following, Saul strode the fifty cubits to the pen where his oxen were kept. No doubt or uncertainty now, no headache or tension, nor need of magic or necromancers, Saul was King, God's anointed, at one with Its power and all that existed. Everything was unfolding, as his holy vision had shown him. Every detail had not been revealed, but the next steps and the final victory over Nahash were crystal clear. What was to transpire between would be revealed in good time, as he needed to know.

Saul went into the pen, led the largest, most handsome bull through the crowd and into the nearby field. He believed this sacrifice was to be of a different sort. Not the usual burnt offering favored by Yahweh and his priests in Nob. In fact, though such an offering was normally required and expected, Saul had no intention of making it. In fact, what he was about to do was not a 'sacrifice' at all, but an affirmation guided by his connection with the Covenant and the vision It had sent.

The crowd, which had doubled in size and was still growing, became quiet. Among them, standing not far from one another, were Hafiz, the Philistine Captain, and Janina, the King's mother. The Captain, who'd been re-assigned to monitor the King's court, was dressed in mufti. Janina, hearing the uproar and seeing the growing multitude, had walked with her students of the Teaching to the pen. As the crowd grew and jostled, Hafiz and Janina were pushed so close, their shoulders touched. Looking into one another's faces, they smiled politely and then, as the crowd continued to swell, were pushed forward.

Saul tethered the ox. He stroked the animal with his left hand and held the big ax in this right. The animal looked up at him with large mournful eyes. He had been Saul's favorite, a young, handsome, virile stud, but very gentle. Saul's heart seized with sadness. Shutting his eyes, the King inhaled deeply, felt the stillness in his heart, and leaning forward, touched his lips to the animal's warm, moist nose. "Blessed art thou," he intoned, standing erect, "oh Lord our God, King of the Universe, Who ordains a time for all things; a time for life." He raised the ax and gripped it with both hands, then bought it down with all his might, splitting the ox's skull. "And a time for death." Blood gushed from the wound covering Saul. The animal pitched forward on to its forelegs, wobbled then collapsed, dead.

Dripping with crimson, his white robes damp and glistening red, the King turned to the quiet multitude, now grown to a many hundred souls, and said, "Yahweh is with us, but we must be with *Him*. He can do for us, only what we allow him to do *through* us. He has placed the vision and will in each of us, but it is we who must use it." Nods and soft murmurs of approval greeted Saul's words. "And it is not enough if only a few of us use the power; all must use It. What I do now, I do to unify the twelve tribes and to bring our people together so that we may put an end to these unprovoked attacks."

Turning to the ox, Saul hacked off its head with four mighty strokes and held it aloft; blood dripped to the ground and splattered him. Turning to face the multitude, he called, "Melchor, Council

Member from Ephraim! Come forth; take this to the elders of your tribe. Inform them of the attack on Jabesh and tell them the King of Israel commands every able bodied male to gather here in two days time so that we can save Jabesh and defeat Nahash."

Trembling, Melchor, stepped forward, bowed before the King and took the bloody message.

"Go now!" The King commanded and the shaken man ran off. The King then walked behind the ox, and with super-human strength, heaved it over, cut off its lingam and balls and called, "Zeror, Council Member from Judah, come forth take this to the elders of your tribe."

In this way, King Saul divided the ox into ten more parts, one for each tribe and sent them forth as summons and warning. Throughout this gory ritual, the crowd, now in the thousands, was still. Everyone knew that this was a re-enactment of the terrible maiming of the Levite's wife nearly two hundred years ago that had led to the near extinction of the Benjaminites. Now the King used his own tribe's dark history, to rally the Nation. Would it work, Janina wondered?

At first, when her son had cleaved the beast's skull and the blood gushed forth, Janina had been horrified. Remembering the tenderness that had preceded it, how the King had patted the animal, bent to kiss it and nearly cried, Janina thought, no, there was more than simple brutality there. Knowing her son's love of animals, the act seemed like a last resort, perhaps not even his own idea. It must have come to him, Janina thought, been given by Spirit. Saul was bright, even cunning, but the brilliance of this strategy of slaughter, its ability both to consolidate the tribes and fight Nahash, unifying the past and the present, shame and hope, was not of him. It was as he had said, the Power working through him. If that *was* indeed what it was, it would work.

Captain Hafiz stayed to the very end and left with the last few clumps of people. He too, had been impressed by King Saul's strategy, but not for the same reasons as Janina. He knew nothing of the history of the Benjaminites, though he would learn. What impressed Hafiz was the King's boldness and vision. Hafiz knew that as long as the Hebrew tribes were divided, they were no threat to the Philistines. Their new King seemed to understand that, too. It wasn't a case of saving a city; it was a move to build a Nation. If King Saul's strategy worked, the Philistine monopoly on iron and smithing might not be enough. Still ruminating, the Captain mounted his horse for the long ride to Gaza. He'd have plenty of time to compose his report on what he'd seen and what he thought it meant.

# Chapter Seven

"Food is not yet a problem," Abner said, "but it will be if we don't deploy soon. Sanitation is our biggest problem now." He peered through the dust and smoke, blazing sun glinting off his bronze armor while he talked with Saul, Joel and Jonathan, all of them baking in the heat in front of King's tent. All four dripped with perspiration, had to lean towards one another to be heard above all the clamor, but were otherwise an island of relative calm in a roiling sea of armed men.

"How many do you think have responded so far?" King Saul asked.

"Hundreds of thousands," Jonathan said, enthusiastically. "Half the men in Israel must be here, Father."

"What do you think, Abner?" The King asked. "You are my commander."

Abner smiled and put a hand on Jonathan's shoulder. "This boy's not a bad leader, cousin."

Jonathan smiled up at him. "I'd estimate close to 300,000. This is good and bad, my King."

Saul nodded. "It is as we said long ago, before I was King, 'who will lead them?'"

The others dipped their heads in agreement.

"I have my Ephramites," Joel offered.

"Good men, but only 500," Jonathan said.

"And we have 1,500 of my mercenaries," Abner said.

"A total of 2,000 experienced warriors, with little leadership experience," the King observed.

"That would come to each of them if we made them captains over 1,500 soldiers," Abner calculated. "But," he said, "just as they have come with their own rations for ten days, so too, have they come with their own tribal leaders. We will have difficulty replacing them."

"We need have no difficulty," the King said, "for we will not replace them. We will simply distribute our 2,000 men, those who will become the core of our standing army, proportionately among the tribes as military advisors and liaisons."

"Brilliant!" Abner said and the others agreed.

"Go now, Joel and Abner; bring these 2,000 here to me so that we may make our plans known to them and consecrate them to our purpose." The two men bowed and departed.

"The stench of so many unwashed bodies and so much waste is awful, Father!" Michal said, joining them. She wore a shining bronze helmet and a heavy leather breastplate that highlighted her budding breasts.

Saul kissed her cheek and nodded. "In future we must have better arrangements. But," he smiled warmly, opening his arms to his warrior son and daughter, "aren't we blessed that so many have responded to my call?"

Michal thought her father was like a child with a fresh millet cake, enthused and eager. It was good to see him that way. "Indeed, we are blessed," she agreed.

Then, looking troubled, Jonathan asked, "Why have you not sent word to Jabesh that we are coming to relieve them?"

"We dare not alert the Ammonites to our plans," Saul said. "They certainly have spies in Jabesh."

"They probably have them here, too, don't you think, Father? You would, in their shoes."

Saul tousled his son's hair. "Indeed I would and do, even now, my son. We have spies in Jabesh and among the Ammonites. You are a good tactician, Jonathan, brave and cunning." The young man beamed. "I will rely on you. Of course, the people of Jabesh know we are coming, as do the Ammonites. What they do not know and cannot know is the manner of our coming."

Jonathan grinned and nodded. "Stealth, trickery and surprise are our greatest weapons, are they not?"

Michal hugged him and nodded, and Jonathan smiled into his father's beaming face. It was good to see him so alive and enthusiastic.

"When Abner and Joel return we will finalize our plans, meanwhile, leave me, my children."

Joel returned to the King's tent before Abner. He found his friend the King pacing, still in an expansive confident mood, but with a little of that familiar habitual doubt eating away at its edges.

"Ah, Joel," Saul said, opening his arms to hug his friend. "We are making good progress, but are not quite ready. Where is Samuel? I need him."

"I don't know about Samuel, but the preparations seem to be as they should be at this stage, Saul, uh, your Majesty."

"Saul, please, old friend," said the King. "We are boyhood friends and kin by marriage." The King looked away. "Did you see Samuel on your way here?"

"No. I did not see him, and thank you, Majesty, for acknowledging our ties of friendship and kinship." Joel dipped his head. "Do you remember the time we were exploring in the Shephelah?"

"I do old friend, I remember it well. We found an iron shield and you threw the javelin further than I did."

"I can still throw further than you."

"Indeed you can!" Saul asserted jovially. "That's why I want you at my side."

"Thank you, Majesty," Joel bowed his head.

"I wonder where Samuel is?" The King mused.

"Sire, I remember the Shephelah a little differently." The King looked at him quizzically. "I remember that you were good, better than most, but not better than me." Saul nodded. "I remember that you were strong, as you are now, smart, as you are now and, one to inspire loyalty and trust, as you do now."

"Thank you," said the King.

"You need not thank me, Saul. I speak the simple truth. You are the same great man now as you were then. But Saul, my oldest and dearest friend," Joel stepped forward and gripped the King's shoulders and stared into his eyes. "Instead of being grateful and appreciating the many gifts God gave you, you focused on the few things you lacked."

The smile slipped from the King's face as he listened intently. "And...?"

"And... " Joel said, bucking up his courage. "... And you're doing that now, with Samuel."

"What do you mean?" Saul asked, hands on hips.

"I mean Saul, my King, Samuel is a man as you are a man, and God is with you, too."

"But Samuel... " the King started to say.

Joel waved his hands interrupting. "Samuel is special. I give you that. I care not for him, but it is not he I wish to discuss, but you. I beg you, Saul, focus not on your fear of the Lord, on your doubts of his patronage, but upon the reality of what he's placed in you, in your head, heart, and hands. You are blessed my friend; you have wonderful children, a fine family, and smart and loyal friends. Where are these but gifts from God?"

Saul's eyes smiled into Joel's and he nodded.

"Is it not written that it is done unto you as you believe?" Joel asked.

The King nodded.

"Doesn't that mean that your fear of God and your doubts about his love create more fear and doubt? Look around you! See the multitude that has come to your call. See me and Abner, Abadantha, and your wonderful warrior children, Michal and Jonathan."

"Did someone call us?" Michal said holding the tent flap open for her brother, then stepping through herself. She looked robust and cute with her cheeks flushed and her helmet off and her long auburn hair braided into a knot at the top of her head. "Uncle Joel," she said throwing herself into his arms.

Saul cleared his throat. "Ahem, a moment, Michal. Joel and I were indeed talking about you and your brother; and, Joel was right! Thank you." The King patted his friend on the shoulder, and then turned to his children. "Joel reminded me of my many blessings, you among them. When I feel my blessings, and am grateful, I am with the God of the Covenant, and when I am fearful and full of doubt, I turn to the rituals and formality of the Scrolls for comfort." He turned to his friend. "Thank you, Joel! May you always be about me to remind me."

"But, Father," Michal interrupted. "May I say?"

"Yes, of course."

"As I understand what Grandmother Janina and Aunt Abadantha have taught us, and I think you already know this, too, but perhaps have forgotten." She looked up at her father from a slightly bowed head and lowered lids so not to seem aggressive and offend him. Saul smiled, nodded and gently tilted her head erect. "In times of great difficulty and stress," Michal continued, "it often *seems* one must make a choice of either the Covenant or the Scrolls, but in truth, both are always available, two aspects of the One God. It is not either/or, but both/and."

Not to be out-shown by a girl, especially one younger than he, Jonathan said, "Yes, Father." He paced and gestured. "You remember in the story of Devorah and Barak, Devorah, embodied both the Scrolls *and* the Covenant."

"Indeed," Abner said, as he entered the tent and joined the conversation.

"Devorah embodied both, the war-like, iron power of the Scrolls and the compassionate, humanity of the Covenant. But, at another level of the story, Barak represents the danger of either/or thinking of relying solely on one or the other." He saluted and the King returned his salute. "Each aspect has its place, its time and its season."

"But," the King said. "I am prone to the Scrolls. As Joel pointed out before you arrived, Abner, too much into my fear and doubt and not enough with my blessings." He opened his arms to his children, who stepped into them.

"There is truth in what you say, Cousin," Abner said. "Joel and I have known you all your life. But now there is also reason for you to doubt and be fearful."

"Indeed, Majesty," Joel said, stepping towards the King. "You are the first King of Israel! We have never had a King before. You have had little to prepare you; nothing! We are invaded and have no army."

Saul nodded.

"More than enough to worry any man, Father," Jonathan said. "Do you remember a conversation we had before your coronation?" Saul looked a question at his son. "About experiencing God's Oneness, about the peace of submission to His will, surrendering doubt and wondering what that would feel like?" King Saul's eyes shone with sad recognition. "Since then I have come to realize that perhaps because we are men, you and I may never know that experience of Oneness that Abadantha and Janina have, that total loss of self and deep surrender, the blessing of faith and certainty."

Jonathan looked away, voice choked. Saul touched his shoulder. "But I want to feel it, Father! I *want* to, as I know you do, especially at a time like this. We must go on, Father, without it. But even so, you are not alone." Jonathan gestured broadly, to include them all. "We are your minions, Sire; we are your men." He winked at Michal, who slapped his arm. "It is our job to help you stay balanced, sort through the challenges and choose aright."

Tears of joy started in the corners of the King's large brown eyes. He was a big man, a head taller than everyone else, but still had the soul of an innocent babe. "Oh, God," he prayed silently. "Thank you for this! Oh, Abba, have mercy on Thy servant; fill my heart with gratitude, peace and virtue. Guide me, for of myself, I can do nothing."

He cleared his throat and walked to the maps on the table, some of parchment, others of sheepskin. He pointed and touched his finger to the place. The others gathered around him. "Here is Jabesh."

"And here," Michal said, leaning forward, making a half circle around her father's finger, "are the Ammonites."

"Given the inexperience of our commanders," Saul said. "It is very risky to divide our forces."

"But, Sire, you, yourself, said we would appoint my experienced warriors and Abner's to leadership positions. Surely that will suffice?" Joel turned to Abner for confirmation.

Abner agreed, nodding vigorously. "Our spies tell us we have perhaps 70,000 to 80,000 more men than the Ammonites. But ours are, as we have said, farmers, armed with what... " He paused and looked around him. "Sticks, rakes, and hoes."

"Half of them," Jonathan said, frowning.

"And the other half?" Abner asked.

"We have perhaps one hundred thousand swords, bronze swords at that, which will shatter against Ammonite iron. And maybe twenty or thirty thousand men at the most who know how to use them."

"We have enthusiasm and the Lord God Yahweh on our side," Michal said, then blushed as they all stared at her.

"We must use our greater mass to overwhelm them," Saul said. "That is why we need to concentrate our force, not divide it. Yet, we have few sling men and fewer archers, so we must employ a more mobile strategy and cannot plan on luring the enemy into a set piece trap."

"Indeed," Abner said, leaning over the largest map and pointing. "But look here, Sire. The Ammonites have divided their forces!"

The King leaned forward, hands on the table, staring at the map as Abner pointed.

"Our spies tell us, their greatest numbers are thickly encamped around the city's walls, but they have two substantial outposts here, in the east, and here, in the south. Were we to divide our force into three, two smaller forces for each of the outposts and one large one for the troops surrounding the city… "

"Yes, Sire," Joel said. "Do you see? We could put our best trained and armed people at the front of our two smaller columns and they could be like the head of a spear, punching through the enemy's defenses."

"I see it," Jonathan said. "And," he, too, leaned forward, "if we coordinate our attacks, make it seem as if one of our columns had failed and broken and run, we might be able to lure the troops inside the city to come out and give chase. Then… "

"Then," Abner said. "The main body, which we will have kept out of sight, can fall on them from behind as they chase our fleeing column."

"Yes!" The King said. "Once assured the bulk of the Ammonites have left the siege, our main body chasing can send part of its strength into the city to hold it." The King stood and smiled. "Of course, our column that seems to be fleeing will turn and we will have the Ammonites in a pincers, trapped between us, where our mass of poorly armed men can hack and beat them to death!"

"I would put the main body here," the King pointed to the map, "in the west, behind those hills." The others dipped their heads in agreement. "Which column shall flee and turn? That is the most sensitive job."

"I will take that column, Sire," Abner said. "And I think it should be this one, here, in the east." He patted Joel's shoulder. "And with all due respect to your brother-in-law, rather than have my spearhead, my best people and arms to the front, I will have them to the rear, ready to turn and fall upon the enemy."

Joel nodded enthusiastically. "And when we polish off our outpost we will join in the rout!"

Michal was standing back from the maps, hands on hips. "And which column shall I be with?"

The King started to dismiss his daughter's question, but looking more carefully at her face and marshal pose and letting the firmness in her voice settle in his mind, he said, "You shall be with me, Michal; and I will be grateful for your presence." The young woman smiled, and stepped forward to hug her father. "Jonathan," the King said after releasing himself from Michal's hug, "you will go with Abner."

"Yes, Father! Thank you, my King!" Jonathan clearly thought that was the place for him.

"Joel," Saul continued, "You shall command the southern column." Saul paused, thinking. "I think this southern column does not need the same strength as the eastern force, because Abner's column will have to stand and fight alone for a short time before Michal and I can fall on the Ammonites from behind."

Michal pulled herself more erect and smiled. "Therefore, let's give Abner the extra strength. Agreed?"

The two generals nodded and Joel saluted smartly, then looked away.

"Something on your mind, old friend?" The King asked.

"Yes, Sire. Do I have your permission to speak freely?"

The King nodded.

"I think that Abner would agree with what I shall say." Abner's face was non-committal. "We have no choice but to liberate Jabesh and defeat the Ammonites; and our battle plans are sound." He looked searchingly into the King's face. "But, it is the Philistines we must really deal with."

Saul scowled and Joel turned to Abner for support.

"Father, Joel is right!" Jonathan said, voice burning with passion and anger. "We have tolerated them for too, long!"

Abner agreed, though more dispassionately. "The Philistines occupy our land, Saul; they have since we were born, do now. They have a military governor in Gibeah, not far from your father's estates."

Jonathan cursed and spat. "Why do we allow it, Father?"

Saul put his hand on his son's shoulder to soothe him. "It has been this way for generations. The Philistines are stronger, better organized, better armed." The King looked slowly from one to the other. "We *will* deal with the Philistines; we have to. Now that I am King and begin pulling the tribes together, they dare not leave us alone." Saul sighed and smiled a quiet, sad smile. "I thank you all and am grateful for your good counsel. But I am sad when I think of the Philistines, because I know it will be an endless series of battles, some of which we will win, but fighting that will last my entire reign."

Although the King wanted to hear words of solace and even disagreement, he heard nothing. Everyone was silent; the truth of his words, incontrovertible. "Fine," he said. "Let's be about the business of today, the Ammonites." He brightened a bit. "That, at least will be quick and decisive." Then his face darkened again. "Of course, that victory shall put more pressure on the Philistines to deal with us."

"Unless we deal with them first, Father," Jonathan said.

Saul nodded. "One thing at a time, Jonathan. Abner, Joel, go forth and divide our force as we discussed. Distribute our experienced warriors in command positions. Remind everyone we will be fording the Jordan under cover of darkness. Our northern brothers may be unfamiliar with this and fearful. Reassure them that the Lord God Yahweh is with us. When all of this is done, summon me; we shall pray and then take up our positions. I want us to be in place shortly after dusk tomorrow. Abner will begin his action, two hours before dawn the following morning." The King saluted, the others returned his salute and left the tent.

Saul paced, restlessly, his headache had returned and butterflies danced in his stomach. He wondered, where was Samuel?

From their position in the western hills overlooking Jabesh, they were hidden from the view of the Ammonites surrounding the city. King Saul and his daughter were able to see for a distance of nearly three miles and observe almost the entire area of the unfolding battle. Michal had never seen anything like the sweep of huge columns of maneuvering men. Neither had her father for that matter, and both of them were in awe and a little frightened. Michal's energy was contagious and, although he was not as enthusiastic as his daughter, the King was eager to engage.

In the distance directly ahead of them, Abner's column had ceased its forward movement and individual units to the rear were forming phalanxes. Just below them, the thousands of Ammonites in front of Jabesh swarmed into two columns and rushed towards Abner's soldiers.

"When do we go, Father?" Michal asked.

"Look there," Saul said, pointing to Joel's column as, with the loud "THWACK!" of colliding men, shields and armor, it flowed into the Ammonite outpost in the south.

"It's like watching the confluence of two streams," Michal said. "Oh!" she exclaimed, "Oh! Oh, how terrible! They are being hacked to death! Joel's men are hacking off heads and arms and legs!"

The curved, slashing swords in the hands of Joel's trained five hundred, even though made of bronze, were deadly and dripped with blood and gore.

"The Ammonite's were totally unprepared, Father. Oh, what horror! The blood is everywhere!" Michal turned away and buried her head in her father's chest. The King stroked her armored head and shoulder. "It *is* terrible, Michal. You need not look anymore, and you need not go when our turn comes."

"No, Father, it is my duty. I am a royal princess. I will know what must be done and will do it!"

The King leaned down and kissed her cheek tenderly. "You are a blessing to me, Michal. Look now, Joel is nearly done with the southern outpost and he turns to the city. We go!" The King gave the signal and the ten men with ram's horn shofars, the war trumpets dating to Moses' time, sounded the charge. He and Michal pulled their circular slashing swords from their scabbards, and surrounded by thousands of other screaming Hebrews, rushed and tumbled down the hills.

As they neared the city's western wall, a column of two thousand men broke off from the charge, dispatched the Ammonite guards at the gates and swept into Jabesh to mop-up the remaining Ammonites. King Saul's main column swept on, still many yards from the Ammonite army running ahead of them. Michal was running, waving her sword and screaming as loud as she could, when suddenly, perhaps one hundred yards ahead of her the enemy column slowed down and with a huge "THRUMP!" seemed to stop and stand still.

Abner's troops must have turned and engaged them! Oh, how well their plan was working! Michal looked around for the King and saw him well ahead of her, leading the charge, as with another "THWACK!" her own column fell upon the enemy. The impact rumbled and reverberated back to her and she was knocked to the ground. Dust filled her mouth and nose and eyes and she would surely have been trampled to death by her own people if the team the King had secretly assigned to protect her had not surrounded, shielded her, and scooped her up. She was too grateful and disoriented to take offense or to resist as they moved back and away from the battle.

Jonathan heard the shouts, the thunderous crash of Joel's column against the Ammonite's southern outpost, and the shrieks of pain. He was afraid. His eyes teared. He couldn't stop swallowing, his mouth was so dry, and his heart beat as if it would burst through his chest. "My first battle is moments away. I might die here, or be maimed or crippled. Please, Lord God Yahweh, not maimed or crippled. Death if it be Your will, but not maimed or crippled."

The column ceased its forward motion. Abner came running by, followed by the shofar men, horns blaring, rallying their soldiers. "Turn, men! Turn! We engage! Swords out; prepare to fight!" and as the others obeyed, Jonathan did also, fear forgotten. "I must be with Abner," he thought. "I must learn how to fight and how to lead." Pushing through his fellows, Jonathan came to the outside of the column, pulled out his sword, and ran screaming after Abner. Just as they engaged the on-rushing Ammonites, Jonathan reached Abner. In spite of the hellish noise and dust, Jonathan heard Abner's voice as if in the calm silence of the King's tent. "Good man, Jonathan! Your father would be proud! Stand by me, back to back, we will fight here and win King Saul's first great victory!"

"Form up, men!" Abner shouted and the shofars sounded a series of short blasts, signaling his command. "Form your phalanxes!" Quickly, with Abner's skilled warriors in command, the entire column, some hundred thousand men, formed into a zigzag series of hollow squares, each two men deep becoming the famous Assyrian phalanxes, a battle maneuver the Hebrews used well. The phalanxes were like rocks in a stream of on-rushing Ammonite soldiers. The first three or four phalanxes broke in the onslaught, but the others held, and as the Ammonites lost the momentum of their charge. The phalanxes held; the Hebrews moved from the defense to the offense and began hacking up the scattered Ammonites.

The discipline and effectiveness of the phalanxes was exhilarating! Jonathan had never seen their likeness in human cooperation. They seemed almost like a force of Nature to him. He and Abner rushed between the phalanxes, encouraging and praising the men, fighting their way from one unit to another. Jonathan's sword arm and wrist were nearly numb, he was covered with blood and carnage but he was learning.

The stench was beyond anything Jonathon could imagine, not just the sweat, blood and vomit, for soldiers, like other men when afraid or badly wounded released their bowels, and the stink of shit and urine mixed with vomit was everywhere. It was difficult to stand upright, much less move forward in the litter of bodies and hacked-off limbs. An Ammonite came at him, shrieking, eyes wide, spear thrusting. He lunged to his left, but too late. The spear grazed his side and he dropped his sword. As the Ammonite slowed and turned for another thrust, Jonathan crouched, pulled out his long dagger, braced it against his knee and let the Ammonite's forward motion impale himself on the three-foot blade. Blood gushing from the writhing dead man, spurted into Jonathan's eyes, nose and mouth. He coughed, spat, rolled beneath the dead man's weight and passed out.

When he woke beneath the body, perhaps thirty minutes later, the battle was nearly over. Jonathan pushed the dead weight off him, wiped the gore from his face, and got to his knees. He was terribly thirsty, as thirsty as he'd ever been in his life. As he slowly stood up, he realized he'd pissed and shit himself. He was momentarily ashamed, then despite his shame and disgust, he gulped in the stinking air and felt grateful, so very grateful, to be alive.

It was still difficult to see; he kept wiping his eyes while stumbling along. Only water would get them clean. Finally, he gave up, stopped wiping, accepted the pain and poor vision and hoped he was not blinded. Moments later, as he moved toward a clump of shadowy figures, Jonathan heard his name called. It was Joel!

"Jonathan! Thank God!" Jonathan recognized the voice but could barely recognize Joel's face. "Here," Joel said. "I have water." He put the skin to Jonathan's mouth. "Drink!"

Jonathan nearly passed out from the bliss of its gushing wetness!

"A moment; enough, here."

Jonathan felt the water spilling over his head and face and into his burning eyes. "Oh, God, thank You!" He thought, rubbing his face. His eyes ceased burning; he blinked and could see! He hugged Joel. "Is the King well, and my sister?"

"They are well, and we have won a great victory!"

Jonathan hugged Joel again. "We have captured, Nahash, the King of Ammon, along with 100,000 of his warriors, much food, many women, and thousands of iron weapons, perhaps enough to equip 15,000 men!"

"Then we can attack Philistia!" Jonathan exclaimed.

"Easy, nephew, easy! Not so fast, we have to lick our wounds and consolidate."

"What were our casualties, Joel?"

"It is still too early to say with certainty. But I would guess only ten or twenty thousand dead and an equal number wounded."

"A great victory indeed!" Jonathan said.

"Yes. But remember, each of those dead probably left a family, wife, mother, children, sister, elders, who now will depend on the King for their welfare. Each one is a precious life. Each one wounded or maimed will never be the same and may also become dependent on the Crown."

"Yes, Uncle, I had forgotten that. Many will be wailing all across our country. It is a high price, but at least it yielded victory." Jonathan gripped his side, tried to staunch the seeping blood, rocked a little then grabbed hold of Joel to steady himself.

"Let's look to that wound of yours," Joel said, dropping to one knee. He poured water on it, probed a bit then picked up some moss and smeared it over the ooze. "This will staunch it for now. It is not deep; it will have to be cauterized." Joel stood. "I saw Abner not far away. Let us join him, and then find your father and sister."

Michal and the King were overjoyed to see Jonathan. They were bruised and dirty, but otherwise in good shape, as Joel had said. They had been talking with Abner about what to do with the thousands of prisoners and how to divide the spoils. After greeting and hugging, it was decided that the Crown would take 50%, the generals 5% each, 2 % for officers and the remainder to be equally divided among the mass of men.

Abner was pleased. "The Crown will need its share to look after the families of the dead, take care of the wounded, establish its foundations and, build the Army. We must have a standing Army. We cannot rely on these conscripts."

"Agreed," King Saul said. "That is why I would share the spoils with our fighters. I want them to see the value in what they do when they are not tending to their private affairs."

"Even with a share of the spoils, that will be difficult to accomplish, Father," Michal said. "Already, there is grumbling about going home."

Joel agreed. "Most of these men fought by clubbing, kicking, and wrestling the enemy. They are not soldiers and do not want to be soldiers. Surprise and the sheer weight of our numbers carried the day for us."

"It is true, Sire," Abner said. "Our tactics and the excellent use of our experienced warriors made the difference." He shook his head. "By all means, give the farmers, shepherds, bakers, butchers, olive growers and wine makers their share, but we can't count on them now. It will take a generation or two to breed a tradition of professional soldiering."

Saul knew they were speaking the truth, but he was terrifically frustrated. "I don't have a generation or two! Our enemies surround us now!"

"We are the next generation, Father," Michal said. "Jonathan, me, and all our brothers and sisters."

"Yes, yes, I know;" King Saul seemed distracted as if listening to a voice only he could hear. "I want to build our House on a firm foundation. I am not sure of the future; I want to be sure, must be sure." His voice became a barely audible, harsh croak. "What will become of the House of Saul?" His head throbbed.

"We have nothing to lose by asking and accepting those among our men who want to join," Abner said. "I also want to recruit the best of the Ammonite prisoners. They are soundly defeated; we will not fight them again, so we have nothing to fear from them, nor they from us. Perhaps they would like to join us in the fight against the Philistines."

Saul brightened a bit. "Yes! Good idea. And the rest of the prisoners?"

"Slaves," Joel said. "We need repairs to the Temple in Nob. We need fortifications at Gibeah. We need a palace for our King. We will need food and materials for our new army. We will need storage facilities for the taxes of grain and oil. The defeated Ammonites will do all of that for us so it will not be necessary to burden the tribes with labor."

A strange light shone from Jonathan's eyes and he pulled himself more erect. "Will we really have all of those things, palaces, forts, an army, Father?"

Catching his son's vision and new sense of power and destiny, King Saul also stood taller. "Yes, my son; indeed we will!"

Jonathan smiled an inward smile imagining how it might feel to have such power and glory. Would it be an adequate replacement for the experience of Oneness he sought? The bliss of selfless surrender: would it fill the aching emptiness he felt deep within him?

But, in the days that followed, the rains were heavier and the weather cooler than normal. Good for the grapes, olives, and vegetables, but not good for construction. The Ammonite prisoners lay idle, penned up, contributing nothing while consuming valuable grain and the resources to guard them.

Jonathan and Michal were frustrated, but the King seemed not to mind. He drifted back into the life of a gentleman farmer, tending his vineyards, breeding livestock, and supervising sowing, hoeing, and weeding, his kingly duties seemingly forgotten. Jonathan burned with the vision of monarchical glory and victory over Philistia. Michal shared his vision, but not as intensely. Her experiences during the war changed and softened her ambition.

Michal used the cold damp days to sit with her Aunt Abadantha and go deeper into the Covenant, while Jonathan, feeling like a trapped animal, paced and railed against God for allowing the Philistines to oppress them. While Michal talked of dealing with Philistia by aligning with Spirit and feeling at one with It, Jonathan paced and silently railed against God for allowing the Philistines a monopoly on iron-smithing. Jonathan had little patience for the philosophy of the Covenant, despite his love for his sister and the new respect he felt for her since the battle at Jabesh. He understood God to be distant and almighty, not one with him. Yahweh was separate and much more powerful than he, Jonathan, was. There was nothing to 'align' with, only some very powerful, magical thing to be feared, appeased and sacrificed to.

Always good with numbers, maps and diagrams, Jonathan drew up plans for fortifying Gibeah, once the Philistines were driven out.

*Saul*

The idea that the hated, heathen enemy occupied the very town Saul, King of Israel, called home, that was for all intents and purposes, the capital of Israel, the land promised him by the Lord God Yahweh Himself, tore at Jonathan's soul, weakening him physically and emotionally.

So torn was he, that the young prince would mount his horse and ride to town to harass the Philistines there, the mercenaries, mostly Moabites, merchants and administrators, and the Governor himself. Jonathan was not arrested nor hindered in any way, because the Philistines were not yet ready for the war that would surely follow such action. Jonathan knew this and thus his provocations. Saul's six other children, with the exception of his son Ish-Boshet, were uninterested in their father's life as King of Israel.

Another thing that not only bothered Jonathan but made him deeply concerned for his own future, especially given his father's brief, half whispered croak about the future of the House of Saul, was their inability to recruit a standing army. Leaving this undone was both unthinkable and dire. Unthinkable, because Jonathan couldn't understand why, given the chance, most men would refuse to serve in the new nation's army. Dire, because without a standing army of at least 30,000 men, not only would they be unable to protect themselves from marauding tribes, they would be unable to launch offensive actions against the Philistines.

Jonathan swore he would find a way to liberate the land, with or without a standing army! The system of tribal militia they used to beat the Ammonites, and had used since the exodus would have to be used again, and again, until the people realized they needed something better. At least now, they had the heart of a standing army, with Joel's 500, Abner's 1,500 and 1,000 Ammonite mercenaries.

Prince Jonathan went and trained with these men every day. They were becoming proficient not in one weapon, but in the full range of weapons–double edged swords, their own curved slashing swords, long and short daggers, spears and javelins, battle axes, slings, bows and arrows. They were learning the tactics of the nations that surrounded them, including Assyria and Egypt, taught by mercenaries from those nations. Every one of them had fought at Jabesh and many places before Jabesh. They were professionals in King Saul's service, well paid and fiercely loyal. Some had families, many of which lived in new quarters erected near the King's compound. They had horses for the leaders, but no cavalry or chariots. Those would come in time, but they practiced tactics for countering chariots and cavalry.

Jonathan's growing militancy and King Saul's drift from his monarchical responsibilities was a concern for Joel and Abner as well, and also for Abadantha and Janina. It seemed the further Saul retreated from being King, the more militant Jonathan became. Two weeks after the victory at Jabesh, with the situation showing no signs of fixing itself, Abadantha and Janina had a serious talk as they walked and surveyed the new construction.

"Will you talk with him, mother?" Abadantha asked.

Janina laughed, sadly. "I would if it would do any good. No, daughter, you have much more influence with him than I."

"It cannot be me alone telling him," Abadantha said.

"Talk with your husband," Janina suggested. "If Joel agrees, perhaps have a Sabbath dinner and invite Abner and the King. Speak with Abner beforehand."

"Yes!" Abadantha was pleased and enthused. "I think that will work, and I'm sure the others will agree!" She leaned forward and hugged her mother.

# Chapter Eight

"How do you like the barracks the prisoners are building for our new Ammonite mercenaries?" King Saul asked Joel. They stood in the expanded great room of the King's palace; all the families, nearly 30 people, milled around talking and shouting. It was almost time for the Sabbath blessings.

"Fine, Sire," Joel answered. "But other than that, the prisoners are doing nothing; they're idle. Only a handful of them are working here on your palace and on the barracks. There's a lot more they could be doing."

King Saul turned away.

Abner touched his shoulder and walked him to a quiet corner. "Step back for a moment, Sire. Imagine yourself on a mountaintop looking down on our land. Imagine you can see for miles and miles. See the olive groves, the fields of wheat, barley and millet, the vineyards, the roads, small towns, the weaver, butchers, artisans, priests, cities, flocks of fowl, sheep and herds of cattle and oxen. Now see the people, the children, elderly, men and women. See them at work and play, singing and dancing, smithing, thrashing, planting, weaving, selling, trading, cooking, birthing and dying. See all this in our promised land as God might see it."

King Saul shut his eyes, visualizing all Abner described, seeing as God saw. A slight smile of appreciation played in the corners of his mouth.

"All that you see needs a government, a steady, wise and compassionate hand to guide, preserve and prosper it."

The King dipped his head in agreement, eyes still closed.

"*You* are that government, Sire; you are King Saul, the anointed of Yahweh, first King of this Promised Land."

The King opened his eyes and looked sharply at Abner.

"Abner speaks the Truth, Brother," Abadantha said, walking up to them. "You're life cannot be as it was. You can no longer content yourself with your private estates when the Lord has given you *His* estates to care for. The House of Saul must be a good steward in the house of the Lord."

Saul smiled, leaned forward and kissed his sister's firm, sweet smelling cheek.

"The picture Abner paints," Joel said, joining them, "is good and it is the image we want to hold in our minds; it is our goal, our purpose. But it is only a partial picture, Sire, incomplete. It lacks the Amalekites, Philistines, Moabites, Egyptians and Assyrians."

The King crossed his arms, staring at Joel.

"The people yearn for a government that can both prosper *and* protect them, Sire," Joel continued. "The people yearn for *you*. You are their King, Sire. They, we," he gestured inclusively, "are depending on you to be the best King you can be." He leaned forward to add emphasis to his words. "We know you cannot do it all yourself. No one expects you to! But we do expect you guide things, to make the laws, policies and plans for the entire nation in all its aspects—political, religious, military, agricultural and trade, and to appoint good men to serve in your name."

Abner too, leaned forward. "Joel is correct, Sire. You can also think of it like the army. You know and understand the army. Every aspect, supplies, intelligence, training, strategy and tactics, must be considered, must have a team of leaders responsible to the General. You are that General, Sire. As King, you can no more ignore politics or agriculture any more than a general can ignore intelligence or tactics. The vision that you hold in your heart, the same picture Joel and I painted a moment ago, is your, our, the Nation's over-all mission."

"You are subtle, beloveds," the King said, hands on hips, smiling. "And I appreciate your delicacy; after all, I am King. But I see now that I have been remiss in my duties. I appreciate your forbearance, but King Saul is not as fragile as you seem to think. I can take the unvarnished truth from my family and closest advisors; and in fact need it desperately and rely on you for it. Thank you for returning me to the path."

He walked to a small table in the corner followed by the others, picked up the thin simple circlet of gold that served as his crown, that up until now he had disliked wearing and had taken it off when he'd entered the room. Now he set it on his head. "I am Saul, King of the Promised Land, and will rule it!" The room was quiet; everyone had gathered 'round the King. "I am God's anointed and will act as such. I will never again remove this crown in public. I am your King and you," he gestured inclusively, "are my loyal subjects." He paused, energy shifting, and looked down. "I am not perfect; you who know me best know that. I will make mistakes. But I know, no matter what, I will be able to count on you, that you will always be my loyal subjects."

"Long live King Saul!" Abner said. Everyone joined in. "We, his faithful subjects pledge to serve him loyally no matter what mistakes he might make!"

The King bowed deeply from the waist and led them to the heavily laden Sabbath table. "After our Sabbath feast, we shall come together in counsel to structure the Nation's affairs more formally, to appoint good and loyal individuals to oversee them, and to aggressively pursue our building and construction activities, the first of which will be to complete this palace!"

After the Sabbath ceremony, the celebratory meal, and the King's promise to take hold, Jonathan felt a bit more centered and a little more calm. As the others left the table, he sat and watched the house slaves clear it. One in particular, Shasheesha, an Ammonite they'd captured, caught his attention. She was demure enough and respectful, but it was clear from her demeanor—head up, nose in the air, that she hadn't been a slave in Ammon. She caught him looking at her and stared back, almost arrogantly, before looking away. Her body was full and comely beneath her austere, white servant's robes, full breasts thrusting against the rough woolen fabric. He wondered if that rough cloth stimulated her nipples.

She wasn't very tall; the top of her head came to Jonathan's chin. Shasheesha's hair, a long, lustrous black, was bound in twin braids. What would it feel like? It shines so; what would it be like to unbraid it and feel it's softness on his chest and erect penis? And those large striking eyes, wide apart and a bright, smoldering brown. When she looked at him with that look, as she'd done a moment ago, he thought he could feel raw power surge directly from them into his heart. And how easily the small nose set into the perfect oval of her face flowed into those full lips tinged with red, as were her toenails, in honor of her patron, the Goddess Astarte, full lips Jonathan yearned to touch with his own.

As he watched the sway of Shasheesha's generous hips against her robe, what would it be like to be that robe? And the way the robe clung, outlining the seductive swing of her shapely buttocks, revealing the cleft between into which he longed to bury his face, Jonathan erected. It had been a long time since he had lain with a woman, not in the weeks before Jabesh, and not in the days since. The preparation for war and its horrible reality had disrupted the normal pattern of his life. Now in the war's aftermath, Jonathan was feeling the pent up longing and deep, unconscious frustration that came from it.

Jonathan thought Shasheesha was aware of the effect she was having on him. As she reached for the bowls in front of him, she brushed his bare arm with her fingertips, felt him tremble and looked into his eyes provocatively, holding them with her own. A moment later, feeling him tremble, she backed away, carrying the bowls, a hint of her scent lingering in the warm, moist air. Jonathan blinked and shook himself, inhaling deeply, savoring the odor, then, willing his erection to subside, stood and looked around. He saw his grandmother, aunt and sister watching him, smiling. He walked over to them, the last of his erection disappearing.

"The slave is quite attractive, isn't she, Brother?" Michal asked. "Too bad the female warriors in our family can't have their pick of the male slaves."

Jonathan smiled and dipped his head. "Indeed, Sister. A warrior like you deserves her pick and any man would be lucky to lie with you!"

"Thank you, brother!"

"What have my ladies of the Covenant been talking about, aside from me? Planning to go into the Council meeting?"

"We are," Abadantha said.

"But you, Jonathan," Janina said, "are a much more interesting topic!" The three women laughed and Jonathan thought, not for the first time, how young his grandmother looked when she laughed. "In what way?" he asked.

"In the family way," Michal answered.

Jonathan raised his eyebrows in an unspoken question. "You seem not to be interested in taking a wife and starting a family. The slave woman is attractive in a foreign way, darker and fuller than our woman." She ran her hands over her body, forcing her light azure robe to outline her lean form. "But she is no substitute for a wife."

"Who's to say?" Jonathan asked. "She has the look of a princess about her, doesn't she?"

Ahinoam joined them. "She does, and the hands and skin to go with it. She's done more work here, since she's been a house slave, than she's done in her entire life until now. Still, son, what I overheard and brought me to you, does need to be dealt with. You must take a proper Hebrew wife and continue our line. The House of Saul is depending on you!"

"Yes, Mother," Jonathan said, testily. "We have had this conversation before and I agree with you. I will marry when the right alliance presents itself, perhaps with one of the wealthier families in Samaria. Now," he turned in the direction the slave woman had gone, "all I want to do is to lie with a woman, any woman, perhaps that slave woman, in peace!"

"The Council is beginning!" Joel called from the Assembly Hall. "Please join us, come, attend the King and give him the benefit of your counsel."

As they began walking into the Assembly Hall, Jonathan turned and thought he saw the Ammonite woman smiling at him from the kitchen doorway.

At first, Jonathan found it difficult to concentrate on the Council. His thoughts kept drifting back to the suggestion of the woman's lush curves beneath her robes and her carmine tipped toenails and lips; and he erected. But this Council held the promise of finally moving forward on all he valued most, so for now, Jonathan resolved to seek out the slave woman later and think of her no more.

"We have a number of pressing concerns," the King began, "that I would like your counsel on. But I see them all relating to one single over-arching goal establishing the House of Saul on a solid foundation. Such a foundation would mean establishing an administrative framework for the monarchy independent of the twelve tribes, and would eventually subordinate the tribes to it. All the programs and projects we might initiate–the standing Army, what to do with the prisoner/slaves, constructing public buildings, collecting taxes, constructing fortifications, can be seen to support the one over-arching goal."

Everyone was nodding. "Yes, Sire," Abner said, looking around the long, wide table at the others. "I agree, and I think we all agree. It is good to hear you state the situation so clearly."

"We will need to involve the tribal elders in our planning," Janina pointed out.

"Indeed," King Saul replied. "But they will have less real influence than those of you in this room. We will want the younger men and women, such as Jonathan and Michal, in the true positions of power. The elders will be honored and allowed to save face, but we will enable the next generation."

"Yes, Father!" Jonathan said. "Thank you. If I may say, I think that Abner has the Army well in hand." Abner dipped his head. "To support his work, that both Joel and I are already involved with, we will want to consider which of our cities to fortify. With the proper fortifications, and a bit of training, the conscripts and tribal militia will serve as reliable garrison troops, freeing the Army for more aggressive action."

Saul stood up beaming and opened his arms for his son to come to him. "Brilliant!" the King said, hugging Jonathan. "Magnificent! Is it not Abner, Joel?" They too, were proud of the young man. Perhaps the House of Saul would be established on a firm foundation after all.

"We have a number of viable locations already near cross roads, in defensible positions and close to perennial water sources. Some have been fortified in the past and have ruins and other materials we can employ."

Michal nodded enthusiastically. "And where we don't have existing materials we can always have the slaves bake bricks and carve rock!"

"I know we don't have the time and manpower to fortify all the likely locations," Abadantha said. "But we can create sectors or regions with strong positions supported by still stronger positions in the center, like mothers and daughters." Everyone chuckled at the metaphor but saw the truth in it, and King Saul smiled broadly and heaved a great sigh of relief.

"Who needed Samuel now? he thought, "With all of these loving advisors?" Their comments were not as knowledgeable as those of his Council members, not as shrewd as Abija's or Joel's, nor as clever as Melchor of Ephraim's, Zeror of Judah's. But they were nonetheless insightful, and better than that, they were entirely well meaning. Saul did not have to guard against hidden agendas and potential treachery with these people.

"I very much like your 'mother and daughters' idea, Sister," King Saul said. "And building on that, I think we can take an incremental approach. We need not clear the land of Philistines before we begin."

Jonathan frowned. "We can clear them from sectors where we are strongest, build there, and then move on to the next."

"Like taking a bite of an apple!" Michal exclaimed.

"Exactly," her father said. "We re-claim the Promised Land, one bite at a time."

"I like it!" Abner declared.

"Me, too," Joel agreed.

"I fear it will be too, slow, Father," Jonathan said.

"Slow, but not too, slow," Abner responded. "Besides, the Philistines will view our moves to establish and fortify administrative and military centers of the House of Saul, as provocative."

Jonathan nodded. "They may attack us, even if we don't attack them."

"Yes," the King said. "Asserting my power over the entire nation and all the tribes is a serious threat to them. We will have to strengthen communication between our 'mothers and daughters,' and that will mean better roads, which in turn will mean more trade and commerce, and more taxes to be used for the building."

"Our 'mother' cities," Janina said, "will become centers not just for military and administrative affairs, but for religious and cultural activities as well."

Everyone was nodding. "Good, very good!" King Saul said. "Now let us decide which of our towns and villages shall be 'mothers' and which 'daughters.' He unrolled two large sheepskin maps that had been on the table before him.

"First," Abner said, "although I love the concept of mothers and daughters," he dipped his head to Abadantha, who smiled back, "I suggest other terms; perhaps 'royal' cities for the mothers and 'regional centers' for the next tier, the daughters." A buzz of conversation ensued.

"Does anyone object to royal cities and regional centers?" the King asked. No one objected. "Good," the King said. "Please continue, Abner."

"Thank you, Sire. I think we all know we have two royal cities already, Hazor in the north and Jerusalem in the south."

"Neither of which is even remotely under our control!" Jonathan's words were harsh.

"Presently," Abner said, "neither of which is *presently* under our control." He looked at King Saul then around the table. "We plan not only for today but for the future of the House of Saul." He looked directly at Jonathan. "Do you not claim Hazor and Jerusalem for the House of Saul?"

"I do claim them!" Jonathan said.

"Then we will be planning and working to make that so. For now, I suggest we content ourselves with what we have here, in Gibeah, which we will treat as an almost royal city and the other regional centers, Lachish in the south, and Megiddo in the north."

"Yes!" King Saul said.

"Please don't forget, my son," Janina said. "That all of this will require many people, many *educated* people, scribes, commissioners of varying kinds for trade, agriculture, and taxes, architects, not to speak of the priests and military leaders."

Saul dipped his head. "May I ask you, Mother, to supervise our educational activities, perhaps with Abadantha and Michal's assistance? Education is indeed a multi-generation effort. In the meantime, I fear we shall have to import the skills we need from our more sophisticated neighbors such as Egypt and even Philistia."

The three women nodded their acceptance. "I'd like to focus on a basic level of skills, such as reading, writing and mathematics" Abadantha said, "then allow the military and priesthood and other specialties to do more specific training."

King Saul tilted his head in assent.

"I know most children cannot be spared from the work of their families. But I'd like to offer education to all our children, at no cost. That would mean the royal treasury would have to pay."

The men in the room murmured.

Abadantha held up her hand, "which would mean taxes, but, Sire, education will be the foundation of the House of Saul!"

"You and our mother and Michal work out the details and bring them to me," King Saul said, standing and stretching. Everyone else stood, also. When the King stands, everyone stands. "It is late," he said. "Thank you all for your excellent counsel! We have taken giant steps forward tonight!"

Almost from the moment Jonathan stepped out into the cool night air, his thoughts returned to Shasheesha, were *drawn* to Shasheesha. Why, he wondered? He needed sex, but this feeling, this pull, was something more than sexual arousal, though there was that aplenty. Something about the woman beckoned him; her body was excellent, her scent strong and inviting. But there was something more, a quality of she herself, her personality or will, that Jonathan found fascinating.

Without thinking, he walked towards the slave quarters. "Come to Me. Gaze upon Me." He heard her voice in his mind, though he'd never heard her voice. "I am so desirable. You want Me; you must come to Me!" "Yes," he said aloud. A guard stepped forward and saluted. So engrossed was he, that Jonathan hadn't even seen the man, though he'd been there all along. Embarrassed at being surprised, he returned the guard's salute, took a few steps forward, then stopped.

"What are you doing?" He asked himself. "Shasheesha." "Yes, Shasheesha, and if the guard saw you who else might see you? She's not sleeping alone in the slave quarters you know, many other female slaves are there, too; they'll see you and talk. Shasheesha. She'll still be available tomorrow. Go to bed now. Ask about her tomorrow. This is part of your training; treat it as such. Learn from it. Yes, but, *Shasheesha*. Go now, go to bed, tomorrow you will be more clear-headed. Yes, good, tomorrow." Jonathan turned, passed the guard and went to his room in his father's palace, and dreamt of Shasheesha.

If Jonathan had gone on, into the slave quarters, he most certainly would have been seen, but he also would have seen that in the furthest corner of the long, grim and dirty chamber, behind a curtain made of worn canvas, Shasheesha was alone, leaning over a small flame, fondling a small doll made of woolen cloth and straw, caressing it and stroking it sensuously as she gently hummed and whispered to it, "Come to Me, gaze upon Me, I am so desirable."

So desirable, and Jonathan did go on into the slave quarters and was not seen in his dream. He found the sensual Ammonite woman alone lying asleep on a straw pallet in the furthest corner of the long, grim and dirty chamber, behind the curtain made of worn canvas. No one saw him; no one else was awake. He stood over her, saw the swell of her breasts beneath the thin woolen robe, and watched their gentle rise and fall as she slept. He felt tender, more than passionate. As he knelt to kiss her cheek, her large eyes opened, full sensual lips parted and she asked, "Are you worthy to be my lover?"

Jonathan was taken aback. "Worthy? *I?*" He was on his knees, looking into her large, laughing eyes. "How dare you? I, worthy? I am a Prince of Israel; you are a slave, taken in battle; are you worthy of me?"

"*I?*" she said, mimicking him, leaning up on one arm, large laughing eyes drawing him in, enchanting him. "I, *taken*? No one can take Me. I am a priestess of Astarte, the Goddess of Love. No man takes Me, but I take all men." "Save but one," she thought, "my Master Dathan. Men serve the Goddess by serving Me." She sat up and her robe fell away, revealing large shapely breasts, pink aureoles and erect reddish nipples. Entranced, Jonathan leaned forward to put his mouth there, to taste her sweetness and slake his sudden, fierce desire.

She put a hand to his chest to restrain him, and though he could easily have overpowered her, so great was her spell and his subservience to it, he was restrained. Her eyes, larger now, serious and without the mirth of a moment ago, bore into Jonathan's, ensnaring his mind and penetrating his soul. "You are open to Me now, Prince," she intoned. "My words are your thoughts; you have no thoughts of your own. You are empty save for My words, and crave My words to fill your emptiness. Do you understand and accept all Shasheesha tells you?"

"I understand and accept all Shasheesha tells me," Jonathan said.

"Service and obedience," Shasheesha chanted in her husky voice, eyes glowing. "Service and obedience is what worthy men offer the Goddess. Are you worthy?"

"Service and obedience," Jonathan repeated, his dull eyes staring into her glowing ones.

"Yes," Shasheesha replied, making a series of hypnotic passes across the kneeling man's passive, immobile face. "Service and obedience to the Goddess through service and obedience to Shasheesha, Her priestess. Are you worthy, Prince?"

"I am worthy, Priestess," Jonathan's voice was a dull monotone.

"Will you render service and obedience to Me?" she asked, leaning up and forward, offering him her beautiful breasts. His eyes dropped from hers to drink in her beauty. Feeling her vagina oozing with the thrill of conquest, the priestess of Astarte cupped her breasts, swayed them gently before Jonathan's wide hungry eyes, hypnotizing him further. Then, satisfied the man kneeling before her was in a deep trance, she gently released her breasts, messaging their already stiff nipples, growing ever more aroused, ever more potent and enchanting.

"Speak to Me, Slave," she said in a voice like a slap.

Recoiling as if from a real blow, Jonathan stared into her bottomless eyes, but said nothing.

Shasheesha stood, robe slipping down to her bare feet, the curly hair covering her warm, strong-smelling vagina touching his nose. Blinking, Jonathan reached to brush the wiry tickling hair away. "No," Shasheesha said. "No. Leave it; put your arms at your sides." Jonathan obeyed. "Good, boy," she said. Her voice had a pleased, upbeat lilt that Jonathan liked and wanted to hear more of it. "Just smell; inhale deeply; fill yourself with My odor, the scent of Astarte. The smell of My sex arouses and enchants you. You cannot get enough of it. You want to breathe deeply, to fill yourself with it; and with every breath, your desire to be worthy, to render service and obedience to Me becomes stronger!"

Jonathan obeyed. His penis, now fully erect, throbbed painfully and his balls ached.

"Good, boy," Shasheesha praised again; and Jonathan felt proud and grateful for Her praise and glad he had pleased Her.

"Now," she said, "you have not told me you want to be worthy of Me, that you will render service and obedience to Me." She reached down and tousled his hair as if he were her pet.

His stiff penis jumped at her touch and he sighed. What bliss, his entranced mind thought. But at what price? He was a prince. She was the slave, not he. But no, here he was on his knees inhaling the nasty odor of her warm sex. He must be the slave, not she.

"Yes, I want to be worthy of you, Shasheesha," he said, dreamily, taking in her powerful scent with deep breaths, "I will render service and obedience to you, Shasheesha, Priestess of Astarte."

She patted his head again. "Good, boy," she said. "You are My good boy, My good slave boy, aren't you?"

"Yes," he said, still hungrily filling himself with the heavy odor of her vagina. "I am your good slave boy."

She stepped back and out of her fallen robe, revealing red-painted toenails. "Bow down before your, Mistress and Owner, slave! Grovel before Me. Kiss My smelly feet!"

He obeyed. He was fascinated by the dirty new smell from his Mistress's endlessly enchanting body. The gleaming polish on Her toenails. (Hebrew women did not use polish or rouge.) The sensation of his cock rubbing on the floor as he groveled below Her. The whole idea of what he was doing, the self-abasement, the willing surrender of his rank, status, and pride to a foreign female slave, a priestess of Astarte, the enemy of Yahweh, this sexy, powerfully charismatic, and enchanting woman *made* Jonathan obey.

He wanted to orgasm. His Mistress knew and would not allow it. "No," She said. "Your orgasms belong to Me now, slave, and are to be used as a sacrifice to our Goddess, Astarte. You understand you belong to Shasheesha and Astarte now, don't you Prince Jonathan? She is your Goddess and you are Her worshipper."

"Yes, Mistress," Jonathan said, between passionate kisses and licks of her feet. "I belong to Shasheesha and the Goddess Astarte and am Her worshipper."

The priestess snapped her fingers and her new slave stopped what he was doing, awaiting Her command. "Kneel up!" The slave obeyed. "Gaze deeply into My powerful, hypnotic eyes." The slave obeyed. "Feel yourself sinking deeper into submission to Shasheesha, your desire to serve, obey and please Shasheesha blotting all else from your heart." Shasheesha sat down on her straw pallet, opened her thighs and leaned back on her hands.

Jonathan gasped, at first repelled, then fiercely aroused by the sight of Her hairy, juicy vagina oozing softly glistening milky fluid from between its soft, succulent folds. Its strong, hot erotic odor wafted up to his nose in the chilly night air, merged with the shameless display, the rounded contours of her creamy buttocks with the slightly brown stained skin around her pink rosebud. He had never experienced a woman this way, the essence of her femininity revealed in all its potent glory. Hebrews made love chastely, often wearing their robes. This was a revelation to him—the wonder and power of Astarte. He was both in awe and disgusted.

"Down on all fours, slave!" his Mistress commanded. He obeyed. "You are Shasheesha's slave dog, now. Crawl to your Mistress, put your face into My sacred mound, symbol of Astarte's might, and render service to Her there!" Jonathan obeyed licking, sucking and kissing as Mistress directed, his own need forgotten. Her orgasms were numerous and powerful and as normal consciousness returned to her, she directed the slave to orgasm also. He obeyed, experiencing the most profound sexual culmination of his life, a feeling of total release, surrender and submission, the experience of Oneness he had craved for so long, and then, at Her command fell into an intense, deep sleep.

Humming, Shasheesha reached her hand between her thighs into her warm syrupy vagina, withdrew it and wiped her dripping, reeking juices on what would have been the doll's face, chanting gently to it, "You are Mine, you are Mine, you are Shasheesha's slave, My adoring slave." The fire was burning low now and the first light of dawn shimmered in the cool air. Shasheesha shivered and sighed a deep, satisfied sigh. It had been a splendid, sexy night's work, Dathan would be proud of her. Now it was cold and time to dress. Still holding the precious doll, Shasheesha stood and slipped her thin woolen robe over her voluptuous body. Soon, she thought, soon we will be restored to our former glory! No plain woolen robes or slave quarters. Soon, her new slave, the Hebrew Prince Jonathan, would come to her openly, take her as his concubine and soon after that, she, Dathan, and the almighty Astarte would be powers in the new, emerging state of Israel. Shasheesha sighed contentedly, fell asleep and dreamt of Dathan, the handsome Ammonite warrior chieftain, who ruled her as her Master.

Princess Shasheesha and Prince Dathan had been captured together, hiding in a cave on the evening following the battle at Jabesh. They were trying to make their way north to the Assyrians, when a Hebrew patrol found them asleep in each other's arms. Dathan made no secret of his identity and the next day, demonstrated his strategic and tactical prowess to Abner by showing him on the Hebrew maps, the mistakes the Ammonites had made. Though the man was a prisoner, stripped of rank and treasure, soon to be a slave, he remained proud and arrogant and Abner knew his value. He asked Dathan if he would like to serve as a mercenary in the Hebrew army. Dathan agreed in exchange for his own living quarters, a command and access to the palace slave quarters. Abner agreed.

It had been Dathan who arranged for Shasheesha's private

space so they could make love and worship Astarte. He suggested to Shasheesha that she enchant Jonathan. Dathan had been training with Jonathan, liked him and admired his military prowess. He saw Jonathan as a brave, intelligent, but sexually immature young man, ripe for the enchantments of Astarte. Dathan wanted the Prince under their control, not only so their day-to-day lives would be better but so they might rise to their former power and prominence. He was also sexually attracted to the young Hebrew Prince, the Ammonites having no restrictions on sexual preferences, seeing him as handsome and desirable.

As Jonathan had walked toward the slave quarters after the counsel, King Saul lingered in the Council Chamber, pacing. They'd done well tonight, very well! So why did his head throb so?

Ahinoam came back looking for him. "Come, my husband," she said, going to him to soothe his furred brow. "Sit and let me soothe you." Saul sat and let her minister to him. Her touch was warm and gentle, but helped only a little.

"Elmira said something might be growing inside your skull," Ahinoam said.

"The old midwife?" Saul asked. Ahinoam nodded. "What could grow inside a man's skull?" he said, not completely ruling out the idea.

Ahinoam felt lighter, grateful he considered the possibility, glad to be of help to her man. "It might be a boil or a bruise of some kind."

Saul nodded, but said nothing.

Ahinoam's lightness ebbed away. "Will you go to your sister, tonight?" she asked, continuing to lightly message him, knowing he often did go to Abadantha at times like this.

"Jealous?" Saul asked, standing and letting her hand fall away.

"A little."

He embraced her. "Forgive me, Ahinoam; that was nasty. I have no wish to hurt you. You are a good wife to me. You have given me a wonderful family and are most understanding." Saul hugged her more tightly, feeling a profound sense of gratitude and regret at the same time, hoping that fierce Yahweh would forgive and have mercy on him for violating His edicts and loving his sister more than his wife.

"Truly, I am sorry for the hurt I cause you. My choice is not about you; it is about me... and Abadantha. You know that, don't you?" He held her at arm's length, searching her tranquil eyes with his pained ones.

She nodded and hugged him. "I know that, Saul. It is how I have borne it all these years. You have been a good husband and father and I am grateful."

"Thank you for your understanding and compassion, Ahinoam."

Sighing, she dipped her head, turned and walked out of the chamber.

Saul's head was better, not all right, but better. He'd have to tell Ahinoam and thank her. As he left the chamber, Saul saw his son coming from the direction of the slave quarters, going to his rooms in the other side of the palace. The King waved but Jonathan was walking with his head down, distractedly, and did not see him.

Joel, Abadantha, and their children lived in a new wing of King Saul's expanding palace, in rooms near Janina's. The night was so exceptional, cool, quiet, and filled with stars, that King Saul hoped his sister might be on the verandah. As he made his way there, walking outside the walls, he received and returned salutes from seven sentries, all of whom smiled at him and bowed deeply from the waist. Saul was proud of these men, and the rest of the palace guard, all of them who had been selected from among Joel's well-trained and seasoned group of five hundred.

Abadantha *was* on the verandah, leaning against its low wall, gazing up at the stars. Saul thrilled at the sight of her. A single candle flickered in the room behind her and the sounds of Joel's snoring mingled with the soughing of the wind. She looked down, hearing Saul's approach before she saw him. Becoming more alert, she pulled her cloak more tightly around her and stood erect. Anticipation, not fear, shone in her face. Saul vaulted the wall and they embraced. "I thought you might come tonight," she said, her warm, scented breath spilling across his face.

"How good and wise you are, Sister," King Saul said, kissing her mouth roughly.

Dantha returned the kiss, but reluctantly. "Softly! Softly," she said. "We do not want my husband, your friend, to awaken."

"You think he does not know?" Saul asked, releasing her and stepping back.

"Yes!" Dantha said. "I think he does not know. Joel is a man of great integrity, if he knew, he would at the least separate from me and cease to serve you; at worst, he might try and kill us both."

Saul grunted, recognizing the truth in his sister's words. "But Ahinoam knows," he said.

"Yes," Dantha agreed. "She knows and has known since before you married her. That is a different set of facts and understandings than Joel has." Saul grunted again. Dantha continued, "Joel knows you and I have a special relationship in sharing the Covenant. He does not know about the sex and special rituals." She paused and paced; suddenly feeling chilled, she pulled her robes more tightly around her.

"It is a splendid night," Saul said. "The kind that, when we were younger, we would honor with a ritual of gratitude." She sighed and he put his hand on her shoulder. "Remember, how we would leave our father's house and go into the hills," he gestured, "these very hills, talk of our total oneness with Spirit, sexual and emotional, then make a small fire to offer up my seed?"

Dantha, face grim, had been looking intently into her brother's eyes. Now as the memory of those simpler times suffused her, she smiled gently. "You didn't have many headaches in those days, Brother," she said.

Saul's eyes widened with awareness; he hadn't made that connection before. "You're right!" he said and smiled. "Perhaps the relief and peace I experienced during our rituals accounts for some of that."

"Perhaps," Dantha said. "I don't think so, though."

Pain shot through King Saul's head, from behind his left eye to his right ear, and he cried out, reaching up to soothe it. Then, as quickly as it came, it departed, leaving nausea and dizziness in its wake. Saul rocked, staggered then breathed deep to steady himself. His sister stepped closer to allow him to lean on her. A moment later, he was able to stand on his own. "Ahinoam said Elmira told her that something may be growing inside my skull," he said, sighing and taking another deep breath to steady himself.

Abadantha nodded. "I have heard of such things. What do you think, Brother?"

"I don't know," he said. "What could be done if it were true?"

"The Egyptians have doctors who can open skulls and cure people."

The King was both hopeful and skeptical. "How many do they save and how many do they kill? I'll wager they kill more than they save," he said, answering his own question.

"You are King now, Saul. If we were to send to Egypt, I'm sure one such hakim would come to you."

Saul nodded, another of a hundred things for him to think about and decide. He'd come to his sister for peace and relief, to perform one of their rituals. Now, he was tired, it was late and he was left with one more important thing to think about, one more important decision to make. He sighed, kissed Abadantha chastely on the cheek then eased himself over the wall to return to his wing of the palace, leaving his sister staring after him.

King Saul walked twenty paces and was overwhelmed with the same kind of regret and gratitude he'd felt hours earlier with Ahinoam. He turned back and saw the lone candle go out; Abadantha had gone to bed. "Sleep well, Sister," he whispered. "Sleep the sleep of the just and the innocent. You have all my gratitude for your steadfastness and for awakening the Covenant in me." King Saul turned and continued walking to his own wing of the palace.

"Oh, Father, Mother God," he prayed, "ever present, ever loving, ever giving, ever forgiving Life. Thank You! Thank You for my life and the lives of those around me. Thank You for this glorious night! Thank You for my trials and tribulations, my decisions and choices. Help me to see them differently, as opportunities to go within, to surrender my puny understanding and replace it with Your loving wisdom. Not the pronouncements, commandments, and rituals of the Scrolls, but by the vibrant, living, energy of Your Presence! Oh, please, Father, Mother God, it feels so good, so right to be with You.

Please, not for my sake alone, but for the sake of Your people Israel. Thank You! I know it is done unto me as I believe. I have planted these seeds believing and pray you will not hold my un-belief against me."

# Chapter Nine

In the days and weeks that followed, it seemed to King Saul as if his prayer on the evening of the Sabbath Council Meeting had been answered. His headaches had not left him but they were less intense. He dispatched ambassadors to the nations around Israel and instructed his ambassador to Egypt to inquire about skull surgeons. Jonathan seemed to become gradually more distracted while developing an unusual relationship with Dathan, the Ammonite mercenary, and while this worried King Saul, he said nothing because Jonathan seemed competent as ever in the performance of his duties.

Saul's mother and sister moved rapidly ahead with developing the basic educational system that would become the foundation of his House, using their already strong network of Sisters of the Covenant. Michal divided her time between working with education projects and military training with Dathan and Jonathan. Abner and Joel went together with strong detachments of their best, most professional soldiers to Hazor, Judah, and the regional centers of Lachish, and Megiddo, to establish garrisons, train the militias in those areas, build fortifications and provide security for the administrators, artisans, traders and priests King Saul sent out to establish the royal presence of the House of Saul.

As they moved forward to achieve their respective missions, Janina and Abadantha, Joel and Abner became heads of rapidly growing networks of supporting organizations that spread throughout Israel, and into neighboring lands. Janina and Abadantha tightened the structure of the Sisters of the Covenant to form a hierarchy of leaders both functionally and geographically. Education about the one, innermost God was their mission, but they empowered their regional leaders and subject matter experts, such as those in math and reading, to make most of the decisions. Word of the Teaching of the Covenant spread and people in many foreign lands requested teachers or missions.

Abner and Joel also reached out to foreign lands. The structure of the Army was in place. It needed a great deal of work, of course, but what they were most in need of were mercenaries to fill its ranks. They and their men had served as paid soldiers in the armies of Assyria and Moab. Though they had no illusions about the depth and breadth of the loyalty of such soldiers, they saw the discipline and skills of these men as superior to those of the conscripts available to them. They had no compunction, and little choice, but to recruit outside of Israel. Good generalship would mitigate the likelihood of mass desertions.

As all of this flowed around him, King Saul coped by taking time every day, often many times a day, to pause and commune with the ever present, ever forgiving, inner-most God. Needing no temples or rituals, he simply paused, breathed deeply, shut his eyes momentarily, and asked for guidance, surrendering his limited, incomplete view, asking for God's complete one. On these occasions, the King listened more than he begged, promised, or cajoled, and came away renewed and clear.

He was grateful and indeed, had much to be grateful for. Even Samuel seemed more supportive and engaged. How perverse, Saul thought when he thought about it, which was less and less. Now that he didn't need the old man, Samuel was often there, by his side, advocating for his Master, the God of the Scrolls. Even his corrupt sons, Joel and Abija, and the other Council members seemed more acquiescent.

Initially hesitant to support their King's efforts in education, and administration, the tribal elders began coming around as the military presence made itself felt, the militias became more disciplined and effective, and bandits were driven from the highways and villages into the hills. The increased construction and attendant increase in the use of skilled craftsmen, trade, and business stemming from the

King's aggressive use of the Ammonite prisoners to build public edifices, temples and fortifications, also helped the emerging men of commerce influence the tribal elders to mute their concerns.

As commerce flourished, few complained about the increased taxes of grain and oil. New granaries and storehouses for olive oil built in Hazor and Judah and the regional centers of Lachish and Megiddo fueled the growth further, as did the increased trade with Egypt and Moab as King Saul traded the grain and oil for gold and silver. Ambassadors from these countries as well as all Israel's neighbors, including Philistia, were received at the King's palace in Gibeah and sought residences in that city, bringing with them their retinues, gods, foods, music and styles, while also increasing the price of land and houses. In the retinue of the Philistine ambassador was Captain Hafiz.

A new group of men and women who saw their lives and the lives of their families and communities improving was emerging in Hebrew society. These people understood the role the King played in these improvements and their loyalty to the House of Saul was strong. This group leaned toward the Covenant instead of the Scrolls, lived in the expanding cities and had more money to spend. This in turn stimulated growth in art, music, poetry, pottery, silver and goldsmithing, weaving of finer garments, and more elegant architecture.

Slowly, as the House of Saul prospered, the King began taking himself more seriously, pausing less, getting less guidance. He began to think that he, himself, not his covenant with the Spirit within, was doing the work. Samuel was with him more often and under the old man's influence, King Saul began favoring the rituals and formalities of the God of the Scrolls. He became more concerned with appearances and the trappings of royalty, choosing to let these carry his rule instead of his relationship with God. Of course, the scope of a King's duties and responsibilities naturally contributed to some increase in concern for appearances and formality. To his inner circle, those he relied upon most and who loved him most, Abner, Joel, Abadantha, Janina, Ahinoam, Michal and Jonathan, King Saul's emphasis on these more superficial issues was almost wrong, beyond what was required and painful to them.

They had experienced the gradual shift to prosperity as a wonderful time filled with a sense of purpose, vision, joy, and teamwork they all shared. Their work was the work of a lifetime; it energized them, and mattered to the entire nation, not just themselves. The work seemed blessed, its success pre-ordained. The King's behavioral shift toward appearances, formalities, and intrigues was gradual but the stress of these changes affected his inner group badly. Each felt it in his or her own way.

Abner had little patience for the formal audiences and presentations at Council Meetings and the need to be diplomatic and inclusive about balancing the varying interests of the tribes. Consequently, he saw King Saul less, and when he did see him, their conversations were strained and defensive, and the King's personal involvement in the development of the Army, his personal knowledge of the officers, tactics and regulations, something that would matter during the next war, was limited. Abner was deeply concerned about this, but had not yet found a way around it.

Joel felt much as Abner did, but somehow forced himself to develop the skills of a courtier, taking precious time away from his work with the Army and supervising construction, to await the King's pleasure and serve him by meeting with recalcitrant tribal leaders to sell them the royal military and construction programs. Joel buffered Abner, whom Joel believed was a much better general than he was, thus enabling Abner to go forward almost unimpeded. The strain on Joel was great. He found himself short tempered with Abadantha and their children.

Abadantha and the King used to be able to take an occasional evening for themselves, and though Dantha did not need these rendezvous the same way Saul did, she missed talking with him about the Covenant and suffered as he drifted away from it. Now, the King gave royal entertainments late into the evenings with voluptuous, foreign female musicians, dancers and jugglers, some of who found their way to his bed.

Janina and Ahinoam actually spent more time with the King. The increase in formality made demands on the King's mother and wife that had not been present before. They complained to one another that their time with him was shallow and unsatisfactory, full of diplomatic niceties and meaningless conversations.

Michal thought her father changed, but did not mind. She enjoyed the pomp and ceremony, the status, new clothes and increased influence that came simply by virtue of her position. She strove to maintain her earlier, simpler tastes and values by working with Janina and Dantha, and training with Dathan and Jonathan, but felt them ebbing away nonetheless.

Jonathan was perhaps the most afflicted and most in need of his father's guidance, but lacked it, not because King Saul had shifted, but because he had. Jonathan's dream of Shasheesha had become his reality.

The next morning, upon waking from his dream of enchantment and servitude, Jonathan heard Shasheesha's siren call, "Come to Me, gaze upon Me, I am so desirable."

"Yes, Shasheesha," he whispered, penis rising to salute her.

"Are you worthy? Will you offer service and obedience to Me?"

"Yes, Shasheesha," he whispered, standing, erection bouncing before him as he walked to the washbasin to lave cool water. "I am worthy; I will offer service and obedience to You."

As he splashed the cool water onto his face, a semblance of normal consciousness returned and he looked down at his stiff penis. It felt good to be erect and thrusting forward as he moved. Yet it was a good thing he was a prince and lived alone. Had he been a soldier and lived in the barracks, he'd have to explain. *Shasheesha.* Was she really the way he'd seen her in his dream? He'd never experienced a woman that way, smelly, moist, hot, curvaceous, secret places revealed, offered, ready to be tasted and licked, sniffed and worshipped with his mouth.

Jonathan shuddered and his erection stiffened further. What would it be like to actually *do* those things? God, he wanted to! Would Shasheesha actually let him see her that way, make love to her that way? She did in the dream. But there was a price. Yes, he had to become her slave and the Goddess Astarte's slave. How exciting; forbidden fruit was the most thrilling! When he thought about giving himself to Shasheesha and Astarte as a slave, to bow down naked before them and to grovel, Jonathan's penis jumped again. There were still a number of logistical problems to be worked out. Splashing more water on his face and chest, Jonathan turned his mind to those so his erection would subside and he could finish dressing.

On his way to the dining hall, he prayed, to Yahweh or Astarte, that Shasheesha would be one of the servers. She was. They were practically alone, only he, Dathan, and five other officers were present. Light and fresh, cool air streamed in through the four large casements on either side of the long rectangular chamber. Shasheesha stood in the kitchen doorway at the opposite end of the room. "Come to Me. Gaze upon Me; I am so desirable."

"Yes, Shasheesha," he whispered, penis rising up to salute her.

"Are you worthy? Will you offer service and obedience to Shasheesha?"

Jonathan took a seat opposite Dathan at one of the small, rough-hewn tables scattered around the large banquet table in the center of the room. They exchanged greetings. The Ammonite was in splendid condition. Jonathan admired his broad shoulders and rippling muscles gleaming with oil. Dathan wore the Ammonite training uniform, a short grey woolen kilt with a leather harness over the shoulder and belted round his waist that Abner had adopted for the Hebrew Army. Though dressed the same way, Jonathan felt that his smaller wiry frame was not nearly as impressive as Dathan's. I wonder who puts the oil on him, Jonathan thought, staring at Dathan's rippling muscles. Shasheesha approached them, wearing the same thin white slave's robe she'd worn the night before; and as the night before, it did little to hide her full curves.

"She is quite lovely, isn't she?" Dathan asked, watching the Hebrew Prince slip into trance at Shasheesha's approach.

"Yes," Jonathan said, startled out of his staring reverie, "quite lovely, and special somehow, too."

"Indeed," Dathan agreed. "See the way her eyes sparkle and seem to grow larger as she gazes at you."

"Yes," Jonathan said.

"She was a princess and powerful priestess of Astarte in my country and enslaved many men, bringing them to the Goddess' service. She even enchanted King Nahash. He brought her to Jabesh to appease the Goddess."

Dathan snorted. "A lot of good that did. Now she is a slave; I am a mercenary, and the King is dead."

"I dreamt of her last night," Jonathan said, simply.

Dathan looked knowingly at him. "Good for you. I have been her lover and she is magnificent. Was your dream exciting?"

Dathan? Shasheesha's lover? Jonathan knew he ought to be jealous but somehow he wasn't. Now Shasheesha stood beside Dathan, absorbing Jonathan's will with her glowing, staring eyes.

"Answer Prince Dathan, Slave," she said softly. The other officers left the dining hall. As Shasheesha waited, she massaged Dathan's shoulders sensually, rubbing in the oil, making his flesh shine. Jonathan's penis was erect. He wanted to leave; wanted to stay; wanted to obey; wanted to resist.

Shasheesha watched the struggle on Jonathan's face. Continuing to stare arrogantly into his eyes, nose in the air, full lips pouting, she gave Dathan's shoulders one more sensual rub then walked round the table to stand next to Jonathan. "I want to make this easy for you, slave. I have no wish yet, to embarrass you. Once you belong to Me completely you shall embarrass yourself to please Me. But for now, until you are more deeply in My power we will keep appearances normal."

She leaned closer to him, made two hypnotic passes across his glazed eyes, and exhaled her saliva-scented breath across his face. "Inhale deeply, slave; you who were once Prince Jonathan. Fill yourself with the scent of your Mistress's warm and arousing breath." The slave obeyed. Shasheesha bent and reached a hand down to grasp his penis. "Good boy," she praised, and his heart raced with joy. "My slaves must always be erect in Shasheeshah's presence, saluting their Mistress. Isn't that right, slave?"

Jonathan tried to speak, but could not. His heart leapt and his mind was a blur. He seemed to be struck dumb by the contradictions he was feeling. The public nature of the setting meant that anyone could walk in, and see what was occurring with Dathan, sitting calmly before him. Shasheesha lifted her hand to strike her new slave and awaken him to his true place, but Dathan leaned forward and grabbed her wrist.

"No, Shasheesha," he said softly, calm eyes staring into her surprised and angry ones. "No, not here and not now. You must be completely alone with him. Take him to my room and finish what you have begun so well."

Shasheesha lowered her hand and Dathan smiled into her eyes. "I am proud of you; you have done well." He gestured to the entranced Hebrew. "Your powers have not diminished, they have grown stronger. But as you said, we want no public displays until we are completely ready. Abner must win a few more battles first; my place will be secure. We shall act then. Meanwhile, take him, enslave him and keep him enslaved."

Shasheesha bowed deeply from the waist. "Yes, Master." She snapped her fingers, returning the Hebrew prince to normal consciousness. "Would you like barely cakes or porridge for breakfast this morning, Sire?" she asked. Dathan smiled, said goodbye and rose to leave.

Staring at the Ammonite's gleaming flesh, Jonathan looked from him to Shasheesha and back to him and answered the question. "It was a very sexy and exciting dream, Dathan," he said, "much like the one I just had." As Dathan nodded and walked away, Jonathan turned to Shasheesha. "What would you recommend I have for breakfast, Mistress?"

Shasheesha looked about her and seeing they were alone, leaned forward pressing a breast into his face. Jonathan could feel her erect nipple beneath the thin cloth. "Nothing," she said, "but to suck on this. Come," she said, stepping back and taking his hand. "Let us obey Dathan. Come; we will go to his rooms where you can worship Me properly."

"Yes, Mistress," Jonathan said, smiling into her face, near normal consciousness in his voice and eyes.

As part of his arrangement with Abner, Dathan had two rooms set aside for his private use in the north barracks. The space was sparse and set off from the rest of the building by a hanging mat woven of rushes. The barracks were deserted at this hour and Jonathan felt a momentary stab of guilt that he was not training with the others. Shasheesha led him to the sleeping rug in the furthermost room and gazing into his eyes, returned him to trance.

"You are Shasheeshah's complete and utter slave," she said, voice husky and sensual. "I have only to gaze into your eyes to control you. You want Me to control you, don't you, slave?"

"Yes, Mistress," Jonathan said, eyes glazed, speech slow. "I am Your complete and utter slave and I want You to control me."

"Good, boy," she praised and Jonathan's heart and mind filled with joy. "Good slave boy. You live for My praise, don't you slave boy? You live to please and serve your Mistress Shasheesha." She made a series of hypnotic passes across his face, and he went deeper into trance.

"Yes, Mistress, I am your good slave boy and live for Your praise and to please and serve You."

Shasheesha reached up her hand and slapped his face, viciously, once, twice, three times. Jonathan blinked and began to slip out of trance. "No," his Mistress's voice was stern, confident and had to be obeyed. "You will remain in trance and take your punishment." The slave's eyes ceased blinking and stared straight ahead, as his Mistress slapped him again. "You embarrassed your Mistress in the dining hall, slave!" She slapped him again. "A slave must never embarrass his Mistress; a slave obeys, instantly. Do you understand? Speak, slave! Beg your Owner's forgiveness; beg Me to punish your further!"

Jonathan dropped to his knees, tears forming in his eyes. "Please, my glorious Mistress, my Owner, forgive Your slave boy for offending You! Please, I beg You! This slave had no intention of embarrassing or offending his Owner. Please, forgive and punish your slave so You feel appeased."

Shasheesha smiled. Dathan was right! Her powers were not diminished. In fact, they seemed to have increased. Never had she had such a profound effect on a man in such a short time. She slapped him repeatedly and he rocked with the force of her blows. "Stay still!" she commanded the slave. "Do not rock." He obeyed. Perhaps it was because of their cultural differences. She had never enslaved a

Hebrew before; perhaps this young man's beliefs in God and ways of lovemaking made him more susceptible to her fleshy hypnotic power.

Her hand hurt; she stopped slapping him. His glazed eyes stared straight ahead out of his red face. Her vagina was overflowing. "Now, My good slave boy, your Mistress will reward you for being so obedient and accepting your punishment." She lifted her robe and pulled it over her head. Naked before him, her wiry pubic hair was level with his face. Without being told, the slave inhaled deeply, filling himself with the potent aroma of his Mistress's power. She patted his head. "Good slave boy," she said. "You adore the smells of Shasheesha's body, don't you?"

"Yes, Mistress Shasheesha."

"Good, continue; breathe deeply." The slave obeyed. "Feel yourself sinking deeper into submission to Shasheesha, your desire to serve blotting all else from your heart and mind." Shasheesha sat down on Dathan's sleeping rug, opened her thighs and leaned back on her hands.

"Tell your Mistress what you see, slave."

Jonathan gasped, barely able to speak. It was like the dream but better because it was real. The same emotions of disgust and arousal raced through him. Mistress Shasheesha leaned forward, slapped him, leaned back and he found his voice. "I see the font of my Mistress's feminine power." He inhaled deeply, "I smell my Mistress's feminine power. I am disgusted and aroused. I see Mistress's hairy, juicy vagina oozing softly glistening milky fluid from between its soft, succulent folds. I smell its strong, hot erotic odor wafting up to me; and I am in awe of the shameless display of the rounded contours of Mistress's creamy buttocks and the slightly brown stained skin around her pink rosebud." He was panting and masturbating.

Mistress Shaheesah kicked his hands away from his erection. "No," she said, "only with My permission and I have not yet given My permission. What does looking at My sex and smelling it make you want to do, slave?"

"Slave wants to worship Mistress's sex with his mouth! Oh please, Mistress Shasheesha, allow slave to bury his face in Your vagina to smell, kiss and lick it. Allow slave to sniff and lick and taste the brown stained valley between Your magnificent buttocks, to smell, kiss and worship Your pink anus."

"Down on all fours, Slave!" Mistress Shaheeshah commanded. He obeyed. "You are My slave dog, now. Crawl to your Mistress, put your face into My sacred vagina, symbol of Astarte's might, and render service to Me there!" Jonathan obeyed, licking, sucking and kissing as his Mistress directed. For a while, she held his head in place, but as her climax neared, she dropped her arms to her sides, and lay, legs splayed, in sheer bliss, her buttocks slightly elevated to give him access to her there.

Jonathan was also lost in ecstasy, his experience so much better than his dream! The moist, hot, slightly foul odors filled his nostrils; the damp ooze and slime clung to his lips, cheeks and nose. The salty, tangy, sometimes sour tastes stung his tongue and polluted his mouth. Pre-cum oozed from his sore penis and pent up semen throbbed in his testicles. He was in pain, but beyond pain.

At last, he was whole, complete, fulfilled! He was a slave serving his Mistress. Only She mattered, only Her will and Her body, Her pleasure, and his need to serve it mattered. Her moans and squeals of pleasure, her juices, smells, and flesh drove him on, beyond his own needs and previous limits. A new world opened before him. Nothing could stop him or hold him back. His desire and arousal armored him, made him immortal in Her service. Was this what it meant to serve God? Was Shasheesha, God? Perhaps. Abadantha said God was in everyone, everywhere, equally present. Perhaps, he thought, this was the God in him connecting with the God in her; perhaps his eager and willing submission to Her was his eager and willing submission to God.

Just as the pain in his penis and the pressure in his balls became almost too great to bear, Shasheesha began to buck and thrust her hips up and down and side to side. Even more milky, salty, slightly sour liquid spilled from between the folds of her labia. She thrashed and screamed and shouted. Her orgasms were numerous and powerful and as normal consciousness returned, she directed her slave to lick her clean. She sat up, ready to give him permission to orgasm.

"Your orgasm consecrates you to My service and the worship of

Astarte. From now until the day you die, you shall live as Shasheesha's most obedient servant and willing slave. You shall strive always to be worthy of Me, offering your obedience and servitude. I shall rule over you and you shall find fulfillment, joy and peace as My most willing and obedient servant."

Jonathan began moaning.

"Can you wait longer, slave?" Mistress asked. Jonathan only moaned. "Very well, slave. Cup your hands and shoot your semen into your hands, now!" Jonathan obeyed, screaming in agony and ecstasy as he rolled to his side, spunk exploding into his cupped hands. "Don't lose a drop!" His Mistress commanded. "That is sacred to the Goddess." Jonathan's screams subsided, but he continued twitching, shooting semen into his hands. It was the greatest orgasm of his life; it wiped his mind clean and started him on a new path.

"Listen, slave. Hear and obey; outwardly, your life will not appear very different than before today. You will still be Jonathan, Prince of Israel. You will love and honor your father; you shall be a superb soldier and commander. You will even honor Yahweh. But inside, everything is changed. In your heart of hearts, you belong to Shasheesha as My most adoring slave, constantly thinking of ways to please and serve Me. My pleasure and contentment are paramount to you. You will know no greater pleasure or satisfaction than to hear words of praise from My lips. The warm, moist, dark and smelly places of My body are holy to you and you shall worship Shasheesha and Astarte there and as a reward for your worship and service, you shall experience orgasms even greater than the one you are having now. Do you understand and accept all that I have told you, slave?"

Slave Jonathan had rolled from his side to his knees and now knelt before his Mistress, spunk-filled hands extended to Her. "Yes, Mistress," he said. "I understand and accept all You have told me."

Mistress Shasheesha stood, reached across the table, and removing the protective leather sack covering the worn, ceremonial silver goblet, held it out to him. He looked into it. "Those are My own vaginal juices from this morning, My morning urine and My Master's urine."

Dathan's urine?

"Add your semen to the cup." He obeyed.

"Lick your hands clean." He obeyed; the taste of his semen was slightly bitter. Shasheesha then poured wine from the decanter on the table into the cup and stirred it with her middle finger. "You will drink this to complete the ceremony," she said, extending the cup to him.

He took it, looked deeply into her eyes, nearly fully conscious, almost fully aware, and drank. "Drink slowly, Slave," Mistress said. "Feel the warmth and might of My power and your submission to it suffuse your body, heart and mind." He drank more slowly, looking into Her smiling eyes. She made a series of hypnotic passes across his face. "You are at peace now, slave, at long last you have a Goddess who will love and care for you, one who appreciates your devotion and servitude." Jonathan felt the truth of her words. "My eyes, gestures, and voice will put you into this blissful condition and My eyes, gestures, and voice will bring you out of it. You need not think or worry or concern yourself with anything. When I summon you to serve Me, you will be My slave; when I return you to the normal world, you will be the brave, Prince Jonathan, loving son and brother, brilliant strategist, ferocious fighter. Do you understand and accept all I have told you, slave?"

"Yes, Mistress Shasheesha." Jonathan's eyes were clear and alert, his voice steady and smooth.

"Good slave boy." She paused, tilted her head and looked obliquely into his eyes. "You know what Dathan and I are doing to you, don't you?"

"Yes, Mistress."

"And you want it? You willingly submit to becoming our slave?"

"I do Mistress."

She stroked his still inflamed cheek. "But why, why do you want to be My slave? You have everything."

"You arouse me, Mistress. I have never known your like; never experienced anything like You and what You do to me. I want more, must have more and will be your slave to attain it."

Shasheesha stroked his cheek again, more tenderly. "Yes, My good slave boy; yes, Shasheesha understands and accepts you as you are, welcomes you as you are. You have but to love Me completely, with your whole heart, feel deeply and drink daily, constantly, of your passion for Shasheesha's body and pleasure, and remember how wonderful it feels to give yourself completely to Shasheesha and to serve My smelly, warm, dark, hidden places."

"Yes, Mistress; yes, my Goddess!" he said with deep awe and reverence.

"Good, My most devoted slave. Now, when I snap My fingers, the last remnants of your trance shall disappear. You shall return to normal consciousness, retaining the memory of all that has transpired between us, longing, in your heart of hearts, to serve Shasheesha again. You shall be eager, but with no stress or sense of urgency, knowing that your time to bow down and serve My most feminine needs will come when I command."

Shasheesha snapped her fingers and Jonathan blinked as normal consciousness returned to him. He thought of Her all that day, not constantly, but often as he drifted in and out of trance. He also was obedient to Her programming, becoming noticeably fiercer in the day's combat training and more loving to his family during the evening meal. In moments of perfect lucidity, when he was able to see himself as if from above, Jonathan saw that he was like a two sided coin, effortlessly flipping between heads, family, and tails, military training. The only overarching constant, was the wonderful, all consuming loss of self that came from obeying Shasheesha and serving the hidden, hot, dark, smelly places of Her body.

He wanted to go to Her, to please Her, but resisted, remembering that he was not to go to Her unless She summoned him. Late in the evening of his first full day as Her slave, She summoned him. He was lying half-asleep when he heard Her. "Come to Me, My obedient one; come. Renew your vows; serve and adore Me. I am in Dathan's rooms." Dathan's rooms? Where was Dathan? Jonathan got up, threw a light cloak over himself and stepped outside.

A new moon riding high in the cool night sky cast silvery shadows across the compound. He tried to avoid the guards, but Joel's men were too well trained and too professional to be avoided and he encountered five of them before reaching Dathan's rooms. His hands shook and his breathing was shallow as he gently pushed the reed mat aside and stepped into the first room. A small candle in the next room guttered in the breeze, casting flickering light, on the entwined bodies in the room ahead of him. The smell of human musk and hot sex was strong in the cool air.

"Remove your robe and bow down, slave; the place you are about to enter is sacred to you." He obeyed, goose bumps popping up on his skin as his penis erected. As his eyes adjusted to the flickering candlelight; Jonathan saw his Mistress Shasheesha on her side facing him and Dathan on his side, facing away from him. They were both naked, well-oiled bodies gleaming eerily, both moaning softly as Dathan's massive penis slid in and out of Mistress's softly glistening vagina.

"Crawl here to Me, Slave," Mistress said. Jonathan obeyed. The smell of their sweat, musk and sex grew stronger as he neared them. Dathan's muscular ass cheeks shone magnificently in the reddish light as they thrust gracefully into Shasheesha's sodden vagina. The power of his muscular flesh was beautiful to behold. Dathan seemed unaware of Jonathan's presence, though the slave's face was now just inches from his massive thrusting organ.

"Yes, that's it, Slave." Mistress's voice was soft, but not to be denied. "Watch our Master's magnificent penis serve My sex. Feel its power; admire its beauty. See how juicy I am, how I have opened wide to receive Him. Come, lay flat on your belly here; put your face against My damp opening, smell Me, feel My warmth. You want to serve Me with your mouth, don't you, slave? You want to join our Master in worshipping Me; but you are a slave and your penis can never touch Shasheesha's holy of holies. Your mouth can, you can use your slave mouth to worship your Mistress's vagina. Do you want to do that, slave, to use your slave mouth to worship your Mistress's vagina?"

"Oh, yes, Mistress! Please allow this slave to use his slave mouth to worship your sacred vagina."

"Do so, then!" She commanded; and as before, she gave him specific directions about how to use his tongue to add to her pleasure. "You may also lick Master Dathan's penis, slave." Jonathan shuddered and hesitated. He was not that way; he could not lick another man's penis! "You can and you will," Mistress said. "It is not for yourself, out of your own desire to lick his penis that you do it, it is in service to Shasheesha, in obedience to My will. You belong to Shasheesha now and must obey. You want to obey, want to please and serve. Lick the Master's big cock as it goes in and out of Me; taste Me on him. Obey! You must obey, want to obey, will obey!" He obeyed, finding a deeper sense of pleasure and ecstasy as another part of his identity dropped away.

She reached a hand down to him and patted his head. "Good slave boy," she said, "excellent slave boy, good boy. Shasheesha, your Mistress and owner, is so very pleased with you!" His heart leapt with joy at Her praise.

Dathan grunted, feeling the new sensation on his massive shaft. "Is that our slave boy Jonathan?" he asked, between moans. Jonathan heard Dathan's voice through his trance as if from a great distance and thought about replying, but felt his Mistress's hand on his head, restraining him. He then heard Her say, "Yes, Lord, it is Your new slave boy Jonathan, learning to serve You." Dathan grunted affirmatively.

Jonathan hesitated again, stopped licking Dathan's penis as it slid in and out Shasheesha's holy of holies. She tugged on his hair. "Resume, slave, resume serving your Master's mighty cock! He is My Master; therefore, he is your Master. You will serve Him as you serve Me; your desire will be to Him as it is to Me." Mistress's voice became lighter, more coaxing. "You will find joy and pleasure beyond anything you have ever known, slave. Have I not guided you aright? Is not your obedience and service to Shasheesha a delight to you, doesn't it fulfill and complete you?"

It was true. It was as Mistress said. His obedience and service to Her was a delight; it did fulfill and complete him. He resumed licking his Master's cock; and it was as Mistress said. As he thought of being slave to the mighty Ammonite warrior, a deeper wave of sensual enchantment swept over him. Another barrier had fallen; he was Dathan's slave, too, the slave of slaves, how deliciously wrong yet how totally fulfilling.

A moment later, Mistress orgasmed. Master slowed his thrusts but continued to move more gently inside her. Mistress's creamy juices dripped from His gently moving penis, and leaked from the sides of Her vagina. The slave greedily licked them up, moaning with pleasure. Mistress orgasmed again and this time, Master orgasmed with Her. He twitched as his semen shot into Her holy of holies and she moaned with pleasure. More heavy, creamy liquid flowed from the sides of Her vagina. "Catch it all, slave boy," Mistress commanded. "That is sacred unto you. It is your Master's seed. Savor it, taste it and enjoy it as you lick it up and swallow it all. Now, as you serve him thus, you are truly His slave and He your Lord and Master."

Jonathan obeyed, feeling the power of Her words and the potency of his Master's semen. He felt renewed, reborn, satisfied as he'd never been satisfied before, and when his Master removed His cock from Mistress's vagina, Jonathan opened wide and lunged for it, taking it all into his mouth so as not to waste a drop. He sucked eagerly but slowly, cleansing Master's penis, tasting Mistress juices on it, experiencing an agony of ecstasy, a delight and bliss beyond anything he'd known before.

Mistress and Master sat up, but the slave continued sucking, groveling on his belly, shifting his position to keep his lips sealed around his Master's now limp penis.

"Enough, Jonathan," Master Dathan said, patting his head, "enough, My good slave boy! Kneel up." Jonathan obeyed, his throbbing erection bobbing before him, his eyes shining with devotion as he looked from one to the other. "Look into My eyes now, slave boy," Master commanded. Jonathan obeyed, feeling the same sensual hypnotic power there as he did in Mistress's eyes.

"I am pleased with you, slave boy," Master praised, sending thrills of pleasure up and down Jonathan's spine. "I know you must orgasm soon and we will use that to further consecrate you to Our service. Know that your servitude to Shasheesha and I shall last your entire life. We and we alone, are the center of your existence, your desire to serve and obey us will know no bounds. Yet, as your Mistress has instructed you, you shall serve as Our slave only when summoned. Otherwise, you shall remain a Prince of Israel, a fierce fighter, brilliant and brave tactician and loving family member." Dathan made a series of hypnotic passes across Jonathan's face, causing his slave's eyes to glaze further. "Your success in these roles is for Our glory and adds to Our power over you. Do you understand and accept what I have told you, slave?"

"Yes, Master," Jonathan said, shivering with the pleasure of anticipation and the realization that he adored his Master, loved the sound of His voice and thrilled to calling Him 'Master.'

Shasheesha handed Dathan the worn silver ceremonial goblet. Dathan took it and held it to Jonathan's nose. "Do you know what this cup contains, slave?" Master asked.

Jonathan inhaled the scent of stale urine. "It is your urine, Lord, and that of my Mistress."

"Yes, slave, very good. Now you will orgasm directly into the cup, drink it down completely, but slowly, and be consecrated to Our service as Our slave forever. Are you ready to do this, slave?"

Jonathan's penis was sore and beyond ready, his balls throbbed and ached. "Yes, Master, thank You, Master. Your slave is ready, Master."

Dathan handed the cup to his slave. Jonathan took it, positioned it and stared into his Master's smiling eyes awaiting the command.

"Spill your seed into the cup and be consecrated to Us as Our slave forever!"

Jonathan obeyed and it was so.

# Chapter Ten

Wars and the rumor of wars swirled around the House of Saul. Egypt attacked Moab in the Sinai; Assyria clashed with the Hittites around the Caspian Sea, and the Amalekites raided Hebrew territory east of the Jordan. But the Philistines in Israel were strangely quiet. King Saul used the relative calm wisely to advance the consolidation of his House and Kingdom. All the initiatives launched on that Sabbath eve, plus other related initiatives, were bearing fruit.

The educational programs launched and overseen by Janina and Abadantha were oversubscribed and available in every Hebrew community as well as in some Philistine and Moabite communities as well. Janina and Abadantha led train-the-trainer seminars, made inspection trips and managed the day-to-day administration.

The standing Army stood at 6,500 men, 1,200 of them crack marksmen with bow and arrow. They even had 400 cavalry for patrol and skirmishing. The militia training was going quite well too, and as Jonathan had foreseen, militia were able, on the basis of regular rotations, to permanently garrison King Saul's two royal cities and the three regional centers, leaving most of the Army free for aggressive action. The building and fortification program was so successful and popular that King Saul became known as the 'Master Builder,' a title he delighted in.

An Egyptian surgeon had come, examined the King and found an excess of fluid around his brain, which he drained. The King's headaches were much improved though still present and the surgeon warned, before returning to his homeland, that more severe headaches were likely to return, as he had been unable to remove whatever it was that was causing the excess fluid in the first place.

Jonathan became ever more deeply enslaved to his Master and Mistress, craving their domination, groveling before them and serving as their complete and utter slave, worshipping them as his God and Goddess, begging them to use him and to let him lie beneath their smelly feet and anuses and even serve as their toilet. He was totally enthralled and shameless in his devotion to them. Although he spent every evening in their service, he awoke in his own bed each morning refreshed and vigorous, the perfect son and brother, and perfect Prince of his people, fierce in combat, wise in judgment, calm in command.

Jonathan did all he could, within the bounds of propriety, to set up a household for Shasheesha, first taking her as his concubine, then building a small suite of rooms for her next to his own in the King's compound. The rooms became a temple where he was able to serve and worship Her and his Master, Dathan, in ever more elaborate and fulfilling ways. In one corner was an altar to the Goddess Astarte, and in another, a shrine containing the worn ceremonial silver goblet, which they used almost every night. Jonathan also actively supported Dathan's suggestions for improving and developing the Army. Though Dathan's competency and credibility were beyond reproach and needed no support from Jonathan, the masterful warrior enjoyed and encouraged the support of his slave.

Dathan was also extremely proud of his slave's military prowess; he was, perhaps prouder of Jonathan than King Saul was. Jonathan was a master of all weaponry, the traditional Hebrew curved sword, the double-edged iron long sword of the Philistines, the short sword of the Egyptians, bow and arrow, battle-axe, dagger and knife, sling, javelin and spear. He could also fight from horseback, and his grasp of strategy and tactics was superb.

Only one thing worried Dathan, even with all his hypnotic conditioning, Jonathan remained too headstrong and his hatred of and deep desire to go to war with the Philistines might undo all Dathan's careful maneuvering. Dathan wanted to fight Philistia, saw it as essential, as everyone in the Hebrew military did. He simply wanted to be sure it was done correctly. The distribution of Philistine military power divided and fractured the Hebrew's ability to fight a single, strategic battle and win, as they did in Jabesh. They would have to fight a series of perhaps eleven campaigns, *campaigns*, not battles, to dislodge them.

Dathan thought Abner and Joel were good generals, aware of the difficulties and would help contain Jonathan's lust for war. They had a plan for dislodging the Philistines that began with driving them out of Gibeah with Jonathan and himself leading that action. Dathan wanted things to unfold as they'd planned, and didn't want his headstrong slave to start something he and his Hebrew colleagues could not finish.

Michal complicated Dathan's efforts, fueling Jonathan's hatred and headstrong rush to war with Philistia. Her dislike of the Philistine's was deeper than Jonathan's. As she trained with them, Dathan saw how she influenced Jonathan, how loud and aggressive his slave's war talk became after spending time with Michal. Dathan thought Jonathan was too easily influenced by women, and smiled at the irony. Not that Michal lacked credibility; on most things she spoke wisely and her advice was sound. After all, she had fought well with her father at Jabesh. But her talk of war each morning as they trained, undid Dathan and Shasheesha's programming of the previous evening.

Perhaps, Dathan thought, they would have to enchant and enslave Michal as well, to quiet her. She would make an excellent slave too, attractive and energetic. It had been a long time since Shasheesha had a maidservant, if only for the evenings. Dathan thought if he and Shasheesha commanded their slave to bring his sister to them and offer her up to them, he would obey. But, should they? And, what if he refused? After all, she was his sister. What if they couldn't enslave and enchant Michal? She was quite strong and willful. No, Dathan would leave well enough alone for now. Besides, he and his slave were preparing to leave on an inspection tour of the royal cities and regional centers, so their usual evening training rituals would not be available for reinforcement and it might not be possible to have any evening rituals at all.

As it turned out, Dathan's concerns were well founded but not for the reasons he thought. He and Jonathan were gone for nine days and slept with the garrison troops so were unable to have any rituals. Unable to induce his slave's trances the way Shasheesha could, and though their journeying was successful and they found the garrisons well manned and the militia alert, well equipped and eager, Dathan feared the trip was nearly a failure from the perspective of Jonathan's enchantment. Nearly. Ever resourceful, Dathan developed a subtle, perhaps more powerful, means of reinforcing Jonathan's enchantment, invoking the deep memory of his surrender to Shasheesha and his fulfillment in her service.

Dathan had seen Shasheesha seduce and enslave many men. He knew that Jonathan's enchantment was deeper and more profound. It was spiritual, more than physical. Jonathan experienced his God in his submission to Shasheesha. If he were able to have Jonathan relive that initial experience with Shasheesha, when Jonathan realized she was as God to him, Jonathan would go into a trance, perhaps deeper than the one induced by the physical rituals the three of them performed.

Dathan tried numerous combinations of touch, gesture, words and phrases during the first two days of their journeying, watching his slave's face, body, and breathing for signs of efficacy. By the third day, he discovered that a touch on Jonathan's shoulder and the touch of his lips on Jonathan's ear, he could whisper the command, "surrender to Shasheesha and fulfill your longing to know your God. Give yourself fully; become Her slave and relive your experience of total oneness as Shasheesha's slave!" Those words would induce a light trance, which Dathan could then easily deepen with further commands, touches and gestures. By the time they returned to Gibeah, Dathan was able to place Jonathan into a very deep trance by simply touching his shoulder, touching his lips to Jonathan's ear and whispering the command.

Not only did Jonathan and Dathan inspect the military facilities, they also visited the Covenant schools, administrative buildings and storage facilities. They noted the condition of the roads, wells and water storage facilities, grain fields, vineyards and artisan shops. As a result of Janina and Abadantha's work with the children, a slight shift from the Scrolls to the Covenant, away from the worship of Baal and Astarte was beginning, and though the priests approved the reduction in idol worship, they grumbled about the smaller tithes and poor attendance at services.

Immediately upon their return, King Saul granted his son and Dathan an audience. Michal was there, as was Ahinoam, Janina and Abadantha, Abner and Joel, the same group, with the exception of Dathan, that shared Sabbath dinner almost a year before. Thanking him for his excellent work, King Saul dismissed Dathan, saying he wanted only to be with his family. Worried, but without recourse, Dathan bowed and departed.

Jonathan noticed changes in King Saul's throne room, though it had only been a month since he'd been there. The throne itself was new and larger, carved of precious aromatic cedar wood, and the two smaller thrones on either side occupied by Janina and Ahinoam were also of new softly gleaming cedar. The King, his wife and mother looked quite regal, dressed in rich new robes of orange and blue in the Assyrian style. Two bare-chested scribes sat on plush cushions next to the smaller thrones, and next to each of them, stood a large burly heavily-armed and armored member of Joel's Palace Guard. Plush, velvety purple-dyed wool draperies hung behind the thrones, regally framing the whole scene.

Joel, Michal and Abner were standing before the King and each in turn, hugged Jonathan. All four of them wore short swords, were dressed in leather and metal armor and had shiny battle helmets on. It felt good to be home, Jonathan thought, good to be here with those he really cared about and those who really care about him. He could tell his mother, aunt, and the King, wanted to hug him too, as he wanted to hug them, but the formality of the atmosphere prevented it; there'd be time enough for that later.

"A good trip, my son?" the King asked, smiling.

"It was indeed, Majesty. They are calling you, 'Saul the Master Builder'!"

The King laughed out loud and clapped his hands together. "Excellent! Excellent! And am I not indeed the Master Builder?"

"You are, Sire. Granaries, storehouses, wells, roads, administrative buildings, gates, ramparts, and fortifications are rising everywhere we went. The people are growing prosperous and are grateful, Father."

King Saul leaned back in his throne, nodding. "And what of the schools?" Janina asked. "And the Covenant?" Abadantha echoed.

"We had no time to visit the schools, but we rode past them and they were active, most with classes and groups gathered in the courtyards. The best measure I have of the success of your efforts, Grandmother and Aunt Abadantha, is the fact that nearly everywhere the priests complained about declining tithes and poor attendance at the temples."

The women smiled and nodded judiciously. "We must be careful of priests grumbling," King Saul said. "The God of the Scrolls is my Master; I rule in His name."

"True, my Lord," Abadantha said, reaching out to touch his hand. "But we here know it is the power within, our connection with the Covenant, that doeth the work and worketh the blessings."

The King dipped his head in agreement. "But still," he said, "appearances must be maintained, the Temple and the priests served."

"On our return to the city, we noticed armed Philistine soldiers stopping and even harassing travelers and traders," Jonathan said. "This is your capital, Father, your royal city... "

Michal interrupted, stepping forward, hand clenched on the hilt of her sword. She said, "The time has come to act, Father! Jonathan's report of progress is good news. The foundations of the House of Saul are being well laid. It is time to remove the enemy from our midst!"

King Saul looked at Abner. "What say you, my general?"

"I say, yes, the time is right. I say we clear Gibeah of Philistines and send the governor back to Gaza!"

Jonathan, Michal, and Joel cheered. "It will mean a long, protracted series of battles, Abner," King Saul said, softly.

"I know, Sire," Abner said. "But Jonathan's report confirms my own intelligence... "

"And mine," Joel said. "We are in gaining strength and they are not expecting an attack. Why wait for the inevitable, Sire? Let us attack them before they attack us.

King Saul stroked his short beard and nodded. "All of you make a strong case. Yes! All right! How shall we proceed?"

"I have already drawn a plan for this eventuality, Sire," Abner said. "I can review it with you in more detail later, but essentially, it calls for keeping three thousand troops, including the cavalry, in reserve, two thousand in ready, active reserve, prepared to march at a moment's notice, and attacking with one thousand troops.

"Normally, I would recommend Joel to command the attack, but the enemy reaction is so difficult to gauge at this point in time, I think it advisable that he command the ready reserve. I therefore recommend Prince Jonathan to lead the attack."

Jonathan was astonished and looked it. Abner patted his shoulder. "You are ready, my Prince. More than ready. I have watched you training with Dathan these last months and I have the utmost confidence in your ability to fight and lead."

Jonathan dipped his head, face red with embarrassment.

"And I shall go with him," Michal said. "As his shield barer!"

Ahinoam did not want Michal to go. She stood. "I am worried about you, my daughter. Must you go?"

"Yes, mother. You know how I feel about the Philistines. Don't worry; the God of the Covenant will protect me." Michal smiled radiantly, from her heart. "This is nothing; God has greater things yet in store for me."

Michal was so sure of herself and radiated such calm authority, that Ahinoam sat down, lips slightly parted as if to say more.

"I approve," King Saul declared. "I am in no need of the details, Abner. I trust you." He stood and turning to the scribe on his right, stretched out his arm and pointed down to the man saying, "So let it be written, so let it be done!"

# Chapter Eleven

Jonathan's action against the Philistine garrison in Gibeah was swift and sure. He'd worked with Abner, Joel and Dathan on the plan of attack for months, and they'd actually been practicing the street-by-street take-over of Gibeah, the capture of the fortress and the elimination of its garrison on their routine walks through town. His thousand men were divided into five squads, each with a specific mission. He himself led the squad that would take the fortress.

To ensure surprise, Jonathan's attacks began three hours after King Saul approved them. Dathan, feeling less worried and much relieved, commanded the squad that attacked the Governor's compound. The Hebrews rolled forward like a tide in the ocean sea, irresistible and relentless. Completely unprepared, the Philistines were routed in less than two hours, with only three Hebrew dead and 42 wounded. Two hundred Philistine mercenaries, mostly Moabites serving under Philistine officers, were captured, another two hundred were butchered, and three hundred wounded.

With the fortress in their hands, Jonathan and Michal raced to the Governor's compound, scene of the stiffest resistance, to join Dathan in rallying their troops to over-run the compound. A lifetime of rage, fear, hatred, and frustration boiled over in King Saul's children. Covered in blood and gore, they butchered everyone they encountered. Jonathan himself killed the governor with a sword thrust to his heart after he, Dathan and Michal eliminated the bodyguards the man cowered behind. For the first time in one hundred and forty seven years, Gibeah, the seat of the House of Saul, was free and in

Hebrew hands. Many horses, iron weapons, chariots, and a great deal of taxes, were liberated.

None of them had anticipated how swift and strong the Philistine reaction would be. Clearer about what was at stake than King Saul, the Philistines assembled a massive expeditionary force, including a cavalry corps and three thousand chariots, invincible against Israel's foot soldiers, and dispatched it to re-impose their authority and quell the Hebrew attempt to establish an independent kingdom. After moving through the Bethoron pass, the Philistines established a fortified base at Michmash.

Abner told the King that the Philistine choice of Michmash was a daring but well calculated move. By pushing to the eastern side of the Judean plateau from their seaside city states, the Philistines now commanded the ascents to the mountains of Benjamin from the Judean desert, the traditional staging area for the Hebrews, bottling up King Saul's soldiers. Michmash also straddled the eastern branch of the watershed road, the main north-south artery and flanked its western branch, in easy distance to block it. Worse still, by making their base in the very heart of Benjamin, the Philistines openly challenged the King's personal authority and competence.

King Saul took personal charge of the Army and called for a levee, summoning the militias. So swift and wide spread was the Philistine activity that the militias were required to protect their own cities and tribes, and only Samaria was able to send five thousand of its troops, leaving the Hebrews badly outmatched in both numbers and equipment. Wide-ranging Philistine flying squads raided territory that had been secure only days before, thoroughly demoralizing the Hebrew people.

So great was the threat, that large numbers of King Saul's well-trained regulars had no choice but to desert him, returning to their homes to protect them.

Abner's spies shadowed the Philistines and warned of even greater disaster as, sensing the Hebrew's weakness and disintegration, the Philistines decided to accelerate the destruction of the fledgling kingdom by dividing their force into three large columns to devastate the countryside. To counteract their weakened center, the Philistines kept a blocking force in an outpost at the passage of Michmash, the saddle that connected Michmash with Gibeah via the western branch of the watershed road, between the heights of Wadi Suweinit and the foot of Michmash hill. Though well situated, Abner sensed an opportunity in the Philistine's Michmash positions.

Suffering fierce headaches, and personally wounded by the desertions and the invasion of his tribal homelands, King Saul, was barely able to function. Supported by Abner, Joel, Jonathan and Michal, the king moved what was left of his Army, perhaps nine hundred men, out of Gibeah to challenge the Philistines, in positions directly opposite Michmash, at Migron. King Saul dared not attack even the weakened Philistine camp, but hoped to mitigate the extent of the enemy's raids into Benjamin and the Hebrew hinterland. It did not work out; the situation at Michmash became a stalemate and the Philistines ravaged unhindered.

So demoralizing was this state of affairs in areas traversed by the Philistine flying columns, that Hebrews, believing this to be the end of the House of Saul, went over to the enemy, supported them with food and water, served as auxiliaries, and even established temples to Baal and Astarte.

Now Samuel, who had been in favor of Jonathan's take-over of Gibeah, and who had been secretly pleased with the king's drift to the Covenant, came to Migron. Frightened by the speed of the Philistine counter attack and rapid collapse of Hebrew arms, the old prophet recalled Saul's unwillingness and reluctance to be King. Samuel saw in Saul a disgusting lack of confidence and competence that had brought about this current disaster. Ignoring the recent progress that had been made relying on the Covenant, the slave of Yahweh heaped guilt upon King Saul, blaming him for not being Yahweh's most loyal servant and failing to anticipate the Philistine reaction.

At his wit's end, and deeply disappointed again by Samuel's failure to support him when he most needed it, King Saul was wracked with guilt. He threw himself on the ground before the prophet, kissed the hem of his robe and begged Samuel to invoke Yahweh's wrath on the

Philistines. "Please Samuel," King Saul implored. "Have mercy not only on me, but on your people. You are Hebrew too!"

Disgusted by his memories of Saul and more revolted by the king's groveling, Samuel said, "Yahweh is a stern and righteous God! He cares neither for individuals nor nations, but for Justice and Obedience. You and the Hebrews have sinned against Him. He expects nothing from the Philistines; they are pagans. But He has a covenant with you and expects more from His people." The prophet scowled and stepped back, pulling his robe from Saul's grasping fingers. "But... very well. I shall return at noon tomorrow to offer sacrifices and ask Yahweh's blessing on this military venture. Many times before, He has given his people great victories, even when they were similarly sinful and similarly outmatched." Samuel strode from the King's tent and out of the camp.

Abner, Joel, Jonathan and Michal felt that waiting for a miracle was poor strategy. They begged King Saul to send a small squad of men to surprise the Philistine outpost at Michmash by going through the Nahal Michmash Canyon between the cliffs. Immobilized by guilt, fear, and repentance, the King said no, he was Yahweh's slave. All this had befallen them because he had neglected to make the proper sacrifices and he would wait for Samuel to conduct them.

The time agreed for the sacrifice came and went and Samuel failed to appear. The situation grew worse hourly, with reports of mayhem, murder and betrayal pouring in from the countryside. More soldiers deserted to go home and save what they could of their homes, families and communities. Those soldiers who remained, even though many of them were sons of the Covenant, grew disheartened by King Saul's inaction, and the inability of their leaders to take effective action. Finally, three days after the agreed time for the sacrifice, seeing his army evaporating before his eyes, King Saul decided he needed to act—at least—to staunch the loss of manpower. Without waiting for Samuel, he decided to offer the sacrifices himself, an act specifically prohibited by the Scrolls.

What was left of the army was assembled for the ceremony. Just as he was finishing, Samuel arrived and again heaped shame and scorn upon Saul. The King again degraded himself before the old man, babbling about defeat and the fall of the House of Saul. But Samuel's heart was hardened, filled with the wrath of Yahweh. There was no room there for the compassion of the Covenant. Pulling himself from his arthritic stoop to his full height, Samuel stretched out his arm and pointed to the groveling King. He said, "For your disobedience today and for your many sins in the past, Yahweh has turned His face from you. From this moment on, you are no longer Yahweh's servant. He will remove you from the throne, and replace you with a man after His own heart." King Saul begged and pleaded but the prophet turned and left him in the dust.

A moan of shock arose from the assembled army when their King fell to his knees before the old man. When the prophet cursed their King, a low growl of anger came from them. Shouts of, "we're with you, Sire!" and "fear not!" punctuated the shocked stillness. King Saul, lying in the dust, seemed not to hear them. Lifting their father, and each taking an arm, Jonathan and Michal, led him to his tent as he babbled, "What will become of the House of Saul? What will become of us? When will I be removed? Who will replace me? What will become of the House of Saul?"

As their King was led away to recover, Abner and Joel spoke to the assembled army, reminding them of their past victories and driving home the point that they were the only effective Hebrew military force remaining in the field and if they disbanded or succumbed, the country and kingdom would surely be lost. Many of the remaining soldiers were believers in the Covenant and had no love or appreciation for Samuel and Yahweh.

A man deep in the midst of the assembly spoke up. "We know God is greater than Samuel's God." Pausing for the crowd to murmur their approval, he continued. "We know we have a covenant with God deep in our hearts, right now. We need no sacrifices and no priests." The murmurs increased. "Let us commune with this, our innermost God. Let us be still and know. Let us understand that in this moment of crisis, even as we know not what to do or how to save our country, God knows and God will reveal the answer to us."

One by one, the soldiers knelt and a great silence befell the assemblage, broken only by faint moans and cries drifting from the

King's tent. When they arose, Abner spoke, thanking them and said if they would persevere and wait one more day, they would win.

As the soldiers drifted away to wait, Joel saw Jonathan and Michal emerge from their father's tent and speak with Abner. Joel watched as they spoke for some time. Then Abner nodded, and seemed to be vehemently opposed to what Jonathan and Michal were saying. The king's children walked away. Dusk was falling as Joel made his rounds of the sentries and saw two heavily armed figures very like Jonathan and Michal disappearing into the Nahal Michmash Canyon between the cliffs heading toward the Philistine outpost.

# Chapter Twelve

Abadantha arrived in Migron shortly after King Saul's children left him. She found him half-asleep in his tent. Kneeling at his side, heart overflowing with compassion and love, Dantha lifted her brother's head and coaxed him to sip a few drops of wine. He drank and gradually, as she rocked him and sang to him, his eyes opened. At first, she saw stark terror there, but as she continued her ministrations, his eyes cleared and he sat up.

"Oh, sister," he said. "How have our sins come to damn us! The mockery we made of Yahweh and the Scrolls; see now how we are punished and not just you and me, but the whole nation."

"Gently, my brother, gently," she said. "You are too much under the influence of that terrible old man. Heed him not; Samuel is the slave of Yahweh and you know Yahweh is but one part of God. You are a true son of the Covenant and the Covenant has been good to you; do not forsake it now! We will persist; you are still King; the House of Saul has not fallen. Ups and downs are a natural, inevitable part of life; you have had victories; you will have defeats. After the darkness, the light must surely follow."

King Saul looked into his sister's eyes, and nodded.

"Ups and downs are natural," Dantha continued. They are not the result of God's intervention. God allows ups and downs, but in spite of the way it seems to men like Samuel, or us when we're fearful, God does not make a particular up as a reward or a particular down as a punishment. Perhaps Yahweh rewards and punishes, but God does not." Dantha brushed her fingertips lightly across her brother's eyelids, closing them. "Rest now, with your head in my lap and think on what I have told you."

The canyon walls were steep and became steeper as Jonathan and Michal moved forward over the rough, rock strewn dry streambed that had carved out the defile. A rising moon cast deep shadows providing excellent cover. Both Michal and Jonathan had studied the terrain during the seemingly endless, frustrating days of waiting for Samuel and even in the deepening darkness, had a good idea of which way to go. The outpost would be just short of a mile ahead on their right. At their present pace, they should hear it in about twenty minutes. Surprise was everything. They'd done their best to muffle their armor and weapons. Each of them had the best of the captured Philistine iron: a double-edged long sword, Egyptian short sword, dagger, and curved slashing sword in leather scabbards on their waist belts. Both carried a bow and twenty arrows slung on their backs, and in their hands, a round dueling shield and javelin.

Their plan was to split up when they reached the outpost and attack it from different directions, west and north being the most surprising, using bow and arrows first. They thought that they could eliminate perhaps six of the twenty or so soldiers before the alarm was sounded. They were the perfect team, in complete harmony with one another's movements, totally trusting one another's competence and both seething with pent-up fury and blood lust.

The dry streambed was rougher than they'd anticipated and it was darker than they'd expected, causing them to stumble and fall often. Fueled by adrenalin, anticipation, and the sense they were destined to succeed, *had* to succeed, Saul's children helped each other up and trotted on. Then they heard the Philistine sentries, Moabites again, talking to each other. What luck! They were in pairs, easier to take two nearly at once. They even had small fires lit; discipline was very lax. They'd pay with their lives.

The pairs called for a change of plan; rather than split up, they'd stay together each taking one member of the pair then move to the next pair. If their luck held, they might be able to get four, maybe even, five pairs. Still wanting to attack first from the west, they wound around the canyon for a few minutes more then climbed carefully to level ground. The first pair of sentries was fifty cubits from them, well within the kill zones of their arrows. Synchronizing their movements, Saul's children drew their arrows, threaded them and let fly, striking their targets. As the sentries collapsed dead, Jonathan and Michal were already circling to the north, bow and arrows at the ready.

Their arrows took ten more Moabite lives, the last three at the 'gate' to the core of the outpost. Inside, fifteen Moabites lay sleeping in four tents. Jonathan going left, Michal going right, they efficiently butchered all but three of them. These three, they disarmed, bound and gagged, walked them through the remains of their colleagues and told them they had been spared to run to Michmash and sound the alarm. Untying and un-gagging them, Saul's children sent them forth, screaming.

Faithful to what they told Abner they would do at this point if they were successful, Michal and Jonathan set fire to the Philistine encampment. The tents, wagons and stores burned brightly, sending flames high into the sky, easily seen by the sentries in Migron. Abner was notified, instantly understood what had happened, and rallied the Hebrew warriors. He explained the plan and told them victory was at hand ready to be snatched from apparent defeat.

After Abner spoke, the ground trembled. It shook, and then opened in places, an apparent earthquake. King Saul's prayers *had* been answered. God had intervened once again to save the Hebrews. The tremors didn't last long at Migron, but they were devastating at Michmash, throwing the Philistines into panic. At first, the Hebrews panicked too, but the soldiers of the Covenant saw the shuddering earth as an advantage for them and believed their prayers had also been answered. They rallied, and Abner's frontal assault on Michmash began. Fearing the earthquake and hearing the cries of Jonathan and Michal's victims, Philistines at other nearby posts were similarly thrown into panic.

Awakened by the earthquake and noise, King Saul, now lucid, was briefed by Dathan and Joel. Wanting to seize the initiative, yet not wanting to offend the God of the Scrolls again, King Saul called upon his priest, Ahiah, to invoke Yahweh's blessings. The priest wanted to conduct a proper ceremony and sacrifice, but Dathan and Joel advised against it, saying there was no time; the situation was urgent. King Saul agreed, cancelled his call to the Scrolls, appealed in his heart to the Covenant, and led his tiny force directly into battle.

Yet, as they prepared to march, a means to combine both military necessity and Yahweh's spiritual requirements flashed through Saul's mind. In the rallying speech to his troops, Saul warned them to fight without stopping to eat or drink. He called Yahweh's curse upon any man who ate or drank before sundown. Shocked, Joel and Dathan asked the King to take back this curse. Troops weak with hunger would not fight at their best. King Saul scowled, turned from them, with his face ablaze in anger, called upon them to keep the faith and repeated his invective—death to any man who stopped fighting to eat or drink before sundown.

The earthquake and Jonathan and Michal's assault had put momentum on the Hebrew side. Great confusion filled the Philistine camps, as many Hebrews who had defected to the Philistines changed sides to fight against them, and in the confusion, Philistines and their mercenaries even attacked one another. The Philistines would be defeated, in spite of their vast superiority. Hebrews everywhere, in the army, the palace staff, fields, vineyards, groves, workshops, and temples, wondered—was it because of Yahweh's intervention or that of the Covenant?

Yet because of Saul's curse, it was a near thing. Everything might have been lost, the House of Saul forgotten, and there would have been no one to blame but Saul himself.

After their destruction of the Philistine outpost, Jonathan convinced Michal, who was slightly wounded, to go back to Gibeah. He continued in the direction of Michmash. As dawn was breaking, he stumbled onto a honeycomb. Being hungry, Jonathan stopped a moment, ate some honey and was refreshed. He then rejoined the main body of the Army to continue fighting.

When evening came, the soldiers paused to eat. All the Hebrew leaders—Abner, Joel, Jonathan and Dathan, agreed the troops needed to rest and sleep. King Saul wanted them to resume the fight during the night, before the surviving Philistines could regroup and escape. As aftershocks rumbled through Michmash, the discussions became heated and a mutiny loomed. Saul's priest, Ahiah, suggested they consult Yahweh. This time, Saul agreed—fortunately, for Yahweh had honored Saul's invective, and fighting further would have been a disaster. Ahiah conducted the proper ritual. They called upon Yahweh, but the God would not answer.

Ahiah said Yahweh was silent because someone in the army had broken faith and stopped to eat. Following the ancient custom that had made him King, Saul commanded they draw lots to find who the violator was. As darkness surrounded them, punctuated by the disembodied moans of the wounded and dying, the remaining hungry five-hundred bruised and battered soldiers lined up. In the glow of two towering bonfires, the starving blood-drenched soldiers filed past Ahiah, each taking a straw. When the lot fell to Jonathan, a deep groan emerged from the exhausted soldiers. Jonathan stepped forward.

Eyes darting from Abner's to Jonathan's, voice quivering, King Saul asked, "Did you eat before sundown today, my son?"

"Yes, Father, I did."

"But Jonathan knew nothing of your order, Sire," Dathan said.

Shouts of, "aye" and, "he didn't know," rose from the increasingly agitated troops.

A chill crept across King Saul's heart, and a frozen calm gripped him. As the King gazed icily into his son's unbelieving eyes, Jonathan knew his father would pronounce the death sentence on him. Anger, white hot and lethal, flared in Jonathan's belly and shone in his eyes. How could this be? He was a hero, how totally insane!

Dathan stepped to Jonathan's side, touched his shoulder, touched his lips to Jonathan's ear and whispered the command to, "surrender to Shasheesha; fulfill your longing to know your God. Give yourself fully; become Shasheesha's slave!" Instantly, Jonathan's eyes became fixed and staring. His breathing slowed and he went into trance.

"You will obey all I command," Dathan whispered. "Maintain a normal appearance." Jonathan obeyed and appeared in normal consciousness, but the reality of enchantment was present.

Abner, Joel, Michal, and Abadantha were readying themselves to appeal to King Saul for mercy. As they prepared themselves, Dathan continued whispering in his slave's ear. "I am most proud of you, my goodly slave and your Mistress, Shasheesha, would be proud of you, too. Remember the glory of your service to Her and to Me."

"Yes, Master," Jonathan whispered.

"Good, you are My good slave boy."

A thrill raced through Jonathan's heart.

"The power of God is in your experience of enchantment, slave. If you are able to reconnect with that power, to relive your experience of it, that connection, in and of itself, might change the balance of energies and shift them from Yahweh to the Covenant and soften your father's heart."

Yes, the slave thought, soften the King's heart.

"What are you remembering?"

Abner had just finished addressing King Saul, who seemed unmoved and Joel began to speak.

Jonathon, audible only to Dathan, answered, "I am remembering my first experience with Shasheesha, my Mistress."

"Yes," Dathan whispered. "Go on."

"I am remembering how totally fulfilled I felt, how complete, when She allowed me to orgasm. I had never known such fullness and satisfaction before, and know it now only in Your service, Master, and in Hers."

"Yes," Dathan spoke in subdued tones, "a powerful experience of Oneness that changed your life." The slave nodded. "When I command, you will relive that experience, only ten times more powerfully." The slave's penis was becoming fully erect, leaking pre-cum. Dathan was also aroused. He touched the bulge in Jonathan's battle kilt. "We do not want others to see or know what you are experiencing."

"Yes, Master," the slave whispered.

"You may not erect or orgasm. You may have the experience of it, but will not do so for others to see."

"Yes, Master."

Joel finished speaking. King Saul appeared to be firmly committed to executing his son. Abadantha began speaking and for the first time, the King seemed to soften.

"Now!" Dathan whispered. "Relive your experience with your Mistress, reconnect with that power!"

*Only Shasheesha's pleasure and my need to serve it matter. Her moans and squeals of pleasure, her juices, smells and flesh drive me on, beyond my own needs and previous limits. A new world opens before me. Nothing can stop me or hold me back. My desire and arousal armor me; make me immortal in Shasheesha's service. This is what it means to serve God. Shasheesha is God. God is in everyone, everywhere, equally present. This is the God in me connecting with the God in Shasheesha. My eager and willing submission to Her is my eager and willing submission to God.*

As Jonathan experienced his psychic orgasm, the blood soaked soldiers, roused by Abadantha's speech and her long, soulful embrace of Abner, began shouting, "free him," "free Jonathan, free the hero of Michmash." Trapped between his fear of Yahweh and his fear of his own soldiers, Saul chose the more immediate fear of his soldiers. Somehow, the energy had shifted and King Saul's heart had been softened. The King opened his arms and stepped towards his son.

Touching his slave's shoulder, Dathan whispered, "Awake and return to normal!" then stepped back to watch father and son embrace formally. Much had changed between Prince and King, almost everything of soulful importance had been rent asunder and the embrace was merely formal and without warmth. Appearances would be maintained, alliances honored, but with the father's willingness to sacrifice his hero son to the father's fear, the filial love and devotion that had been the foundations of the House of Saul, were swept away. The Army cheered, but the lot ritual had lost them the momentum; the invading Philistines were stopped, but not expelled.

Stepping back from his son's embrace, King Saul adjusted his robes and walked regally to his tent. As the soldiers dispersed, Michal raced to her brother and threw her arms around his shoulders, tucking her head against his neck. "Oh, thank God, Jonathan, thank God!" Jonathan hugged her back then took a step away. Holding Michal at arm's length, he looked into her red, tearing eyes, leaned forward and kissed first on one damp salty cheek, then the other. His voice was distant and solemn. "We are most certainly cursed, Michal, to be the spawn of this maniac."

Eyes wide, Michal recoiled as if Jonathan had slapped her. "Surely not, brother," she said, voice shaking.

"He would have killed me, sacrificed me, for no good reason."

Michal nodded, wiping the tears from her eyes and cheeks.

"Our lives hang from a thread, a gossamer thread unraveling even as we speak."

"What will become of us, brother?" Michal asked.

Abner, Dathan, and Joel, had been standing back waiting to offer their congratulations, but allowed brother and sister to have a moment alone, now pressed forward throwing their arms around Jonathan and Michal, hugging and encouraging them.

After awhile, when Jonathan and Michal were alone again, Jonathan looked intently into his sister's face and said, "After what we have seen and experienced this day, the miracle of our victory at the outpost and the treachery of our own father, we must take care to trust only in the deepest promptings of our own souls."

Michal dipped her head in agreement.

"The House of Saul means everything to me," Jonathan said, "as I know it does to you. Hear me, please, I beg you! Duty, loyalty, honor, and family responsibility can be respected, but not at the expense of our own sense of our soul's guidance." Jonathan looked down and shook his head. "To do otherwise will surely bring misery and empty sacrifice." He gripped Michal's shoulders, stared into her eyes. "You too, are in danger! Take care! I am doomed to die with our twisted and insane father, because to me, the House of Saul is everything. But you need not perish."

Michal started to protest, but Jonathan silenced her with a finger to her lips. "You can live on though the House of Saul be destroyed. Promise me," tears streamed down Michal's cheeks again, "promise me you will live on trusting only in the deepest promptings of your own soul, no matter what the effect on the House of Saul."

Michal was choking and coughing. "Promise me, sister!" She bobbed her head and flung her arms round him.

In the dark, alone in his war tent, King Saul tossed fitfully on his camp bed. He still couldn't sleep, even though the noise of the camp had diminished. He nearly fell asleep, but the pain in his head, not just in back where it normally was, but also on both sides, felling like his head was in a vise. He twisted and turned in useless attempts at comfort. Thoughts of Dantha speaking to him of the Covenant and God's unceasing love for him and all people, even the hated Philistine's, often soothed him, but brought no respite this time.

How could he have done that, ordered the execution of Jonathan? He loved the boy, man really, and owed the victory at Michmash and the saving of his House to him. Was he jealous? Did he fear his son would be the one to usurp his throne? The pain in King Saul's head grew worse. No, he thought, tossing, but then yes, yes, God help him he *was* jealous. Yahweh had to be appeased in any event; someone had to pay. It was him or me. No, no. Yahweh might require that someone pay, but certainly, God did not.

The King finally slept and dreamt that Yahweh's next assignment after the Philistines were contained, was to attack the Amalekites and destroy them utterly, taking no survivors and no plunder; a strange touch, for typically slaves and plunder were a soldier's pay.

In the nightmare, Saul assembled his army, made special arrangements to protect nearby innocents, and laid an ambush against the Amalekites. With Yahweh's help, the battle was a great success. Filled with pride and gratitude, Saul decided to keep the Amalekite King, Agag, alive as a trophy of God's favor and love for him; and following his example, his soldiers kept much Amalekite livestock as plunder.

King Saul tossed violently in his sleep. Samuel had come to the battleground. "Ah, stupid, stupid man," Saul said aloud, as Samuel. "Will you never learn?" Now Samuel was apologizing to an angry Yahweh, saying he regretted making unfaithful Saul king; and Saul saw Samuel tossing all night, as he himself tossed, bitterly crying to God for the disaster that was coming on Saul.

Horrified, the dreaming king watched a sad and sorrowful Samuel come to him the next day and heard himself say, "I have performed the commandment of the Lord." Samuel answered, "If you obeyed the Lord, why is this man," pointing to Agag, "still alive and what are all these animals here for?" Saul made excuses, but Samuel was firm against his arguments, pointing out that even if Saul sacrificed all those animals, as his excuse claimed, it wouldn't undo his act of rebellion. Obedience is precious to Yahweh.

Sweat dripping from him, King Saul shuddered, his head throbbed; yet more horror was to come. As Samuel turned to leave, Saul was in the prophet's head and understood that it was over and Samuel thought there was no point in supporting the House of Saul further. King Saul grabbed the prophet's robe. "No, no, please," he begged, urging Samuel to stay. The old man pulled away and Saul clung to his robe, tearing it. Face aflame with rage, his grey hair and white beard floating with static electricity, Samuel said in a steely, guttural growl, "Now has the Lord God Yahweh similarly torn the kingdom from you, and will not change his mind." Still, Saul begged Samuel not to embarrass him by leaving without saying a few appropriate words.

"Give me a sword!" Samuel shouted. Saul handed him his own Philistine iron long sword. "These are my few appropriate words," he said, addressing the Amalekite king, "As your sword has made women childless, so shall your mother be childless;" and plunging the sword deep into Agag's chest, killed him. "This," the blood drenched old prophet said, "is what Yahweh had commanded you to do!"

Saul tossed himself awake. Darkness, thick and heavy clung to him. His body stunk of sweat and fear. Faint eerie reflections of the campfire tore at the walls of his tent. He shook himself, gulped in the stale acrid air and choked. The throbbing in his head had subsided; it was still there but not as agonizing. How much of the dream was true? It felt true, all of it, every horrible, vivid detail, and God, what feelings! He'd never had a dream quite like it before, certainly not one that foretold the future. He called Joel to him. His life-long friend, brother-in-law and general was angry, could barely look him in the eye, but was civil.

"I have had a dream, Joel," the king said. "One I think foretells the destruction of the House of Saul."

Joel looked up at his king and shrugged. "You need no dreams to foretell that future, Saul! Just continue as you are and the destruction of the House of Saul is assured. You are your own worst enemy; only you can destroy the House of Saul. What you did yesterday...."

King Saul finished the sentence. "Was unforgivable, and an act of destruction such as you describe. Yes," he took a step nearer Joel and laid a hand on his shoulder. "I know. I would take it all back if I could."

"But you cannot!" Joel said, shaking off Saul's hand.

Saul shuddered, stepped back. "No, I cannot take it back. I can only go forward; make amends, one deed at a time."

"How could you, Saul?" Joel asked, staring into the king's eyes. "How could you, in the midst of war, beset by enemies on all sides, sow dissension in your own house?" Joel shook his head. "How is anyone to trust you, to serve you, to be your ally when you treat your own son in such a way?"

Shaking his head, Saul sat on his bed, put his hands over his face and cried. Joel fought back a momentary twinge of compassion and left the tent. As the sun rose and the breeze came up and the air freshened, Abadantha came and knelt by her brother's side. The red flames of the campfire no longer tore at the tent walls. Sensing a different presence, Saul stopped sobbing and lowered his hands. He was overjoyed and deeply grateful to see her. Abadantha wrinkled her nose at his smell. "You need a bath, Brother, you stink." She stood and opened the tent flap; crisp early morning light and brisk fresh air streamed into the gloom. "As you always seem to do, Brother, you have done both good and evil all at once."

"Forgive me, Dantha," Saul said, voice shaking, leaning forward for her to stroke his cheek.

"For my part," she said, ignoring his gesture and looking sternly into his eyes, "I may be able to forgive you in time, but it is not for me to forgive you, but your son, your army and your commanders. You have betrayed them, Brother, done them a grievous wrong and thereby undercut the foundation of your support and power."

The King looked down and sighed heavily. "I have made the fall of my House inevitable."

Dantha stood and slapped him. He looked up at her, startled. "Why?" he asked.

She slapped him again. "Enough, Saul! Enough!" she said. "All this wailing and weeping, enough!"

"But, but... " he sputtered.

"But what?" she asked, raising her hand again. He flinched back. "What good does all this moaning and groaning do? You're still King, aren't you?" He nodded. "Does the wailing and weeping make you a better King?" He shook his head. "Then why do it? It only reinforces the impression that you are weak, insane and incompetent."

Saul swallowed hard. "But the prophet said... "

Dantha raised her hand to him again. He fell silent. "That old man? None of your captains believe in him! And neither do most of your troops. If Yahweh were going to dethrone you, wouldn't he have done it by now? How do you even know that Samuel speaks for Him? Hasn't God with His earthquake supported your victory at Michmash? Didn't God give you Michal, Jonathan, and me to serve and support you?"

Saul sat up, deeply ruddy color flowing back in his cheeks.

"Enough, I say. Go forth now and exploit what you have begun! Michmash can be a great victory, the equal of Jericho, if you get out of this tent and attack! Your instincts are good. Fight now! Fight without ceasing!"

Joel was waiting outside the tent. The light gleamed on his armor and the wind whipped at his battle kilt. Seeing the King's new resolve, he was encouraged, but said, "It will not be as it was before, Saul. We here, and our people everywhere, have no choice. You are our king. We are on the cusp of victory. Now is not the time to go crawling to the Philistines and beg them to forgive us and allow us to worship their gods. Yes, you have betrayed us, and yes, it will take time to forgive you, but we have no choice. You are King. The House of Saul is our house." Saul opened his arms. Joel stepped into them and they hugged.

"No doubt, I will betray you again, Joel," Saul said, sadly.

Joel nodded. "And make other, more numerous mistakes. Samuel is not your friend, Saul. You give him too much power over you."

The sounds of the awakening camp—fires crackling, men calling to one another, the clank of armor, filled the air.

"He speaks for Yahweh," Saul said, as the freshening breeze blew his hair into his eyes.

"Even if he does, which I doubt, Yahweh is not God, only one of His aspects. The living God exists in our Covenant with It. As we remember It, It will remember us."

The smell of cooking food drifted all around them. The sun climbed rapidly into the cloudless blue sky and the wind picked up. Dathan and Abner, Dantha, Jonathan and Michal joined them.

"Let us eat and refresh ourselves," King Saul said, "then go forth and finish what we have begun."

# Chapter Thirteen

Although King Saul managed to drive the Philistines from much of the center of Israel, from Hazor in the north, to Hebron, and well past Jerusalem in the south, the Philistines still thrived in their strong, beautiful fortress cities on the coast of the Ocean Sea. They held a strong salient in the heart of the Shephelah, in the Valley of Elah, from which they continued to harass the Hebrews.

After weeks of hard fighting following Michmash, life in Israel gradually returned to the condition of the steady progress that characterized it before the massive Philistine invasion. Education and the Covenant were extended; public works projects resumed; trade, craftsmanship and artistry grew. The small, emerging Hebrew aristocracy of priests, artisans, administrators and soldiers focused on King Saul's court in Gibeah and the never ending warfare against enemies on every side, Moab, Ammon, Edom, Zobah and the Amalekites, continued.

Jonathan was dispatched to the deep southern desert, then the east side of the Jordan River to erect a string of staging points and light fortifications to fend off the constant inroads of the nomads roaming the Negev. He had not forgiven his father, and thought he never could or would. Although he had numerous opportunities to plot against Saul for the throne, he remained fiercely loyal to him.

Jonathan established his headquarters at Hebron, building the neglected outpost into a thriving garrison town. Shasheesha and Dathan went with him and under their loving tutelage his slavery and service blossomed and he became first an acolyte, then a priest in Astarte's service. He had a deep need to worship, not just intellectually, but emotionally and physically, to bow down naked and abase himself and to submit, to sing and dance and to lose himself in mindless obedience and servitude. Such worship refreshed and exhilarated him.

He experienced no contradiction between his sensual, fleshy, sometimes obscene sexual rituals, and his fierce commitment to the House of Saul and the Hebrew state. In fact, the reverse was true, the more dedicated he became to serving and worshiping Dathan, Shasheesha and Astarte, the more potent and effective he became as King Saul's heir apparent. When Jonathan thought about what his life had become and how good and full it was, he remembered how, when his father was about to condemn him, Dathan helped him shift the energies by reliving his enslavement to Shasheesha. Jonathan thought if he were to discuss this shift with his aunt Abadantha, she would find it a wonderful example of the Covenant at work. Dathan continued to live the ascetic life as a warrior prince, but Shasheesha lived like a goddess on earth, having, in addition to Jonathan, five slaves, one male and four females, completely dedicated to satisfying her every whim.

Rumors of Jonathan's enchantment and servitude floated about King Saul's court, but given the strain in his relationship with his son, the king was reluctant to do anything overt to verify them. Michal often visited and fought at Jonathan's side, and upon her returns, King Saul questioned her, but if she knew anything, which he knew she did, she would not reveal it to him. After awhile, fearing their combined power to overthrow him, King Saul decided to keep Michal at court in Gibeah.

Of all the marauding Bedouin that Jonathan dealt with, the Amalekites were the worst. A special hatred between the Hebrews and Amalekites had existed for nearly five hundred years, ever since Moses led the Hebrews out of Egypt. Every Hebrew was familiar with the Torah story of a horrendous battle between the outnumbered Hebrews and the better armed, trained, and more numerous Amalekites. In that tale, the Hebrews could keep the Amalekites at bay and ultimately win at sunset if they fought fiercely all day long.

In that battle things were not going well and Yahweh told Moses that if he kept his arms raised above his head, He, Yahweh, would hold back the sun until victory could be theirs. Moses's arms soon tired and four men were required, two on each side, to help him hold up his arms until Joshua could secure the victory. The Hebrews had nearly wiped out the race of Amalekites then, but the Bedouin persevered, nurtured by their hatred of the Hebrews, to once again become a major threat.

In his dispatches to his father, Jonathan continually asked for more troops to deal with them. Finally, two years after Michmash, on leave to Gibeah, Jonathan went to court to plead with the king to dispatch an army that would destroy the Amalekites once and for all. The king, mindful of his dream, was loath to become more deeply involved with the Amalekites. The pressure for action, not just from Jonathan, was too great and Saul decided to talk with Abadantha about that old, but never forgotten, dream.

"I know not what to tell you, Brother," Dantha said, after hearing the dream.

They were walking in the sun-drenched Palace courtyard garden, Saul's pride and joy. He had taken great care with it, installing a variety of fig trees from as far as Egypt, citrons from the north and east, black mulberries, apricot and apple trees, even a few carob plants and a small vineyard and olive grove. As they strolled, the King greeted his gardeners by name. "Clearly, Yahweh has not deposed you."

"*Yet*," King Saul said, a wry expression on his face.

"Yet," Dantha repeated. "I'm glad to see you making that face. Does that mean you see how nearly brainless your fear is?"

" 'Nearly brainless?' " Saul repeated. "If you weren't my sister, you should be flogged for showing such disrespect to your king."

"Flog me, then," Dantha said, smiling. "But you do begin to see, don't you?"

The king nodded. "Good.

"And all this business with Samuel, my God, Saul, he's a senile old man, who's been living quietly in Nob since Michmash. Why, his corrupt sons aren't even on your Council any longer. Samuel's no threat to you."

The king shuddered. "You seem to be right, but it's not over yet, and now there's all this pressure to do something about the Amalekites, and in the dream Samuel was so clear about what was to be done. Remember, Dantha, Samuel selected me, anointed me and backed me. He has a place in my heart." The piquant sweet smell of the black mulberry shrubs drifted around them on the warm breeze.

"He backed you in the beginning, Saul, but not since." She reached out and touched his chest. "And as for his 'place in your heart,' that is diseased, no longer healthy, and does not fit the facts. The facts are first. At this point, there are similarities between your dream of the Amalekites and the present situation. Two, the Amalekites are our people's ancient foes. Perhaps it is your fate to eliminate them once and for all and Samuel's demand that you do so merely reflects your own wisdom."

King Saul dipped his head in agreement.

"Three," she continued, "making an example of the Amalekites by destroying them utterly is good policy and would serve as an example to all our enemies, especially Zobah. Fourth and last, Jonathan is your heir and one of your best generals. You don't want to go against him. If he and Dathan advise a large scale operation, it is probably the wisest course of action."

"What of these rumors about Jonathan's enchantment, his worship of Astarte and the wild sexual excesses?" Saul was secretly jealous of his son's rumored sexual excess. He wanted to experience them for himself and thought they were reminiscent of the rituals he and Dantha had done years ago.

"What of them?" Dantha said. "Is he any less effective, any less a leader or administrator or builder?"

King Saul shook his head.

"I have heard the rumors and know of Shasheesha and her power over men. As long as Jonathan continues to be effective, I care not. In fact," Dantha paused, leaned forward and looked closely into her brother's eyes, "from what I've heard about what they're doing it sounds a lot like what you and I used to do." Her eyes softened, "You remember that, don't you, brother?" she asked, stroking his arm.

"How could I forget!" King Saul said earnestly. "I miss those rituals, Dantha, and want to do them again; they gave me strength and hope, courage and focus."

"Yes," Dantha said, caressing his cheek, "I enjoyed them too, and they were good for me, as well. Perhaps we should revisit them."

"Oh, yes, Abadantha! Please, let us perform our rituals again!"

"Yes," she said, gazing into her brother's hungry eyes, feeling her power to control his lust well up within her. "Yes, all right, perhaps tonight?"

He nodded vigorously.

"So," she said, walking on, "given how you feel about our rituals, has it occurred to you that perhaps Jonathan's continued success and loyalty to our House may be due to Shasheesha? That in fact his worship of Astarte and his enslavement to Shasheesha and Dathan may be the actual cause of his achievements?"

Saul looked down. "Yes," he said. "But wouldn't that be blasphemy?"

Dantha sneered and smiled scornfully. "Was that what it was when we did it, brother?"

"I'm not sure; it was so good, so healthy and life affirming, how it could it be blasphemy?"

Dantha nodded. "Yet that's what it would be if Samuel were here to name it or if Yahweh were God. But neither is true, is it, brother?"

Saul shook his head.

"I sense the Covenant at work here, Saul. It matters not who or what Jonathan worships, or what we worship for that matter, only that one be a good person and loyal leader; and that Jonathan is, as you are, despite your tortured self doubts.

"Ah for the love of God, Saul, take hold! Cast out the fear; celebrate your life and our love; you've earned it. Go now, meet with your son and fulfill the destiny the dream foretold. Destroy the Amalekites utterly. It will not only strengthen our House by cementing your relationship with Jonathan, it will finally end a chapter in our people's history."

"I would like to make things right with my son," Saul said, eyes alight with hope.

"Yes, my King," Dantha said, standing on tiptoe to kiss his cheek.

"My handsome and manly King. Follow your heart and we will celebrate your rebirth tonight."

They were naked. Dantha's body was still lush and beautiful, a little heavier, the skin not as luminous, but she was still gorgeous to him. As he knelt at her feet, gazing up at her magnificence, he felt the same combination of arousal and deep devotion he'd felt years ago. Her eyes closed as she pirouetted slowly, arms straight up above her head hands flat and touching, allowing him to worship her naked glory. It felt good and right to have him kneeling in adoration before her once again. Why had she let these rituals lapse? Her nipples erected and her vagina grew moist as she felt his eyes caressing her flesh. Oh, this was so good! Her eyes opened and she saw he was fully erect, his proud manhood saluting her aging beauty. We will do this on a regular basis, Dantha promised herself, no more waiting years and years. Then she felt herself taken, in the past it had been a benign spirit, this time it felt more sensual and fleshy. Its voice, her voice, was deep and severe, "Though you be king, you are nothing but a slave, My slave!" it said.

"Yes, Goddess," Saul replied, his voice husky with barely controlled lust. "Your slave."

Dantha's eyes stared, but it was not she who looked out through them. "Yes, My slave. All men are My slaves, though all do not worship Me as you do. Your worship finds favor in My eyes."

Saul was stroking his erection, moments from an orgasm. "Thank You, Majesty. It is a privilege to worship You, an honor, and my destiny to serve and obey You."

"Yes, you are a good servant to Me. Why have you waited so long to attend Me?"

"I know not, Majesty. But I am here now, Highness, ready to do Your will. May I know Your name, Goddess?"

"Astarte."

Saul recoiled and almost woke from his trance.

"Gaze down upon My feet, Slave."

He obeyed.

"Do you find them attractive? Does the thought of serving as My foot slave arouse you?"

Her feet were small and perfectly shaped, Her toenails painted red. "Oh, yes, Majesty! I was born to be Your foot slave."

"Yes, that is true," She said. "You were born to be My foot slave. Lay down flat on your belly, hands at your sides, face at the feet you long to serve."

Saul obeyed, laying on his erection, the pressure of his body on it making him ready to cum.

"Sniff My sacred feet, slave!"

Saul obeyed; the smell was an earthy mixture of sweat, dirt and garbage with a hint of the red paint she'd recently used. The smell and the act aroused him mightily, "Oh, God! Oh, God!" he cried out between whiffs.

"No," She said, "not God, but the mighty Goddess, Astarte. Now, as a clear token of your complete dedication to Me, take your hand, lift My foot and place it on your head." He obeyed and when he felt the pressure of Her foot on his head and She pressed down, he knew he was Her slave forever and orgasmed.

As her brother writhed and twitched beneath her foot, Dantha sighed. She orgasmed and felt Astarte leave her. Slightly embarrassed at seeing the king groveling before her, Dantha nevertheless understood how useful this could be for him. Besides, she enjoyed it! Joel was a fine man and an excellent lover, but there was nothing like this feeling of absolute power that came from having another human being groveling at her feet. Oh! She shuddered. Saul was laying still now, his head still beneath her foot. Thank God, she was able to resist the temptation to abuse her power over him, to make him adore and glorify her in public. These private ceremonies were enough for them both. Dantha took her foot from his head. "Sit up, Saul," she said.

Saul, still slightly in trance, obeyed and gazed adoringly at her with doggie eyes. Ah, Dantha thought, I do enjoy this and from now on, we shall do these worship rituals at least once a week, maybe just before the Sabbath; that would annoy Yahweh. She smiled. Well why not? Wasn't the feminine part of God worthy of worship, too? Of course! Look at Devorah and Yael; hadn't they embodied the Spirit of the Covenant and brought peace, joy and prosperity to their people? That reminded her of the Kenites.

When the trance was completely gone and his demeanor normal, they dressed, and Dantha stroked his cheek chastely. He smiled warmly at her. "Joel told me that the plans for attacking the Amalekites are nearly complete."

King Saul nodded.

"And the Kenites, what about them? Aren't they mingled with the Amalekites?"

"Yes," Saul said, "Abner has dispatched Kenites from among his force, who have family in the area and would not arouse suspicion if seen there, to warn them and help them evacuate quietly." He smiled at his sister. "Leave it to you to be mindful of Yael's husband's people! I am proud of you! We owe them too much, not to take care of them. Devorah and Yael were so close and made all the difference to us, especially to our family and to you and me." He leaned forward and kissed her fully and sweetly on the mouth. She returned the kiss then stood.

"And Moses," she said. "Moses married a Kenite when he left Egypt."

Saul nodded.

"All right, brother, thank you." She reached down, he took her hand and she pulled him to his feet. "When do we attack?"

"After the Sabbath, in two days time."

The next morning, learning of King Saul's plan to launch a major campaign against the Amalekites, Samuel left his home in Zulph and made the long, dusty trek to the King's Court in Gibeah. Shunning the usual public audience, the old prophet asked to see the king alone, in his sumptuously appointed private chambers.

King Saul had wine, honey cakes, and dates arrayed in silver dishes on a polished cedar table. As Samuel entered the room, Saul seated himself and gestured for the prophet to join him at the table. The King saw in Samuel's raised eyebrows and hesitant movements that the prophet was taken aback by the new kingly confidence and the opulent surroundings—silver, cedar, drapes, carpets, rich, luxurious multi-hued robes, a golden circlet crown. Saul knew the prophet normally stood to deliver Yahweh's word, but saw in Samuel's willingness to sit with him, man to man, a good omen. How marvelous, he thought, to be with Samuel and not have a headache! What a wonder!

"It is good you have chosen to make war on the Amalekites, King Saul," Samuel said, seating himself and taking the proffered silver goblet of wine.

King Saul's confidence and sense of well being soared. "Yes," he said, nodding sagely. "The Council and all my advisors said it was the correct course of action. I slept on it, prayed on it and received no contrary guidance." He looked down momentarily as he said this last, swallowed hard then again looked into the prophet's wrinkled face.

"Are you sure, Saul?" Samuel asked, staring into the King's eyes.

Eyes steady, King Saul looked back. "Yes. Absolutely! We will be victorious. We have a splendid plan, even down to getting the Kenites out of the way. And the Army is enthused, eager for rich spoils."

Samuel dipped his head in agreement. "Good about the Kenites—Moses married one, as did Devorah's Yael. They are like our own." He took another drink of wine and nodded approvingly. "You are right. You will win; Yahweh sent me to tell you that."

"Thank you, Samuel!" Saul exclaimed, jumping up to thump the prophet's thin shoulders, truly and deeply happy that both Samuel and God were pleased with him at last. "I appreciate you coming to tell me." But then he realized that Abadantha was right, Samuel was just another player sensing which way the wind was blowing and wanting to be on the winning side. Oh, too harsh, he criticized himself, there *is* something of the Covenant in him; he does truly speak for God at times, not only Yahweh.

King Saul sat down, adjusted his rich, multi-hued robes, and Samuel continued. "It is the *aftermath* of your victory that God has commanded me to speak with you about."

"Aftermath?"

Samuel nodded. "Yahweh has commanded me to tell you that it is His wish that you destroy the Amalekites utterly. God wants you to kill every living thing; wipe them out to the last man, women and child, and all their cattle and livestock as well."

King Saul stared at Samuel. "Why would I want to do that old man?" He stood, hands on hips. "You know the soldiers are paid in the spoils of slaves and livestock."

The old prophet also stood. "You would do it, King Saul, because your Lord and Master, Yahweh, has commanded you to do it."

King Saul felt a shiver of fear, but did not waver. The two men stared at one another, the air almost crackling with their emotional energy. Finally, Samuel turned to leave. "Consider the word of God, King," he said, turning to look over his shoulder.

"I shall, prophet, I shall," the King said, sitting and sipping from his goblet.

Samuel took a few more steps, felt his heart soften and turned back for one more plea for repentance. "It is not too late, Saul. You know you are a sinner."

"How so, Samuel; how much worse am I than other men?"

"Yahweh sees what men do not, oh King! He knows of the incest between you and your sister and of the blasphemy of your enslaved son's worship of Astarte. The House of Saul teeters on the brink, King. Do not add one jot more to the scales against you!"

The King dropped his eyes for a moment, looked up, but said nothing. Sighing, Samuel turned and shuffled from the room. Normally after such a confrontation, King Saul would have had a severe headache, dizziness and even nausea. But now, and since he and Dantha had discussed his dream, he felt only a dull throbbing.

Samuel isn't all there is of God, he reminded himself. I am *not* being singled out for punishment! I too, am a blessed son of the Covenant, no better and no worse than my fellows, despite my kingly rights and obligations. Why those responsibilities alone, in and of themselves, would be enough to give a person a headache! And hadn't the Egyptian physician said all was not right in my head? The King rubbed his temples. This meeting with Samuel was progress. I pray the Almighty God of the Covenant will continue it!

The Israelite victory over their ancient enemy was so swift and so relatively free of casualties and dead on the Hebrew side,

King Saul was certain he was blessed by God, that finally, his grim debilitating back and forth with Yahweh was at an end. This feeling was reinforced by the fact that all the men but Agag, the Amalekite King, were killed in combat as were most of the women and children. Now, surely, Yahweh's command was obeyed. Now, surely, He would not begrudge His victorious army the spoils of a few women, children and livestock? Besides, many of the cattle would be used as sacrifice in His honor.

Agag would be kept locked away to be shown off from time to time as a reminder of the fate of those who disobeyed Yahweh. Now, covered in gore and blood, at the center of the reeking battle field heaped high with the twisted and broken bodies of Amalekites, surrounded by the Army, King Saul and his commanders, Jonathan, Dathan, Abner, Joel, and Michal, gathered large smooth stones to erect a massive monument to their victory. Beside the monument, an altar was also erected, upon which the choicest of the captured cattle were to be offered.

The day had been hot, the dust of battle thick and blinding, the noise deafening. Now, in late afternoon, as the monument was completed and the sun dropped lower in the sky, the breeze freshened. The stench and dust blew away and the light, crystalline and sharp, illuminated the monument and thousands of silent men massed around it. King Saul thought it to be a truly blessed moment.

As the King's battle-hardened priests prepared to make the sacrifice, Samuel strode in from the desert covered with dust, his long white hair and robes billowing in the wind, his eyes flashing red with anger. "The wrath of God is upon thee, King Saul, and upon me," he said to the stunned King. "The Lord God Yahweh is sorry he made you King. 'I repent of having made Saul king,' He said to me, 'and of having you anoint him.' "

"Why, Samuel, why? Have we not done the Lord's will today and wiped out the Amalekites?"

"Were you not commanded to destroy *every* living thing?" Samuel asked. "What is this bleating of sheep in my ears? Why do I hear the lowing of cattle? The Lord sent you forth with strict instructions—

kill *every* living thing. Why did you not obey? Why have you seized the spoil and done what was wrong in the eyes of the Lord?"

"Yahweh is not all of God," King Saul said. "I... "

Samuel turned his back on his King and started to walk away.

"Wait!" Saul called. "I am King! You will listen, old man!" Desperate, feeling the eyes of the multitude upon him, King Saul seized the prophet's robe, struggling to hold him. "Please," the King said, "pardon my offense and come back with me."

"I will not go back with you," Samuel said, "for you have rejected the Lord God Yahweh's command, and the Lord has rejected you as king over Israel."

Part of Samuel's robe tore away in the King's hand. A huge, "Ahh!" issued from thousands of throats. For a moment, neither King nor prophet spoke nor moved. The air was thick with the electricity of their emotions. Then, with fierce red light streaming from his eyes, the old prophet said, "Thus has the Lord God Yahweh torn the kingdom of Israel from your hand, and will give it to another, a better man than you."

Cries of, "No!" and "Never!" and "Get thee hence, old man!" flew from the assembled soldiers. Samuel whirled around. As King Saul stood stunned, the prophet reached across Saul's chest and pulled the King's iron long sword from its scabbard at Saul's side and brandished it above his own head. Saul and his captains shrank back. With a deep groan, the crowd of soldiers fell into an astonished silence.

"Bring me Agag, King of the Amalekites!" the prophet shouted.

King Saul, who had regained his composure, nodded and the frightened Amalekite was dragged forward, defenseless with his arms bound to his sides, heavy chains clanking. "Surely," Samuel said to Agag, holding the sword with both hands high in the air, "the bitterness of death is at hand. As thy sword hath made women childless, so shall thy mother be childless among women." Uttering an unearthly scream, and with supernatural strength clearly not his own, Samuel brought the sword down on Agag, splitting the upper half of his body in two; then wrenching the sword free using his foot to push the writhing body forward, the prophet of Yahweh, soaked in warm, still spurting blood, hacked the king of the Amalekites to pieces.

Samuel dropped the King's sword and fell to his knees completely spent and panting. Shaken, dripping with blood and gore, the King, Jonathan and Michal rushed to the trembling old man, knelt beside him and lifted him to his feet.

"Ha!" Samuel said, looking into each of their faces as he allowed them to lift and steady him. "The House of Saul. I did what you should have done!" Samuel shook himself from their hands. "I have done with you! Yahweh has done with you!" He walked away.

Saul and his children looked at one another, horror, fear and relief battling across their faces. Relief won.

"He will not be missed," Michal said, stooping for a handful of dirt and wiping her hands together to get the sticky blood and gore off.

Jonathan handed her a woolen kerchief he'd been using. "Indeed," he said, "that old man means our family no good, no good at all."

"True," their father said. "He never wanted a monarchy and anointed me reluctantly."

"And has done all he could since, to make your life miserable," Michal added.

"It is good that he is near death," Jonathan said. "Else we should have to kill him."

"Do not speak so, my son! It borders on blasphemy. He is a prophet and still has a connection with God!"

"Father," Michal said, voice annoyed. "You give him too much credit."

"He did anoint me, Michal, and I rule in God's name because he anointed me."

"Yes," Jonathan said, wiping sweat from his brow. "That is true. We must watch him. He could easily anoint another."

Abner, Dathan and Joel drew nearer. "True, my Lord," Abner said. "We must keep eyes on him."

King Saul frowned with distaste and nodded. "But no harm must come to him. Samuel is one our greatest prophets and still has a great following among the people. We dare not offend his followers any more than we must."

Abner dipped his head in agreement, gestured to one of his

officers, and briefly spoke with him. As the man trotted off, Abner rejoined the King. "The House of Saul is victorious this day!" he proclaimed. "Let us continue the sacrifice then divide the remaining captives, livestock and cattle among your loyal warriors."

King Saul bent, picked up his iron long sword, wiped it on a remnant of Agag's robes and returned it to his scabbard. "Let it be as you have said, Cousin." He smiled into Abner's face, and then gestured to the priests to resume their preparations. As the choicest bulls were led forward, a huge cheer arose from thousands of throats, filled the air and echoed from the shadowy brown hills.

The King was pleased. He raised his hands for silence. "Now, my brave and loyal comrades, my fierce warriors, when the sacrifice is complete shall the King's portion of the spoils be divided among you!" The cheers were louder than before and in the wave of love and approval that swept over them Saul, Jonathan, and Michal embraced. Then, with King Saul in the center, they raised their clasped hands and turned slowly in a circle, to even more deafening cheers, exalting the unity of the House of Saul for all to see. But for Jonathan and Michal, it was only a show, for they could no longer trust their father. They served him fully and loyally, but would never forgive him for almost killing Jonathan.

# Chapter Fourteen

As he slowly made his way back to his estate in Zulph, Samuel felt as if he was followed, but each time he looked around, saw no one. Tired, sad, and bone weary, the prophet arrived home to the scorn of his ne'er-do-well sons. Samuel wanted to be left alone. He lay abed for two days tortured by dreams of King Saul as the reluctant young man he'd anointed, then as the rich and arrogant potentate, and Samuel wept.

*"How long will you mourn Saul?"* Yahweh asked him. *"I have rejected him."*

*"Fill your horn with oil and go. I am sending you to Jesse of Bethlehem, for I have chosen a new king among his sons."*

"Please, Master," Samuel begged. "I am old and weary; let me die in peace! Saul may have fallen out of favor with you, but you have left him in place. He is still King of Israel and he will surely kill me if he hears of my mission. Why have you not yet removed him?"

*"It is not for you to question Me, Slave!"* The God's angry voice shook the earth and Samuel quaked with fear. *"Go hence and obey! Saul shall not harm you; you shall die peacefully in your own bed. But, should someone ask what your mission is, take a heifer with you and say, 'I have come to sacrifice to the Lord.' Then call Jesse to the sacrifice and you shall anoint the one I point out to you."*

Aware of Samuel's difficulties with King Saul and wanting no trouble, the elders of Bethlehem greeted the prophet with trepidation. "Is your visit peaceful, O seer?" They asked. Samuel reassured them and invited the entire community to the sacrifice, making a special effort to have Jesse bring his seven sons.

Happy to comply, Jesse was flattered when he and his sons met Samuel privately before the public ceremony. Eliab, Jesse's eldest was so striking, tall and handsome, that Samuel was reminded of Saul and thought he was the chosen one. But Yahweh said, *"Do not look upon his appearance or his stature. I have rejected him. It is not as a man sees that God sees: a man looks into the face, but God looks into the heart."*

One at a time, Jesse brought each of his sons before the prophet and Yahweh rejected each in turn. "Are these all of your children?" asked the tired and frustrated prophet.

"There is the youngest. He is tending the flock."

"Send for him," Samuel ordered.

The day was mild; puffy white clouds drifted elegantly across the powder blue sky. Birds sang in the nearby apple trees, and not far off, Samuel heard the murmur of the crowd gathered for the sacrifice. He sighed and leaned back to wait. "I will be done soon," he thought, drifting off to sleep. "The boy to come must be the chosen one."

*"Arise,"* Yahweh commanded. Samuel opened his eyes and stood. A small blonde child, beautifully proportioned with angelic features, perhaps ten years old, was making his way towards them. *"Anoint him, for he is the one!"*

Without hesitation, the weary prophet obeyed. "Come here, child," he said. "Do you know who I am?"

"No," the boy said. "You're not from Bethlehem."

"That is correct," Samuel said.

"This is the prophet Samuel," Jesse said. "The Lord God Yahweh has sent him here on a mission."

"What is your name, boy?" Samuel asked, taken by the boy's beauty and serenity.

"David, Prophet," he said, bowing deeply.

"A goodly name," Samuel said. "The Lord Yahweh our God has chosen you to be King of Israel. I am here to anoint you."

David's mouth fell open and his blue eyes grew wide with surprise. He looked to his father and to his eldest brother. They too, were amazed and speechless. But then Eliab, the eldest and handsomest, said, "Wait, Prophet!"

Samuel hesitated.

"This boy's mother is not even married to our father; she is a slave woman! How can such a spawn be made King of Israel? Besides, I am the oldest, he the youngest; it is my birthright, I am to inherit!"

Jesse pulled Eliab aside and tried to quiet him, but the handsome young man would not be stilled. "You are senile, old man! God would never pick such a one as this!"

Samuel pulled himself to his full height and his eyes shone red with fury as he stared at Eliab. "Do not blaspheme!" he said. Eliab shrunk back. "I obey the Lord God Yahweh and you would be well advised to do so also." Samuel gestured to David. "Come, boy. Stand here, before me." The boy obeyed. Samuel raised his horn and slowly emptied it over David's head. "In the name of Yahweh, Lord God of Israel, I hereby anoint you, David, son of Jesse, King."

David reached to wipe the holy oil from his eyes. "No," Samuel said. "Do not disturb the sacred oil. Do not wash it off; allow it to dissipate naturally." David bowed his head in acceptance.

"Thank you for your hospitality and cooperation, Jesse," Samuel said. "Now let us go that I may perform the sacrifice."

"But prophet," Jesse said, alarmed. "Is not Saul still King in Israel?"

Samuel looked sadly into Jesse's eyes and dipped his head in agreement.

"Then what are we to do?" Jesse asked.

"Go to the sacrifice," Samuel replied.

"And what of my son, the king?"

"Saul is a fierce warrior," Samuel said, "loyal to his friends, vicious to his enemies. Were he to discover what we have done here, today, I believe he would kill us all."

"And we would deserve it!" said Eliab. "For what you have done, Samuel, not us, but *you*, is high treason!"

Knowing Eliab to be correct, Samuel was anxious to be gone.

Jesse and his eight sons talked anxiously amongst themselves. "When will David assume the throne?" Jesse asked.

"When the spirit of the Lord moves him and makes clear the way," Samuel said, walking toward the altar.

And, in the meantime?" Jesse asked Samuel's back.

"In the meantime," Eliab said, "we keep our family's treachery a secret."

"To Bethlehem?" King Saul asked Abner. "Why would Samuel go there?"

"I am not sure, Sire."

They were in the antechamber to the throne room. Courtiers, soldiers, and administrators hurried by, bowing to the king as they passed. Completely open to the garden on one side, light, air and the scent of growing things streamed in. The space soothed Saul and he preferred conducting business there whenever he could, rather than in the formal throne room.

"All right," King Saul said, "what do you *think* he was doing there?"

Abner's face reddened. He hated it when his cousin got this way. "The official reason was to conduct a sacrifice." The King nodded for him to go on. "He did that."

"And... ?" the King said.

"Well, why go all the way there to conduct a sacrifice?"

"Indeed, why," the King said. "So... ?"

"Before the sacrifice he met with Jesse and his eight sons."

"And?"

"And, I wonder why, Sire, don't you?"

The King dipped his head in agreement. "What do you think, Abner?"

"I think the sacrifice was an excuse to see Jesse and his sons."

"And?"

"Samuel probably anointed one of them."

King Saul put his hand on Abner's shoulder. "It is as we feared, then?"

Abner nodded. "But which one?"

Abner shook his head. "We will have to wait and watch."

The King pulled his general-in-chief to him into a hug. He stepped back. "Thank you, cousin. You have done well. We will wait and watch together." He took a purse from his belt and handed it to Abner. "Distribute this to those who deserve it, and bid them now to keep a close eye on the house of Jesse and his sons." Abner, took the purse, bowed and walked away.

In Bethlehem, David welcomed the solitude of the dry hills, to be with the sheep, his dog, Brigand, and to play the lyre, feeling its notes soothing his rushing mind like rain drops falling on parched soil. He experienced the reality of the Covenant most fully here, composing and singing songs of gratitude and celebration to the One God who ruled his soul and lived and manifested Itself in all Its creation. He was grateful to his stepmother, Nitzevet, for awakening him to Its reality and sheltering him from Yahweh.

But now that shelter was at an end, David struggled, forced to share his soul with the fierce God of the Scrolls. What a contrast! How different from the benign, all- inclusive God of the Covenant. Since Samuel's anointed him as Yahweh's servant, not only did David's mind race and rush, but constant strife and bickering filled the house of Jesse. How much time before word of Samuel's visit and the reason for it, reached King Saul? Then what?

David had admired the King before all of this. He was proud of Saul's numerous accomplishments, and having been born two years into Saul's reign, knew only Saul as king. It felt strange now, exceedingly strange, to fear King Saul and think of him as a personal threat.

Life had changed for David and his family in other ways, too. Once, they had been like the other families in Bethlehem living simple, open and honest day-to-day lives praying, working, bickering, and laughing. Now they had something to hide. As the low status youngest, son of a slave girl, David had been the butt of his older brothers' pranks and jokes. Now he was the reluctant focus of the family's hopes and aspirations. He experienced fewer pranks and jokes, and because of him, not only did the family have something to hide, it had a future to prepare.

Plans were made for David's mother, Embet's, manumission and marriage to Jesse; the future king's mother could not be an unmarried slave girl. It was decided that to allay suspicions of treachery, should any arise, and to prepare to be the future king's military advisors, the oldest of his six brothers, Eliab, Abinadab, and Shimea should go to Gibeah and join King Saul's army. The others, Nethanel, Raddai, and Ozem were to be the future king's administrators and priests. Jesse had wanted to apprentice them to the rabbinical court in Nob, but their mother, Nitzevet, prevailed on him to send them to the nearby Covenant school.

As these plans took shape, the bickering, and with it, the immediate fear that their treachery might be found out, diminished. But each of the conspirators in the House of Jesse, Jesse, Embet, Nitzevet, and each of their children, had to cope with the extreme emotional swings between exultant pride and abject terror in their own ways. David, out for days by himself, was most alone and found some solace in the Covenant with his lyre, dog, and sheep. Not only did his brothers have one another, they had access to news, education, and gossip.

Now David missed that access. His shepherd's solitude didn't soothe him as much as it used to. His mind raced with thoughts of his future role and his need to keep up with tribal politics, economic, military, administrative, and religious affairs. He wanted to be in Bethlehem more and visit other places. Jesse, Nitzevet, and Eliab wanted him out of the way and out of temptation's path. When David did come in, every ten days or so, he plied his family for information on current events and spent days in briefings with his brothers. His liquid silver mind absorbed what they shared with him. Although it was not their intention, the family became an effective school for preparing David to be King.

All but Embet. David's mother was still a house slave at heart, unfit for more rigorous structured activities. She didn't even take well to being David's mother. She hadn't seen him much in the fourteen years since his birth, and when she had, it was as a house slave. She still didn't see much of him, and didn't really know him, so the transition was difficult for her and the rest of the family, especially for David. He was used to thinking of Nitzevet as his mother and

Embet as a servant. As a slave, Embet had most enjoyed talking with the other slaves and servants and found it difficult to change her ways. She liked David and the others, but nothing was as satisfying as a good gossip session with her ex-colleagues. It was from them that Abner's man found the information his Master and King Saul sought.

"Samuel anointed Jesse's son David," Abner told the King. "He is a mere boy, a shepherd. I have gone to Bethlehem to see him for myself. We have nothing to fear from him. The family is ordinary. In fact, three of his brothers serve in our Army and are reckoned by their Captains as good and loyal men."

Saul nodded and rubbed his temples. They were in the busy, breezy antechamber to the Throne Room.

"Your head is bothering you again, Sire?" Abner observed.

The King nodded. "Tell me more about this shepherd boy who is no threat."

Abner stepped back and raised his hands in affirmative protest. "He is no threat... *now*. What may come in time, I cannot say. Had you not banned necromancers, you might know. But with me, Cousin, you need no necromancers. As I said, he is a shepherd and spends most of his time with his flocks, amusing himself playing the lyre."

"The lyre?" the King repeated.

"Yes. I have not heard him myself, but those who have give good reports of his music. They say he literally charms the sheep to sleep at night with his playing."

"Interesting," King Saul said. "And you say his three oldest brothers are already in my service in the Army?"

Abner nodded. "Yes, Sire, they are good men and no threat to us."

"So," King Saul said, "If we bring the boy here to play for me to soothe my headaches, we would have the most possibly dangerous people under close observation."

Abner smiled and dipped his head in respectful agreement. He loved the way his cousin grasped the puzzle pieces and slid them into place!

King Saul smiled in return. "Good! Then send for this shepherd boy that he may play for me."

# Chapter Fifteen

As he looked across the table at Jonathan, Dathan felt true affection for him, despite how their relationship had begun. He'd enslaved the young man only because he'd had to, to ensure his safety and Shasheesha's. Now Dathan was proud of the positive feelings he had for his erstwhile slave and proud of himself for having those feelings; he'd come a long way.

Like most of the priestly Ammonite aristocracy, he and Shasheesha had been accustomed to dominating and controlling those around them with hypnosis and religious sex rituals, turning them into willing slaves, using them, but never feeling anything more than contempt for them. Now, however, Dathan felt something bordering on affection for Jonathan. In fact, Dathan realized, as he watched the Prince in animated conversation with his sister, Michal, there had always been something special about Jonathan. Even as the young man had writhed in sexual frenzy, degraded and debased himself in his yearning and lust, Dathan had sensed a child-like innocence, sincere affection, and an honest direct openness he found endearing and wanted to nurture.

As their sense of safety was established, and Shasheesha had what she wanted, Dathan knew he was appreciated and valued for his skill and talent. He curtailed the rituals and made them less intense, shifting them from mindless obedience every night in the beginning, to genteel worship once a month. Shasheesha still used Jonathan as her personal maid and sex slave once or twice a week. Dathan knew Jonathan adored serving his dominant curvaceous Mistress, but Dathan also knew that as Jonathan neared thirty, he needed, and was ripe and ready for, an honest, truly loving relationship. Sometimes he mused about the effect their enslavement had on Jonathan. Had it stunted his emotional growth? Still, it had definitely accentuated his natural military prowess and leadership skills. Dathan thought there'd been a balance, enslaving the King's son in the way they had, had been a good thing for all of them.

Now, as Dathan watched Jonathan talking with the Princess, he realized he wanted only the best for his protégé. He wasn't sure what that was, and felt a sinking feeling about his inability to guide Jonathan on the next leg of his life's journey.

They were in the great dining hall of King Saul's palace, preparing for the Passover Feast. Having converted to the Hebrew faith three years ago, a rare occurrence, Dathan was honored to be included among the King's family and guests for this splendid occasion. It was his first time at the royal Passover Seder.

As a recent convert, Dathan was centered on serving Yahweh, but occasional conversations with Abadantha, had opened his eyes to another way of thinking about God. In fact, they'd just had one of those quiet, almost surreptitious chats in the garden, before they'd entered the great dining hall. Jonathan and Michal had listened and nodded as Abadantha spoke.

"The exodus we celebrate tonight can be viewed literally, as belonging to our people alone, or symbolically, as belonging to *all* people. That is, as we grow in affection, compassion and regard for all peoples, we have an exodus from the slavery of fearful, narrow, parochial thinking to the freedom of peace and all inclusiveness. The God of the Scrolls would see the story literally as belonging only to Hebrews and thus would keep us narrow and fearful. But the God of the Covenant would see the story symbolically as belonging to all peoples and in so doing, would fill us with peace and compassion." She looked into their faces. "Tonight be aware of which God you serve. The rituals and words are of Yahweh, but the meanings you choose to celebrate in your hearts can be of the Covenant."

Dathan thought Abadantha had a strong point and wondered why they had to talk about it so surreptitiously. Now he noticed Jonathan leaning forward, eyes bright and soft lips moist and slightly parted, staring intensely at someone. Dathan recognized that look as a pre-trance stare in which the subject gathered his inner resources to offer his beloved. Who was Jonathan looking at? Dathan followed Jonathan's eyes and saw a young male, perhaps fifteen or sixteen, fair and sunburned, of average height and weight; nothing special but for his ruddy blondeness. Nothing special to *him* perhaps, but Jonathan obviously felt otherwise. He was smitten, unable to pull his eyes from the boy, watching fascinated as he ate, drank and talked.

Feeling a pang of jealousy, Dathan nudged Jonathan. "Who is that boy?"

"I don't know," Jonathan answered without looking away.

Dathan turned to Ish-Boshet, Jonathan's brother, sitting on his left. "Who is that boy?"

"David," Ish-Boshet said, scowling. "Son of Jesse of Bethlehem, Father's latest treasure. He is a shepherd who plays the lyre and soothes the King's aching head." Ish-Boshet looked at Jonathan looking at David. "Your commander seems quite taken with him; have you noticed?"

"Yes, I have. Has David been long in King Saul's service?"

"No," Ish-Boshet said dismissively. "Not long; perhaps four months."

"Has it been that long, since we've been to court?" He said trailing the last words.

"I'm sorry, Captain," Ish-Boshet said. "I didn't hear you."

"It is nothing, my lord, I was merely thinking aloud."

Ish-Boshet dipped his head and looked away.

"We have been too long absent from Court, Jonathan," Dathan said.

"Yes, Dathan," Jonathan answered, finally pulling his eyes from David and looking at him. "That is true. There are many things of interest here."

"I see that," Dathan answered. "Do you fancy him?"

"'Fancy him?' My God, Dathan, I feel as if my soul had been sundered from his at birth and at long last has found its missing piece! It is more than 'fancy' and it horrifies me, even as it compels me. I have just laid eyes on this boy. I do not even know his name... "

"David," Dathan supplied.

"David," Jonathan repeated. "And have not spoken to him. How can I feel this way about him?"

As Jonathan's pained and wondering eyes touched his, Dathan put a hand on his shoulder. "Perhaps it is as you said, Jonathan, that he is indeed your soul mate; and if that is the case, you *would* feel as you do, even seeing him for the first time, with no knowledge of him. Has he looked back at you? Does he reciprocate your feelings?"

"No, he hasn't. Thank you for your words, I feel clearer, but no better. Why *hasn't* he looked at me? Surely he can feel my eyes upon him?"

Dathan smothered a smile. "Perhaps your eyes lack the power you think they have."

Jonathan looked hard at him then smiled. "You're right, of course, Dathan. Perhaps later, after the Seder we can get better acquainted."

"Yes, my Prince," Dathan said, eyes smiling softly, patting Jonathan's shoulder. "I'm sure that can be arranged."

David liked Jonathan, but not nearly so much as Jonathan liked him. As they talked after dinner, getting to know one another, the astute and sensitive young shepherd felt the powerful affection the King's son had for him. David had become enough of a courtier in his four months in King Saul's palace to know he didn't want to discourage Jonathan's feelings for him. After all, this hiding in plain sight was a dangerous and nerve-wracking game and one never knew when a Prince might be a useful ally. The Princess, Michal, was already such an ally. She too, was smitten with him, and David liked her no better than her brother.

It wasn't that David disliked King Saul's favorite children; he just didn't reciprocate the intensity of their feelings. He liked them well enough; he just hadn't found anyone, yet, who moved and excited him as he moved and excited them. Perhaps it was his age, but David doubted it. Most boys his age were already married, some with children of their own. More likely, the detached inner coolness was a function of his precarious situation. David had to keep his wits about him. If the King knew who he was, that Samuel had anointed him, he would surely slay him and his entire clan.

Sometimes David thought Saul did know. The King would look at him, lips curling in a sneer, eyes flashing red and he'd say, "Play for me!" and David would play. The King would be soothed, and so David chalked his suspicions up to the King's illness. Yet....

The valley of Elah separated the massed armies of the Philistines and the Hebrews. Neither side had the will or resources to dislodge and defeat the other. The stalemate had been going on for close to a year, and from time to time, Goliath, champion of the Philistines, a giant standing six cubits tall, would go down into the valley to taunt and shout insults at the Hebrews, challenging them to send forth a champion to do battle with him.

David's three elder brothers, Eliab, Abinadab, and Shimea, in the militia Judah sent to be part of King Saul's army, endured Goliath's boasts and taunts. The giant was much too formidable to be taken in single combat. In the months before being summoned to court, Jesse sent David to the battlefront, with provisions, loaves of bread and parched corn, for his brothers, and cheeses as a gift to the captain under whom they served.

There on one of the occasions, hearing Goliath's taunts and challenges, and seeing his brothers and the rest of the Hebrew host cower, with no one daring step forth to fight for their honor, David's cheeks burned bright red with shame and embarrassment.

"Come no more, David," Eliab had said. "Tell our father to protect you and keep you at home. Who have you left to look after our few sheep in the wilderness? I know you, my boy, you seek only for excitement!"

Undaunted and angered by their collective shame, David replied, "The sheep are not in the wilderness of Bethlehem, elder brother, but here, in Valley of Elah!"

Eliab grimaced at the sharpness of his brother's retort. "Return to our father, David. You are too young to fight, although you have much spirit. Our father need not fear the deaths of four sons, three are sufficient." David left, but vowed to return.

King Saul did not intend it, but as with two of his children, Jonathan and Michal, he too, felt strong feelings for David the moment he laid eyes upon him. The plan to keep the potential traitor and usurper close, to observe and control him, drifted away as King Saul, like so many others, was instantly smitten. Saul's affection and fondness for David grew as the golden shepherd boy sang his poems while accompanying himself on the lyre. The words and music soothed the King's brain fevers. "He is skilled in speech and handsome," King Saul wrote Jesse. "The Lord is with him."

To honor the shepherd in time of war, as well as to keep him close, King Saul named the teen-aged David his weapons-bearer, a title of distinctive intimacy and importance in the royal household. "David shall remain in my service," the King wrote Jesse, "for he has found favor in my eyes."

David returned the King's feelings. Unlike the more superficial polite regard he felt for the King's children, sons, <u>Jonathan</u>, <u>Abinadab</u>, <u>Malchishua</u> and <u>Ish-Boshet</u>, and daughters, <u>Merab</u> and <u>Michal</u>, David felt true affection and deep appreciation for King Saul. Grateful for the opportunity to serve his king, David thanked God everyday for allowing his music and poetry to soothe the King's pain. Occasionally, the Egyptian physician trepanning Saul's skull, would join them in the King's private chambers, to also be relaxed and to appreciate the way David's songs soothed the King.

"Someday," the physician said, "men will understand how the notes of your lyre, the rhythm of your words and the flow of the melody quiet pain."

As time passed, David did develop stronger feelings for three of Saul's children. He formed an almost instant dislike for Ish-Boshet, the youngest male, finding him arrogant and spoiled. Ish-Boshet returned David's feelings. But as he got to know Michal and Jonathan, David found much to admire and developed a deep affection for them. For their part, Michal and Jonathan, like everyone else, fell under David's spell. Each of them in his and her particular way fell in love with him.

Meanwhile, the stalemate with the Philistines and the effect of Goliath's taunting, were the King's greatest concern. He constantly consulted with Abner. David, being present, absorbed much military strategy and saw how the shifting alliances of tribal politics kept his people from becoming a nation.

"I should go forth and take up Goliath's challenge," Saul said, as he often did. "I am champion of our people; it is right that I go forth." David appreciated the King's willingness, but knew, as the Egyptian physician said for him, "You are not well enough for single combat, my Lord."

David often wondered what kind of God would allow this kind of torture of His people and their leader? He knew what the priests said about it, that Saul had sinned and the people had sinned, that what befell them was their own fault and if they ceased sinning, their travail would be lifted. From what David knew, Saul's 'sins' were more technical and formal, misdemeanors, really, not sins. Surely, a compassionate God would consider that, and if punishment was required, which a compassionate God would disavow completely anyway, then it should fit the scale of the 'sin.'

As for the people's "sins," David was one of them, as Saul had been only a generation ago; how serious were they? True, many kept teraphim, consulted necromancers, and had fallen into the worship of local gods, but they lived in a world of idol worshippers, surrounded by idol worshippers. It was easy to assimilate their neighbors' ways. Even during the Exodus, with God's miracles and wonders still fresh, had they not prevailed upon Moses's brother, Aaron, to make them a golden calf to worship? People were weak and subject to the trials and tribulations of daily living. Wouldn't a compassionate God be more forgiving?

And what of David's own "sins?" He neglected the required worship rituals on numerous occasions and though he'd had ambition before Samuel anointed him, his heart and mind now lusted after the fame and glory. This in turn, aroused his guilt and anxiety because he did not want to succeed at Saul's expense. He admired Saul and all he'd accomplished, and forgave him his human foibles, as he hoped others would forgive him.

Now Abner was with the King and they were discussing another possible flanking movement around the left side of the Philistine entrenchments. After much discussion, both of them wanting to attempt it, they decided that they could not afford the potential loss of men because the tribes were holding back replacements. Again, David was embarrassed to hear that his own Judah was among the most vociferous about ending the conflict with the Philistines as soon as possible, even without a clear military victory.

Judah and these tribes believed that if peace were declared, the Philistines would return to their coastal fortress cities and leave them in peace. Before his experience in the King's service, David would have agreed, but now he knew that only a clear-cut military victory and a continued strong military presence could establish and keep the peace. The territory was too small, the spaces too narrow, and the Philistines, too close. Armed might was all they would or could accept. It was not like the current peaceful relationship King Saul had established with Egypt, such that a physician from the Pharaoh's own service would come and attend him. Egypt was far away and had little trade with Hebrews, whereas the Philistines lived cheek-by-jowl with them, traded and shared the towns, cities and highways and often the same gods and temples.

Abner looked sadly from the King to David. "We cannot tolerate much more of this stalemate, Sire." Then, suddenly, as if seeing David for the first time, the eyes of the King's cousin and General in Chief's widened, and he blinked twice and shuddered violently.

"What is it, Abner?" King Saul asked. David felt as if his covenant had been revealed and shrunk back.

Abner passed his hands across his eyes, took a deep breath, looked again at David and his shuddering subsided. "It is nothing, Sire," the General said. "Nothing at all, just a momentary vision. I am fine."

Later that day, Michal spoke with David. "How goes it with my father?"

"Not well," he said, shaking his head. They were in the Palace gardens, seated on stone benches beneath the gnarled, tall live oak trees, ancient before the House of Saul was founded. Bees buzzed around them, birds called and flitted in the leafy branches and clear, bright sunlight filtered through casting green tinted shadows on the ground below. The air was crisp and cool.

Michal pulled her shawl more tightly around her. "How can you go about in that short tunic, David?"

He reached out and caressed her cheek. "Fear not for me, Michal, it is stout Judean wool."

Michal looked a question at him. "I am embarrassed that Judah will not properly support this war with the Philistines. Are you offended?"

David looked down.

Michal spat. "Were you not from Judah, I'd say the whole tribe was accursed. They have always been jealous of my father and work tirelessly behind the scenes to bring him down."

David smiled wanly at her. "Sadly it is so. But I am not one of those. I love your father as my own, more than my own. He needs no help from Judah, or anyone, to be brought low. He is his own worst enemy."

Michal raised her hand to slap his face; he restrained her easily. "Your loyalty is admirable, Michal, but not well placed. You know, as does the entire kingdom, how he would have sacrificed Jonathan and maybe even you, if Yahweh through Samuel had demanded it."

She knew all too well. Her face flamed and tears started from them.

David was sorry he'd mentioned it. "Forgive me, Michal; you are a fierce lioness, the kind of woman any man would be proud to marry."

Looking longingly into David's eyes, she took his hand, brought it to her lips and kissed it. He touched her cheek, stroked her hair.

"I would be *your* lioness, David," she said.

Jonathan approached. "Watch out, David. A lioness has sharp teeth and claws."

David stood and embraced the king's son. Michal stood and Jonathan embraced her too, then they sat hands in laps, looking softly at one another.

"We both love you, David," Jonathan said. "I think even Father loves you. But only the lioness may bear your children." David's face reddened. Michal looked down.

"Now, now," Jonathan said, "no need for modesty or dissembling among ourselves. We are too high, and like moths and fly too close to the flame; we must help one another."

Michal and David nodded.

Ish-Boshet walked past them, scowling. "Beware, Sister," he said. "And you too, Brother. Be not deceived. This Judean bears our House no good."

David made to rise as Ish-Boshet's hand tightened on the bejeweled dagger in his sash.

Michal restrained David. "How can you say that, Brother? All the world knows the good David that does for our father! Even the Egyptian physician benefits from David's songs!"

"Mark me, Michal," Ish-Boshet said over his shoulder as he walked on. "David *will* betray the House of Saul and mightily disappoint you... both of you!"

As they watched Ish-Boshet stalk away, Michal said, "David was just telling me how embarrassed he is that Judah will not more readily help with the Philistine stalemate."

Jonathan's face tightened. "It seems as if they have a champion of their own in the wings waiting to step forward and take the King's place."

David winced. He was a traitor, but not *that* kind of traitor. It was not for him to organize resistance to a sitting King—at least not yet.

"This stalemate is draining Father's strength." Jonathan looked up at the pale blue sky, and swatted at the bees. "I think I might volunteer to be our champion and put an end to this braggart, Goliath."

"No, Jonathan," Michal exclaimed, "you cannot!"

"Have you seen him, chaver?" David asked.

Jonathan nodded, "Once."

"I have seen him on numerous occasions, even studied him," David said.

"So?"

"So, Goliath cannot be beaten in hand-to-hand combat."

Jonathan saw David's face and eyes. Even the tone of his body had become taut and coiled. Gone was the softness of the youthful poet inexperienced in military matters, and in its place, the hard-bitten calculations of a combat veteran.

"He is too big; his reach is too great and he can throw a javelin a long distance. He must be taken by stealth and from a distance beyond his reach."

Jonathan peered at David through narrowed eyes. "You have a plan, chaver?"

David nodded. "I am an excellent slinger and small."

Jonathan dipped his head in agreement.

"He will not feel threatened by me. I will walk within sling range of him, beyond the range of his javelin with my sling hidden at my side. I will kill him with a stone to the head before he can think to raise his shield."

Michal flung herself onto him. "No! No! Not you! You shall not!"

David stood, shaking her off. "What do you think, chaver?" He searched Jonathan's eyes.

Jonathan put his hand on David's shoulder. "I too, would not want you hurt, but the plan is a good one. Any warrior can see that." He lifted Michal up. "You are a warrior Sister, and a good one. Surely you see the merit of David's plan?"

"Put me down!" she squealed.

Jonathan obeyed. "If David is willing to work his plan, who are we to restrain him?" Michal dipped her head in agreement. "We must let him go with our blessings; isn't that so?"

Michal nodded again, choked back a sob and returned to the bench. Jonathan hugged David, holding him perhaps a moment too, long. "When shall you go forward, David?"

"Soon. With each day that passes, the King suffers unduly and the morale of our Army drops further; every day we have more desertions."

Jonathan nodded. "It is so, chaver. Go with God."

King Saul, Abner and their captains were touring the Hebrew emplacements at the time of day Goliath came forth to taunt the Hebrews.

Goliath goaded them. "Give me a man," he bellowed, strutting up and down the valley floor with impunity, "that he may fight! Is there not one such amongst you?"

The King stepped forward as if to take up the challenge and Abner restrained him, even as their captains shrunk back in fear. "No, Sire!" Abner said. "You have other foes to face, greater and more dangerous than this one!" King Saul dipped his head in agreement, turned and dismissing his fearful captains with a wave of his hand, went with Abner back to the royal tent.

Once inside, the King, dropped his shield, javelin and gripped his aching head. "Thank you, Abner, for restraining me. The pain and frustration give me a death wish to end my torment and die in glorious single combat!"

Abner smiled warily, "And you might yet, Sire. But not today and not here."

Saul stripped off his heavy regal armor. "Aiyee, my head, Cousin! Find David and bring him to me, please. Perhaps one of his songs will soothe me." Abner bowed and returned a few moments later with the shepherd boy. The King was slumped against his cushions; David began a song accompanying himself on the lyre. His strong youthful tenor and the crystalline notes of the lyre shifted the energy instantly. "O Lord my God," David sang, "in Thee have I taken refuge. Save me from all of them that pursue me, and deliver me. Rebuke me not in Thine anger; neither chasten me in Thy wrath. Be gracious unto me, O Lord, for I languish away. Heal me, O Lord, for my bones are affrighted."

A moment later, King Saul sat up, eyes clear, brow un-furrowed. "Would that He would, David," he said. Abner stood to one side, arms folded across his chest.

"But He does, and I would help you too, my King," David said, "and with more than my music."

"What help would that be, shepherd?" Abner asked.

"I am more than a shepherd, General," David said softly, eyes flashing, restraining himself.

"Indeed?" Abner asked.

"I am a slinger, my lord."

"A slinger?" Abner said.

"I didn't know that, David," the King said. "Good for you! And how would you help me?"

"I would be your champion, Sire." David's voice was soft and quiet.

The King wasn't sure he heard correctly. "Our, *what*?"

Abner guffawed loudly, "The shepherd boy said he would be our champion to fight Goliath."

King Saul's eyes were wide as he looked from one to the other. "Is that true, boy? You want to fight Goliath? But that would be certain death!"

"For Goliath, Sire," David said, simply.

"Out of the question!" King Saul said. "I can't lose you!"

"A moment, Sire," Abner said, the derisive laughter gone from his voice. "Let us speak."

King Saul nodded. "Leave us, David," he said with a dismissive gesture. "Wait nearby."

As David bowed and left the royal tent, Abner stepped closer to the King and whispered in his ear. "Let him fight, Sire! You cannot lose."

"What do you mean, Abner?"

"Remember, he is Samuel's anointed. If he dies fighting Goliath, you are free of him and if he kills Goliath, you are free of *him*. Either way you win!"

Saul smiled cunningly. "Yes, Abner, I see it! Still his music soothes me."

Abner stepped back. "Sire! This is a gift from God, a sign. He favors you again; you cannot lose!"

Still reluctant, Saul said, "And if he wins and defeats Goliath? What then, Abner? We shall never be rid of him! He will be a hero."

Abner guffawed and folded his arms. "Sire! Sire! How can he win? He is a shepherd boy—a boy without military experience."

"True," Saul said. "But he is God's anointed."

"As you are, Sire," Abner said simply.

The power of that simple statement was like a physical blow. Saul's head rocked. "Yes," he said, instantly centered and composed. "So I am. Ask David to rejoin us."

David entered and stood before the King. "David, my good servant, I fear your ability to fight the Philistine giant," Saul said.

David dipped his head. "Your concern for your servant is deeply appreciated, Sire. As I kept my father's sheep, there came a lion and a bear that took a lamb out of the flock, and I went out after them. I smote the bear and delivered the lamb from his mouth. I gave chase to the lion and when he rose against me, I caught him by his beard and smote him, and slew him. Thy servant slew both the lion and the bear. And this uncircumcised Philistine shall be as one of them, seeing he hath defied the armies of the living God."

"Your tongue is quick, shepherd," Abner said. "Let us hope you are as quick on your feet and with weapons to surprise Goliath."

"I shall be, General," David said, "and not just with Goliath, Abner."

Abner looked sharply at the boy.

But as for Saul's opinion, the cunning calculations were forgotten in love and admiration of the boy's quickness and confidence. The qualities that he, himself, had always wanted but never had, stood and pointing to his weapons and armor heaped on the floor. "Good and brave boy, though thou art but a youth, and Goliath, a man of war from his youth, I would have you go forth protected. Take my armor and weapons."

To appease the King, a much bigger man, at least a head taller and seventy pounds heavier, David picked up Saul's shield and sword. They were too heavy and unwieldy for him. Saul picked up his chain mail and dropped it over the boy's head and shoulders, not noticing how it nearly collapsed him. Then, in a kind of perverse crowning of his rival, King Saul put his own brass helmet on David's head.

David took a step, nearly fell, and said, "I cannot go with these, for I have not proved them."

Saul scowled, but Abner agreed with David. "He has no mobility in all that, Sire, or the training to use what you have given him. Let him go and fight with weapons he knows."

Realizing how silly the boy looked in the big man's helmet and mail and carrying the overly-large sword and shield, Saul dipped his head in agreement, but looked a moment longer, savoring one last look of the almost familial sharing of strength he meant to convey to the boy by giving him his armor. Smiling sadly, the King took his helmet and mail from the boy and as David laid the sword and shield down, he hugged the golden shepherd to him.

"Fear not, Sire," David said, retrieving his shepherd's staff from its place near the tent flap. "I shall return with the monster's head!"

Abner accompanied the shepherd boy from the king's tent. "Have you heard of the b'nai Elohim—the sons of the gods?" he asked.

David smiled. "Of course. Everyone knows the legends of the Nephilim, the race of giants, bred at the beginning of time when the b'nai Elohim descended from heaven and lay with the fairest women of Canaan." Then the smile faded from David's face as he grasped Abner's meaning. "You think Goliath is one of them?"

Abner nodded. "I do," he said, seeing what he'd hoped to see, as fear spread across the boy's face. "Fear not. I'm sure you also know that in Moses's time, his spies told him that "all the people we saw in Canaan were men of great stature." In addition to that they said, "we were in our own sight as grasshoppers, and so we were in their sight." and that "Joshua exterminated all but a few of them who remained in Gaza, Gath, and Ashdod. So they are mortal you see."

Fear gone, David glared into Abner's eyes. "I never doubted it."

"Good," Abner said. "And you also know that Goliath is your cousin."

David put his hands on his hips and stared at the General. "Even if he is, it will make no difference. He is a dead man."

Abner nodded. "He is connected to you through our great matriarch, Ruth."

David stroked his beardless chin sagely. "Ruth was a great woman. I didn't know my family and hers were connected."

"Indeed," Abner said, appraising the young man and sensing he was still strongly resolved. "Ruth begat Obed and Obed begat Jesse." David dipped his head in agreement. "I knew that."

"Yes, but did you know that Ruth had a sister, Oprah, who mated with a Philistine, a giant, and went to live with him in Gath?" David shook his head, no. "And through Orpah came Goliath. So he is your cousin."

"Your command of genealogy is splendid, General," David said, voice tinged with sarcasm. "Perhaps even surpassing your command of the military arts." Abner scowled. "But, as I said, cousin or not, Goliath is a dead man."

Turning on his heel, David walked through the camp to the Valley of Elah. As he crossed a swift flowing stream, he bent and selected five smooth stones from its bed and put them in his shepherd's pouch. Placing an oblong gray one in his stout leather sling, he whirled the weapon over his head and let fly. The progress of the stone was straight and true. Satisfied, David walked on until he came to the Hebrew emplacements. Greeting the soldiers, many of whom recognized him, David passed through the lines and waited at the edge of the flat, wide-open field in the valley between the opposing armies, hidden behind a clump of thorny shrubs. It was nearly time for the giant to come forth.

David felt a heightened alertness, but no fear. Images of Goliath drifted through his mind, and he felt it was good to review these because he'd have to be very precise about where to deliver the stones. He thought the head would be best, at the place between the eyes, but he couldn't be sure if the giant's helmet protected him there. He'd have to see; but there wouldn't be much time. Others were intimidated by Goliath's eight-foot stature and huge armor covered body. His coat of mail, the greaves on his thick calves, his sword, spear, javelin, were all of the same impressive scale and the shield that was carried by a barer who walked ahead of him. David would pay no mind to all of that, but focus on the giant's helmet.

David heard the giant's bellowing, "Give me a man that we may fight!" before he saw him. Although he wanted to stand and go forth, David decided to remain where he was hidden, make his assessment then go forward into the open. A smile crossed David's face as he thought of his last visit to this place, of who he'd been then, and of how now he knew his fortune was to be found not among his father's sheep, but here on the battlefield among giants and kings.

Goliath appeared and David saw that his helmet would not protect him. Gripping his sling tightly, David stepped into the wide-open space between the two massed armies. Goliath stood nearly 500 yards away. Shouts, laughter, catcalls and the sounds of swords pounding on shields and stomping feet greeted his appearance. At first the giant did not see him, then, seeing him, shouted, laughing, "Am I a dog that you come to me with a stick? Come forth and I will feed your flesh to the birds and the beasts."

Unperturbed, David continued closing the distance between them, mindful to stay outside the range of Goliath's javelin. "You come at me with a sword and a javelin," David shouted back, "but I come to you in the name of Yahweh, the God of the armies of Israel whom you have taunted." Nearing the beginning of the effective range of Goliath's javelin, David stopped, laid down his staff and placed a round smooth stone in his sling. "This day will Yahweh deliver you into my hand, and I will smite you, and take your head off, and give the carcasses of the hosts of the Philistines to the birds and beasts so that all the earth will know there is a God in Israel."

Laughing no more, the enraged giant raised and hurled his javelin in one swift movement and it landed where David had been standing. Anticipating Goliath's attack, David dashed forward, and whirling his sling before the giant could duck or move, let fly his stone striking Goliath squarely between his eyes, penetrating his skull and lodging in his brain.

The giant groaned, wobbled, dropped his sword, and fell straight forward on his face, his bowels releasing. Great shouts of triumph from the Hebrew side and cries of panic from the Philistines surrounded David as he moved up the valley toward the fallen giant. The stink of Goliath's bowels assailed his nostrils, but David walked on, picked up the giant's sword, damp with the dead monster's urine, and pulling Goliath's head up by its hair, he severed it from his body with three mighty whacks. Covered with blood, David lifted the still dripping head with both his hands and turned in a slow circle so all could see. The noise was now deafening. Screaming, the Hebrews rushed forward, smashing into the ranks of the fleeing Philistines. The slaughter was horrible and the day was a great victory for the Army of King Saul.

Avoiding the swooping rush of the Hebrew soldiers, David walked calmly off the field, carrying Goliath's head in one hand through the thick shrubbery towards the Hebrew camp. Abner, who had not seen David's victory, met him at the edge of the clearing. Looking him up and down, seeing him dripping with blood and gore, carrying the giant's head, and hearing the whoops and cheers of Hebrew victory, Abner saw the young man with new eyes. "A great victory for the Lord," he said deferentially.

"Indeed," David said, feeling the slight shift in power and staring into the General's narrowed eyes. "I could not have done it without Him. We are truly blessed."

"The Lord works in mysterious ways," Abner said. David dipped his head in agreement. "We must hurry now and follow-up your triumph. Allow me to escort you to the King, and then I must return to the army."

"*We* must return, Abner, my work is not done yet either," David said.

Looking down and nodding, swallowing hard, Abner led the way through the chaos of the camp and into the royal tent. King Saul sat in a daze, seemingly unaware of the uproar around him. As they entered, he looked up blankly and asked David, "Who are you?" The young man replied, "I am your servant, David, son of Jesse of Bethlehem."

King Saul was speechless for a moment then blinked, his eyes coming into focus, to rest on the still dripping severed head David clutched by its hair. The King seemed unsure of what he looked upon.

"It is the head of the Philistine Goliath, Sire," Abner said.

King Saul nodded slowly. The uproar outside made clear thought almost impossible. The King beckoned David to come nearer. When he did, Saul reached out, cupped Goliath's head by its chin and tilted it back so he could look into the vacantly staring dead eyes. "This is the fate of all who mock the Lord God Yahweh, and challenge His servants," he said. Then standing, he took the head from David, impaled it on his javelin, walked outside and set the javelin into the ground before the tent flap.

Abner and David followed him out. Men were running to and fro, the clamor was deafening and no one was paying attention to them. King Saul embraced David. "You have done well, David, my servant." He released him and stepped back. "I would have you be my shield barer. Go forth now, my shield barer, with Abner and destroy the enemies of our God!" David embraced Saul in turn, bowed and with Abner at his side, rushed off to do battle with the Philistines.

# Chapter Sixteen

They fought for five days without ceasing, driving the Philistines back to their seaside city fortresses. The land promised was once again completely in Hebrew hands. The first royal majlise since the Philistine invasion, twenty months before, was in progress. Four, perhaps five thousand Hebrews from all twelve tribes as well as ambassadors from Egypt, Syria, Macedonia and other neighboring nations, and even some Philistines, were gathered in the royal campground near the palace.

King Saul sat on a rough-hewn, beautifully polished throne made of gleaming cedar, on a raised dais, surrounded by his family, Abadantha, Janina, Ahinoam, Michal, and Jonathan, and closest advisors, Abner, Joel, Dathan, the High Priest, and the Tribal Elders. All were dressed in their finest raiment. They had expected David to be there, but he had not yet appeared.

The multitude was in a holiday mood, milling about at the wine and food stations provided by the King, talking, laughing and dancing as flute, timbale and harp players strolled among them. Dust and smoke floated in the warm, dry air, stinging tired eyes, and clinging to robes and sweating flesh.

Abner leaned close to the King, wiped his damp brow and said, "David wants to make an entrance, Sire, to impress the crowd."

King Saul nodded.

"No, Father," Michal said, overhearing Abner's remark. "David is simply late."

"And you, Jonathan," the King asked his son, "What do you think?"

"I agree with Abner, Father. I love David, but he is a wise politician for one so young."

Michal looked daggers at her brother.

"I too, agree with Abner," Joel said. "At present David is an asset to your House, Saul. But he bears watching."

"I agree with Abner and Joel," Abadantha said.

"As do I," Janina agreed. "But my son, I urge you to tread carefully with this son of Judah." Heads were nodding. "We Benjaminites have a long unhappy history with Judah."

"And remember, Sire," Dathan said, sneering. "He is the son of Embet, a slave woman. A person of no breeding..."

"Speak not of that, Dathan!" Jonathan said angrily.

Dathan's jaw dropped, shocked by the public challenge. "You, yourself, were once a slave!"

That was too much for Dathan. "Perhaps your appreciation for David's deeds and even love for him blinds you to the reality of your situation, Prince, both with him and with me!"

Jonathan did not look away nor bow his head.

Though grateful for her brother's support, Michal still looked lost and overwhelmed by the weight of opinion against her. Saul smiled and put his arm around her shoulders. "I love him too, Daughter, but," he gestured to the others in their circle. "They are right." He lowered his arm and turned slowly looking at each in turn. "Abner and I have had our eye on him for some time and will continue to do so."

The sounds of the crowd intensified, grew louder and became a chant, "David! David! DAVID!" The circle around the King opened, Saul stepped forward to embrace the young man climbing the stairs to the dais and the crowd redoubled its cheers.

The King gestured for silence and addressed the multitude. "This day have I promoted Yahweh's champion, David ben Jesse, to be at the side of my son Jonathan and my General-in-Chief, Abner." Abner and Jonathan stepped forward, linked hands with David and King Saul, then all four raised high their linked hands and the cheering reached a deafening roar.

Later, when the King, Abner, and Joel were alone, Saul said to

Joel, "Your loyalty and judgment are good, chaver. David is more of a threat to my House than you know."

Joel raised his eyebrows at his friend. "Abner and I have determined that Samuel anointed him, six months ago." Joel's eyes widened and his mouth fell open. "Can it be?"

Abner nodded. "After the battle with the Amalekites, we knew the Prophet could no longer be trusted and kept him under surveillance. Two weeks later, he went to the home of Jesse in Bethlehem and there anointed David."

Still, Joel could not believe it. Staring at Abner, he said, "And you have kept him close to the King all this time? Did you not think the King in danger? What if...?"

Abner was slightly offended. "Are you questioning my loyalty and judgment?"

"No," Joel said. "But... "

"Gently, my friends," Saul said, "gently. The facts speak for themselves, Joel. Abner complied with my wishes in this matter. And, as you can see, we were correct. I was in no danger from David and still am in no danger from him."

"If by 'no danger,' Sire," Joel said, "you mean no 'physical' danger, I would agree. But you heard the multitude today. They are mad for him. You may not be killed by him, but your Crown and House are most definitely in danger."

Abner stepped closer to Joel and put an arm around his shoulder. "Yes!" he said, enthusiastically. "Yes, yes, absolutely! You see it, Sire, don't you?" he asked, turning to the King. Saul nodded sadly. "Ah, Sire," Abner said. "You cannot still be harboring affection for this Judean who would steal your throne?"

Saul swallowed hard and looked down.

"No!" Abner's tone and gestures were fierce. "No! He is an arrow, head deep in your chest, one that must be cut out and removed! If you do not remove it, your House is doomed." Abner turned to Joel. "Surely, you can see it, Joel, tell him."

Joel dipped his head in agreement. "Abner is right, Sire. David is a danger to your House, perhaps not at this moment, but soon. The sooner he is eliminated, the better. Each day he grows larger and more powerful in the affections of the people."

"I understand," King Saul said. "And I am grateful, but the time is not yet right."

"But, Sire—" Abner began.

"No, Abner! Enough! I will hear no more about it now." Head throbbing, the King turned and walked away from his advisors, the bright torch light, and stale air into the cool, refreshing darkness. He wandered the royal compound aimlessly, and as the throbbing gradually diminished to tolerable levels, found himself at the stables.

"Father," Michal said. "Do you believe all that they say about David?" She was stroking one of the two new stallions that had come that morning from the Arabian Desert. "I couldn't sleep and came here." She turned to look at him.

He stroked the magnificent horse. "Ah, Michal, you are a joy to me! Such compassion, love, and honesty!" He leaned down and kissed her forehead. She hugged him. "And a fierce warrior, too!" he said.

"I love you, Father," Michal said. "And I think I love David. I believe he feels the same about me."

Saul gently touched her hair and looked deeply into her eyes. "David is an amazing man, Michal. I could wish for no better mate for my daughter. But he is also an ambitious man. What they say about him is true. I am not sure he will wait for me to die of natural causes to succeed me."

Michal shuddered, blinked, but did not turn away.

Her father smiled proudly into her eyes. "Ever the warrior princess. I can only imagine how difficult this situation must be for you."

Michal smiled softly. "It is difficult, Father, but the Lord will guide us. We have no choice but to trust Him and give our lives into His care."

Saul hugged her then, and feeling a bit better, bid her good night and went to his sleeping chamber.

David had felt the chill as he climbed the steps to the dais, even as the multitude cheered and chanted his name. The adulation should

have warmed him, but it did not. His heart froze as he looked into the faces of those he'd come to care about, the King, his family and advisors. Only Michal had a truly warm smile for him. The High Priest and tribal elders stared as if he were a freak, with fixed, formal smiles on their faces, while the elder from Judah winked at him.

David's first blush of pride when the King announced he was to be assigned to Abner and Jonathan, slipped into doubt as the day progressed. Did the King know Samuel had anointed him? Was he trying to put him in harm's way to eliminate a potential rival? Saul would not be half the man nor half the king David thought he was if he didn't know. "I'd know if I were in his place," David mused. But he couldn't be sure; a military promotion after his victory over Goliath was the correct thing to do. He felt friendless and exposed, without allies. And, he felt inferior as the son of a slave woman, a lowly shepherd raised by a stepmother in a country backwater. A crown and a palace would never change any of that.

Now, still troubled and unable to sleep, David roamed the royal compound. His heart jumped in his chest when he thought he saw Michal leaving the stables. A sign, he thought, a blessing of support from the God of the Covenant! Dashing the distance to where he'd last seen her, David caught a glimpse of her entering the palace.

"Michal!" he shouted in a hoarse whisper. "Michal!" She paused, took a step back, turned and saw him. He rushed to her and she to him. They embraced.

"Oh, God, David," she said, "you haven't left my mind since this morning!" She stepped back from the embrace and looked into his face. "Why so sad?"

He looked down, then away.

"You needn't tell me," she said, "I know. You're feeling alone and friendless."

He looked up into her face and nodded, an expression of deep gratitude in his eyes. "I sometimes feel so unworthy, Michal... My mother was... "

She hugged him again, long and hard. His heart swelled nigh to breaking and tears formed in the corners of his eyes.

"My family is of simple stock too, David. We weren't born royal."

Nodding, David stepped back from their embrace, and studied her face. "You ought not to be seen too much with me, Michal. Not only is it unseemly, it is dangerous."

"Dangerous?" she repeated. "What danger could there be?" He looked down. "Oh no, David!" she said. "It isn't true! What they're saying about you can't be true!"

He looked at her levelly, and then nodded. "No!" she insisted. "No! I can't believe you would harm my father!"

His eyes opened wide in surprise and he waved his hands in denial. "You're right! I would never harm your father! Is that what they're saying?"

"Some do," Michal said.

"No," he said, "Never! Saul is King. It is my duty and my privilege to serve him."

"Then what?" Michal asked.

David looked down again. "I cannot tell you now, Michal. Simply know I would never hurt you, your father or any of your family."

"But there *is* something?" Michal asked. He dipped his head in agreement. She looked away, and then opened her arms to him. He stepped into them and with her warmth, felt his renewed commitment to her and her father. A cock crowed.

"We must go to our beds, Michal," David said.

She lowered her arms and stepped back. He bent and kissed her cheek, then stroked her hair as her father had done. "Thank you, Princess," he said, more formally. "Your friendship means a great deal to me."

Seeing the twinkle in David's eyes and catching his mood, Michal bowed formally, saying, "And to me as well, David ben Jesse, Champion of the Hebrews and slayer of Goliath." Then she rushed forward and kissed him on the mouth. He returned the kiss.

"It is not seemly, Michal. I do love you, but it is not seemly. Enough!" He turned abruptly and walked away.

Joel, Abner and King Saul were in the empty throne room, sitting on the steps of the dais. It was twilight and the light was fading.

"Have you noticed how David is still a bit in awe of the finery and formality of court life?" Abner asked. Saul nodded.

"He is but a country boy, Abner, that is natural," Joel said.

"Do you think he is still a virgin?" Abner asked, leering.

"I believe so," the King said. "The way he looks at my concubine, Rizpah."

"She is very alluring and sensual, Sire," Joel said.

"Egyptian," Abner said. "Schooled in all the sensual arts. Even her walk and movements are captivating." Both men nodded their agreement. "If we are seeking ways to bind David ben Jesse to us, what better way than to arrange a rendezvous with Rizpah for him?"

"She is *my* concubine," the King said.

"Better yet, Sire," Abner said. "That will make the boy doubly grateful to you."

"It is worth considering, Sire," Joel said.

"Yes," King Saul said, looking from one to the other. "I *will* consider it."

# Chapter Seventeen

Jonathan was on his knees, bowed down before Shasheesha, hands flat on the floor, face at her succulent red-painted toes, his bare ass in the air, and inflamed penis brushing the carpet upon which Her throne rested. "Praise Me, slave!" the incarnation of the Goddess Astarte commanded. "Kneel up, gaze upon My splendor, feel your deep devotion and endless desire to please and serve Me. Praise Me!" She sat erect on her throne, lush body naked but for two thick strands of precious black iron beads surrounding and setting off her breasts. A thicker strand around her waist accentuated the shapeliness of her hips and mound.

"Yes, oh magnificent One!" Jonathan replied, deep in a sexual trance. "Oh divine Shasheesha, Mistress of my soul, earthly incarnation of the heavenly Goddess Astarte, hear the pleas of Your lowly slave!"

Shasheesha looked down upon her supplicant, smiled, and raised a bare foot to his face for him to sniff. Jonathan voraciously inhaled his owner's foot odor, as a thirsty man would drink water. Shasheesha lowered her foot. The slave began to bow down after it, to continue sniffing its stink, perhaps waiting to be allowed to kiss and lick it, but his owner stopped him with a command. "No! Continue praising Me."

"Oh, magnificent Shasheesha, Your power over me, Your slave and worshipper, is complete and total." He looked into Her smug, self-satisfied eyes and knew every word he spoke was true. "I am grateful to You for allowing this lowly Hebrew male to be in Your sacred presence, to worship and serve You. You are beautiful and almighty!"

The casual, easy grace of Her body flowing into generous naked curves thrilled him. The copper sheen of Her glistening freshly oiled flesh and its hypnotic odor, reached deep into his soul. "Your holy body and sexual power excite me as nothing else on earth can. Thank You, mighty Goddess for allowing this humble male to be Your body servant, to smell and lick Your flesh, to bathe You and to taste and eat the fruits of Your body."

Shasheesha was ready for him to serve her sex. The earnest sincerity of his words and the beauty of his firm naked masculinity had aroused her fully. "Enough, slave!" she said. "Put your face into My holy of holies, bring Me pleasure and do not cease until I command!" Jonathan instantly obeyed.

As he licked her to her third orgasm, Dathan entered the room. He wrinkled his nose at the strong odor of sex, pulled a chair close to Shasheesha's throne, leaned forward, kissed her full lips, sat down, and spoke with her, without fear that his presence or their conversation would distract the slave from his task. "Isn't this the third time this week that you entranced Jonathan?"

"And what if it is?" Shasheesha said, shifting her weight to give the slave access to her asshole.

"But you know he prefers men, me to be exact; are you trying to destroy his mind?"

"Does that," Shasheesha gestured to Jonathan's erection, and his expert lapping, "look like someone who prefers men?"

"You know what I mean, Shasheesha. He can do both, is very responsive to our enchantments, but left on his own, he would prefer men and prefers me above other men."

"Really?" Shasheesha said, before slumping into her throne and softly mewling as the slave brought her to orgasm. "Enough, slave." She commanded. "Sleep now." Jonathan collapsed at her feet. Shasheesha again turned her attention to her husband. "Really?" she said again. "Have you noticed how he moons after that shepherd boy?" Dathan frowned, looked down. "Jealous?" his wife asked.

"I've noticed," Dathan said. "But I don't think they've engaged in anything sexual or that Jonathan even thinks about David that way."

Shasheesha laughed softly, a worldly-wise sneer on her lovely, full-lipped face. "You are fooling yourself, Husband," she said. "You know this man; you've had sex with him, you've seen him serving as my sex slave. You know how potent, naturally erotic and over-sexed he is. It's only a matter of time until he makes love to David, if David wants him to." Dathan dipped his head in acknowledgement. "And you've been neglecting him lately."

Again, Dathan dipped his head. "I don't want to dominate or entrance him. I want him to want me for my own sake."

Shasheesha guffawed raucously. "By all the gods, you sound like a love struck virgin!"

Dathan pushed back his chair and stood. "I do love him and want only the best for him!"

"Then don't neglect him!" Shasheesha said, also standing. "I too, love him in my fashion. I too, want only the best for him. Hasn't he grown in stature and prowess since we have enslaved him?" Dathan nodded. Shasheesha stepped over Jonathan's naked body. Running a hand through her vagina, she removed it dripping with her cum, sniffed it and sighed, then held it out to Dathan, who also sniffed it appreciatively. "I go now to bathe away the fruits of this man's service. Wake him and take him; and if you value him, neglect him no more." As she left the room, Shasheesha clapped for the maids to attend her in her bath.

Dathan stared down at the sleeping Prince, at his still erect penis and beautiful hard body, and felt his own penis erect. Oh, to have those moist sweet lips so innocently parted now, surrounding his throbbing penis! He slipped off his tunic, knelt, kissed Jonathan's cheek and whispered in his ear. "Jonathan! Jonathan, awake! It is I, Dathan."

As the young man blinked and began to awaken, fear gripped Dathan's heart. What if he won't love me the way I want him to, he thought? It hasn't happened yet; perhaps it never will. Better not to risk it now, perhaps some other time. As Jonathan's eyes fluttered open, Dathan gently closed them again and messaged the young man's temples. "Drift again, Jonathan, My good slave boy. It is I, Dathan, your Master."

"Master?" Jonathan's voice was eager.

Dathan's penis twitched. "Yes, My good slave boy. It is I, Dathan, your Master."

"I have missed You, my Master."

"Yes, I know and I am sorry I have neglected My good slave boy." He leaned forward so his massive erection brushed his slave boy's lips and the strong hot scent of his scrotum could fill the young man's nostrils.

Jonathan's penis, already erect, became harder. "Ah, Master," he said, eyes still closed. "Your slave wants to serve You."

"Yes, My good boy, and Master wants you to serve Him. Before you do, Master has suggestions he wants you to hear and obey when you awaken. Are you ready to hear and obey, slave boy?"

Jonathan moistened his lips in anticipation of receiving his Master's mighty penis. "Yes, Master. Tell me Your will that it may be my will."

"Good. Then hear and obey. You will love and serve no man but me, your Master. Repeat!"

"I will love and serve no man but You, my Master."

"You may be attracted to other men and want to love and serve them, but you will not. You are My slave; I am your Owner and you will obey only Me. Repeat!"

"I may be attracted to other men and want to love and serve them, but I will not. I am Your slave; You are my Owner and I will obey only You."

"That includes David ben Jesse."

Jonathan shuddered, hesitated.

"Repeat, Slave; repeat your Master's command!"

"That includes David ben Jesse."

"Good boy!" Dathan praised, leaning over his slave's prone body, touching his erection to the young man's lips. Dathan thought this was a poor substitute for the kind of love he yearned for, but better than nothing. "Now take Me in Your mouth, slave! Take your Master's mighty penis into your slave mouth and serve it. This is your reward for accepting My suggestions. When I cum and you swallow all of My seed, you will have no memory of My commandments, but will simply obey them."

"Yes, Master. Your slave hears and obeys." Jonathan nuzzled his Master's scrotum, filling himself with the scent of His sex, lightly brushed His shaft with soft lips, kissing it, then opened his mouth and began licking and sucking his Master's magnificent penis.

Abadantha and Saul were riding the magnificent new stallions through the hills near the palace. It had rained the night before and the brown earth was alive with tufts of green. The groves and orchards were beginning to blossom. Farmers waved as they galloped by. Puffy cumulus clouds rolled across the sun, casting shadows on their path. They reined in at the stream running through the apple orchard.

"David's popularity with the people grows," Saul said.

Dantha nodded. "And that worries you," she said, "as it should." They were silent awhile enjoying the scent of growing things in the cool air. "What if you were to offer him Merab? She is your eldest. That would make it more difficult for him to turn against our House."

"It might," her brother said. "But it might also bind us."

Dantha dipped her head in agreement. "Yes, it would. But such bonds would be peaceful at least. So far, your strategy of putting him in the vanguard of your armies has not worked. Not only has it not worked, it has had the opposite effect, making him more popular with the people. Have you heard what they sing now when he passes by at the head of a column?"

Saul spit with distaste. "How could I not? It is everywhere, 'Saul has killed his thousands, David, his tens of thousands.'" The King dismounted and helped his sister down. They were completely alone in the cool, sun-dappled stillness. Tying the horses to a low-hanging branch, they walked quietly in the cooler shade. "Yahweh is with him, Abadantha," Saul's voice was muted and melancholy. "He is victorious wherever he goes! He is God's anointed."

"As are you, my brother," Dantha said, standing on tiptoe to kiss his cheek. "The self pity I detect in your voice is ill fitting the first King of the Hebrews!"

"Yes," he whispered huskily, embracing her, filling himself with her warm, arousing scent. She did not discourage him, did not back away, but opened her mouth to receive his tongue.

When the long kiss was done, Abadantha slipped off her robe revealing her still lovely body, bare breasts and the white linen that hid her sex. "The God of the Covenant is with us, my brother Saul. King Saul, King of the Hebrews!"

He shuddered and threw off his own robe, revealing his nakedness and rapidly erecting penis.

"It is like the old days, Abadantha," he said, voice hoarse with desire. Letting her linen girdle drop, she dipped her head in agreement and cupped her breasts. The ritual had begun. He knelt down before her.

"Now have I become the Shehkina, the female incarnation of God. As you love and worship Me, you claim your oneness with the One God incarnated in all that is." She signaled with a nod, and Saul, first King of the Hebrews, bowed down before his sister, still sexy after all these years, his erect penis touching the rough earth, and kissed her sandal-shod feet.

Abadantha became aroused, and her juices dripped, as she looked down upon her naked brother the King, passionately adoring her feet. It had been ten years since they had performed this ritual, begun in their long ago youth, but it had lost none of its power for them.

"I am the love and joy, sex and power, peace and compassion, lust and serenity at the very center of human existence." Abadantha's voice was resonant with a hypnotic power not her own but which flowed through her, increasing and becoming more potent with each word she spoke. "I am the mystery, the unknown and unknowable, the unbounded and unfettered life force at the center of being, free of man-made rules and strictures, yearning to be expressed. I am eternal. I have existed, exist now, and will always exist at the center of your being. Mate with Me, love Me, worship Me, and you will know that this is true.

"Who am I?"

Entranced by her words and the power in her voice, Saul looked up at his sister. "The Shehkina."

"And who are you?"

"Your slave and worshipper."

"And how would you worship your God, slave?"

"I would abase myself before You, oh, Shehkina, bow down before You, and adore Your flesh."

"Yes," the Shehkina said, voice husky, another drop of Her sacred vaginal juices falling on his forehead. "Taste Me now, slave, worship Me with your mouth."

The King hastened to obey, lost in Her scent, the ecstasy of serving Her with his mouth, and the erotic transport to a remembered, trouble-free place of complete oneness and deep, mindless peace. He brought her to orgasm four times, and then she lay down and let him enter her. He came in a moment, her hot, wet sex searing him to his soul. He rolled over and as they lay side by side, Abadantha stroked his damp hair and sweating face.

"Oh, my dear sweet brother!" she exclaimed. "How strange and different it all is now than what it was, and what we thought it would be when we did this the first time, when we made up this ritual."

He smiled into her accepting, warmly glowing eyes. "Indeed, sacred Shehkina," he said. She slapped him playfully. "But the connection it brings us, the peace and renewal, is the same, perhaps greater."

"That is so," she said, leaning over to brush his lips with her own. "We have had good, even blessed lives, though the priests would say we sin and blaspheme. But the true God, the God of the Covenant knows nothing of our puny, man-made laws. For some, this, what we have done, *would* be sin and blasphemy, but for others such as we, who honor the One God in our hearts and live kind and decent lives, it is neither sin nor blasphemy."

Saul sighed. "I have not lived "a kind and decent" life, Abadantha. I have killed and butchered, lied, and stolen, cheated and betrayed."

His sister stroked his cheek. "You are King, Saul, and not as other men."

"And you are the King's sister and his Shehkina," he said, lowering her hand to his still semi-erect penis.

"Ah," she said, voice smiling, stroking him back to life, "*this* is sinful. No man should be blessed with such a penis."

"My friend Joel, your husband, has such a penis if I remember aright."

"He does, my Lord, and though I love him dearly and honor him completely, except when we are joined during our rare interludes, whenever he makes love to me I think of you." She brought her hand to her dripping vagina, wiped it there, then raised it to his nose.

He inhaled deeply, shifting to bring himself into her again. "And he does not serve your sex as I do, does he?"

"No, my Lord, he does not." She sighed as he inserted himself into her. "And what of Ahinoam, your wife; do you think of me when you lie with her?"

"You know I do," he said, grunting as he slid in and out of her.

As they rode back to the palace, they held hands affectionately, like children, until they saw someone on the road. "Thank you, Sister," the King said, "for everything."

She smiled and brushed his hand with hers. "It is been a pleasure, Sire."

"I will consider what you suggested about inviting David to marry Merab. It is a good idea."

Abner, Joel, Jonathan, and Dathan also thought it a good idea. They were in Sederot, their fortified camp at the southeastern edge of the Philistine salient at Gaza, watching archery practice.

"But I would still keep him in the front ranks," Abner said. "The best would be for him to die, and by any hand but your own."

Saul nodded; Jonathan looked away. The King touched his shoulder gently. "I know you care for him like a brother," he said.

Dathan scowled then made his face blank again.

"Why must he die, Father?" Jonathan asked.

"He is a threat to our House. There cannot be two anointed Kings in Israel."

"Would you kill him yourself?" Jonathan's voice was full of pain.

"If I had to," King Saul replied, putting both hands on his son's shoulders and turning the younger man to face him. "And who would *you* choose, my son, your father and your House or this man you love?"

Tears formed in the corners of Jonathan's eyes, but he did not turn away, returning his father's stare. "You and our House, Father. You know that!"

Dathan smiled. Saul hugged his tortured warrior son to him. "Yes, my son," he said, "I know."

Joel cleared his throat; father and son stepped back. "And when will you offer Merab to David?"

The King was about to speak, but Jonathan interrupted him. "David loves Michal," he said with absolute certainty. "He will never accept Merab."

"I suspect you are correct, Jonathan," the King said, watching his son's face. "And she loves him no doubt, much as you do." King Saul looked down wistfully, "and as I did, once." He gripped his head with both hands and shuddered. "Oh, oh," he cried, "peace! How have we come to this?" Joel stepped forward to soothe his friend's pain. Saul shook him off. "No. No," he said. "This will pass." But it didn't pass and Joel led the King to the shade of a nearby tree and sat with him, until it did pass, while Abner, Jonathan and Dathan returned to supervising their archers.

A few days later, David joined them in Sederot with his "men," a loyal, handpicked band of mounted archers, two hundred and twenty in all, mostly Judeans. They had come from skirmishing with a Philistine raiding party just east of Ashdot, to participate in a contest of skill between Dathan's cavalry and his. The atmosphere was festive. Dathan's troop was glad to be in the green hills near the sea, and away from the drifting, brown sands of the Negev, while David's men were fresh from their success driving the Philistines back to Ashdot.

Saul hosted a banquet for his commanders and there was much food, drinking and good fellowship. They and their army were in peak condition, nearing the height of their power. But for the lack of chariots, they were almost the equal of the better-trained and equipped Philistines.

David had aged well. His body had grown harder and more muscular with the rigors of fighting, riding and marching. None of the inner turmoil and stress of the conflict between his love of King Saul, Jonathan and Michal and his need to protect himself and his desire to succeed to the throne peacefully, showed on his face. His blue eyes still sparkled and his smile was ready, warm and inviting. He had become tougher, more serious and focused, more strategic, and more demanding. He hadn't played his lyre in over a year, didn't even know where it was, and at times, felt as if a part of him had been burned away.

Yet a spark of gentleness, love and compassion still burned; for when the King took him aside and offered his daughter Merab to be his bride, David's first reaction was, "I cannot, for I love Michal!" Then he thought, but no, his prayers had been answered, marrying Merab would give him a claim, though distant, to the succession. But no, not a good enough claim, because Saul had four sons. Offering Merab was a bribe, a way to mute his claim. He was Yahweh's anointed, picked to replace Saul. He had an obligation to God, not to be bribed or settle for less than the throne. But he did love Michal! She made his heart sing. She was a true warrior princess, his soul mate. Perhaps he could have her and the throne, too.

He responded to King Saul, thinking of his mother the slave, saying, "Who am I, and what is my life that I should be son-in-law to the King?"

"You are a hero and as such, worthy to be my son-in-law. If you are concerned about the mohar, the bride price, fear not, only be valiant for me and fight the Lord's fight."

David bowed deeply. "Thank you, Sire. I am most honored. Yet I still cannot accept, for it is your second daughter, Michal, the warrior princess, whom I love."

The King looked annoyed. "Michal cannot marry until Merab has married."

David dipped his head in acknowledgement. "Yes, Sire, I know. Now, by your leave, if you will forgive me, I must return to my soldiers." Saul gestured and David departed, feeling lighter.

Later that day, the King called Joel to him. "I want you to be my emissary in this matter of marrying David into my House." Joel smiled and nodded. "He has admitted he loves Michal. A good choice.

If I were he, I too, would prefer her to Merab. Nonetheless, Merab must be married first." Joel nodded. "In the vicinity of Megiddo is the estate of one Barzillai and elder of Asher."

"Yes, Sire, I know of it."

"Good. Go there and see if he will have his son, Adriel, marry Merab; such an alliance would strengthen the relationship between Asher and the Crown and clear the way for David to marry Michal." Joel bowed and departed.

# Chapter Eighteen

The wedding, as was customary, was held on Barzillai's estate. The King used the occasion as an opportunity to show the might and splendor of the royal house of Israel. The entire court, including the ambassadors of foreign powers, Egypt, Syria, Moab, even Philistia, which was not at war with the north, went in great pomp and state to observe the nuptials. There was room only for the King and his immediate retinue to stay on Barzillai's estate. The rest of the court, some three hundred people including slaves, servants, and attendants, overflowed the inns of Megiddo and camped in the hills nearby.

Throughout the three days of festivities, culminating in the marriage ceremony conducted by the High Priest Abimelech himself, Merab, who had seemed pale and withdrawn in the shadow of her more vigorous sister, shone above the other women. She also exhibited extraordinary administrative skills, personally supervising the smallest details of the ceremony, from her dark purple wedding robes, cut in the style of Asher, to the music, food, and placement of the reception tables among the olive groves of her father-in-law's estate. She blossomed, and all that knew her, especially her sister Michal and mother Ahinoam, showered her with approval and admiration. Merab was not Michal, but she was a worthy person in her own right.

Adriel was ten years older than his bride, but lacked nothing in strength and vigor. He had served in King's first army at Michmash, and now ran his father's estates. His special interest was in developing new strains of fruit, by grafting limbs from one tree to another. Though he had first seen Merab only a week before the wedding,

Adriel quickly developed a keen appreciation for her unique blend of gentleness and strength. As he watched Merab at table or strolling in his arbors, Adriel, a man with wide experience in the sexual, felt the stirrings of desire for his bride to be.

Not only was the entire court in attendance, but on the day of the wedding ceremony, people from all over the north, even from Syria, came to catch a glimpse of the wedding party and perhaps savor the local wine or enjoy a honey cake. The King did not disappoint them. His own stewards and provisioners spent many hours preparing tables laden with fruit, sweets and wine for the uninvited guests. Joel estimated that perhaps ten thousand people were in attendance and feasted on the King's bounty.

The King himself, along with Jonathan, Joel, and Merab's brother Ish-Boshet had held the four polls of the chupa, the traditional marriage canopy. David and Michal stood at opposite sides stealing soulful glances into one another's eyes.

Reflecting on the wedding as he returned to Gibeah, the King was glad that the way was now clear for Michal to marry David, but felt regret that he had gone all Merab's life without appreciating her or seeing her talents. Now, save for occasional visits home to Court, he would rarely see her again. She would remain on Adriel's estates. It felt like finding someone he cared for deeply, then losing that person, all in a single day. It made his head and heart throb and ache.

Joel rode beside him. "You are sad, my friend, and in pain." Saul nodded. "It was a wonderful celebration. Are you proud of Merab?"

Saul choked back tears and nodded again. "Life is so strange, Joel," he said, regaining his composure. "Is it not?" Joel touched Saul's shoulder. The King sat more erectly on his saddle. "We will proceed with David and Michal."

Joel nodded and dropped back in the column to find David and his men. "Now Michal is free to marry you," he said when he found him.

"Thank you, Joel. But does it seem to you a trifling thing to offer oneself as a son-in-law to the King?" Joel stared at him.

"Well," David said, "as for me, I am poor and humble."

"But you love Michal! Why lose this chance to have everything—honor, glory and love?"

David shook his head. "What honor and glory will there be without the mohar? How long would our love survive if I am shamed?"

Joel smiled. "Yes, of course, you are correct. But the King has told me he desires no bride price other than that you ride in the vanguard and be valiant in battle."

David shook his head, no.

"The King told me he offered you this for Merab's mohar." Joel said. "He told me to tell you that if you require a fair exchange, he would accept one hundred Philistine foreskins."

David had all he could do to conceal the smile that rose from his chest to his mouth. What ingenuity, he thought! What lengths Saul will go to, to have me killed, and have himself judged innocent! How easy it would be to die by the sword of a Philistine warrior unwilling to be separated from his foreskin. What better motivation for a man to fight to the death?

Yet, he did want Michal, did want to be with her under the chupa as Merab and Adriel had been. David smiled into Joel's quizzical face and thumped his shoulder. "Return to our Master, the King, thank him for his generosity to me and tell him I agree!"

Joel looked hard into David's eyes. Is he feeling guilt as the messenger of my doom? David thought.

Joel smiled. "As you will, David! I go now to tell the King."

As Joel moved his horse to the side, preparing to gallop, David said, "Hold, oh messenger," and, signaling his men to fall out of the column, said to Joel, "Also tell the King I go now to collect his bride price; my loins tingle for the flesh of his daughter!" As Joel rode to the head of the column, David and his escort of fifty men turned east toward Ashdod and its Philistine outposts.

Four days later, David returned to Gibeah in triumph, not with the required one hundred foreskins, but with two hundred foreskins. Before he could formally present the mohar to his soon-to-be father-in-law and claim his bride, word of David's feat swept the city. As he made his way through the streets thronged with cheering people, his trophies on his belt, men, women and children pelted him with apple blossoms and rose petals. The noise preceded him to the palace.

Saul's head hurt and he was nearly out of his mind with anger and frustration. Abner and Joel were with him in the deserted throne room. "No one cheered very much when I became King. And he had fifty men with him, fifty! No wonder he could do it in four days. I had to do everything on my own." Saul paced, twisted and turned as if trying to cast off and escape his own history. "Now this boy has it all handed to him."

"But he *is* brave, Sire,"Abner said, "a fierce fighter and brilliant tactician and strategist. Two hundred foreskins," Abner shook his finger at his cousin. "You only asked for a hundred." Saul was scowling at him. "You set the task; you let him go against Goliath; you put him in charge of your armies; you made him what he is."

The King raised his hand and stepped forward to strike Abner, then, thinking better of it, lowered his arm. "It is Yahweh, not me," the King said. "Yahweh caused Samuel to anoint him. Yahweh gives him the love of my son and daughter. Yahweh blesses all he does with success, while allowing me to bluster and blunder and be made a fool." His face was red and he gripped his head with both hands, bending double with pain. Joel stepped towards him, but Abner waved him away.

"I will no longer stand for it," King Saul said, straightening, less apoplectic, but still in pain. "I too, am the anointed of God, and I *am* King. David is a traitor to the Crown and the House of Saul. Enough hiding and games! He shall have Michal, but then I shall see him dead, even if it be by my own hand!"

"He is very popular with the people, Sire," Abner said.

"He is a traitor!" Saul screamed. "A traitor! We will tell the people. Show them."

"Given the choice, I fear the people would choose him over you," Abner said quietly. The King stared at him for a long moment. He looked away, dipping his head in agreement.

"Let us have the wedding, chaver," Joel said. "We will make it grander than Merab and Adriel's. All the world will see the power and glory of the House of Saul, our strength and unity!"

Joel put his arm round his old friend's shoulders, hugged him to him and looked into his tortured face. "We can make the best of this, Saul," he said, rubbing the King's shoulder. "Worse things have befallen us. Isn't that so?"

The King sighed and looked into his oldest friend's eyes. "Yes, Joel, thank you. Yes, we will make the best of this. Please, go forward and arrange the wedding festivities. After I receive my son-in-law to-be's mohar, I shall go deep into the Negev, perhaps with Jonathan, and dwell there with Spirit for a time." Joel dipped his head in agreement.

A half hour later, when David came to present the King with Michal's gruesome mohar, only Joel and Abner were present to see the King muster his majesty and stare down the young hero's gloating bravado. Both thought it was one of King Saul's finest moments and one of David's worst, a moment that would fuel the King's hatred of Jesse's son until one or the other of them were dead.

After the ceremony, David and Michal were given a moderate house in the royal compound far removed from the King's house. David remained in its vicinity, avoiding court and contact with the King and his new in-laws with the exception of Jonathan. At first, Michal was distressed by her husband's self-imposed isolation, even though she understood and accepted the need for it. But as the days passed and she saw that she was still welcome in her father's house, her distress dissipated.

Saul decided to go to the desert alone. He had thought to stay in isolation and fasting for two weeks, knowing it was usually the second week that brought the most perfect communion with God. But the recurring pain in his head, the harsh, boring conditions, and the softness of royal life, leading to diminished physical capacities, caused him to return to civilization after only six days.

On the King's return to Gibeah, he stopped at Dathan and Jonathan's encampment in Beersheba. The two commanders put on an excellent military review. Chariots, archers, slingers, feted Saul royally as befitted his status. On the evening before he was to leave for his capital, the King and his son stayed up late and drank alone beneath clear desert skies thick with stars.

"I know you love David, my son," the King said. "I loved him once, too." Saul squinted and rubbed his forehead.

"Your head is still painful isn't it, Father?" Saul nodded. "David's music helped you once, why not let him try again?"

Saul looked searchingly into his son's handsome earnest face and shook his head sadly. "He is a traitor," he said, "and must die."

Jonathan scowled and shook his head. "I know the stories. Perhaps Samuel anointed him, perhaps not. David has not wronged you. His conduct toward you has been beyond reproach. If he would be king, he would be king after you are gone."

Saul looked unbelievingly into his son's face. "But the kingdom is for *you*, Jonathan, or Ish-Boshet, not David ben Jesse!"

"I would let the future take care of itself, Father. Has David not taken his life in his hands countless times for you and for Israel? When he slew Goliath, you danced and sang, and shared the rejoicing as we all did. Why would you commit a sin of innocent blood by putting David to death without cause?"

Staring sadly into Jonathan's face, Saul nodded then embraced him. "As the Lord lives, he shall not be put to death. I will let him play for me once again and he shall resume his duties as a captain in our armies." They stood, and embraced, Saul going to his rooms, Jonathan to Shasheesha's suite to serve Her as Her sex slave.

David did play for Saul and soothed him and did fight against the Philistines, but his military victories re-awakened the King's fear and jealousy. Now, as Abadantha and Saul sat in the north arbor, surrounded by the balmy fresh air and sweet smells of apples and tamarinds, they spoke of Saul's concerns about David. "The people are saying, mostly David's people, that when you rage at him you are tormented by an "evil spirit" from the Lord," Abadantha said.

Saul snickered. "I know." He shook his head. "But the people know nothing of the treachery in David's heart, of his lust for power and for my throne."

Dantha dipped her head in agreement. "He is a clever conniver. If the people knew of your forbearance, they would laud you. Still, he is not without his benefits; Michal is extremely happy and his playing soothes you."

"Indeed," the King nodded. "But at times I cannot get my mind off what he might do, that he might rise up against me." Saul dropped his head sadly. "At those times I would kill him." He looked deeply into his sister's eyes. "Perhaps I *am* afflicted... ."

"Nonsense," she said, standing. "You have a growth in your head, a boil; the Egyptian physician told us that. That is what pains you and drives you to extremes. Go now. Don't you have an appointment with David for him to play for you?" Saul nodded and they walked together to their respective suites.

David was already in the King's suite, waiting, stroking his lyre and singing sweetly. This normally would have soothed Saul, but just as he entered his rooms, heard the music and saw his golden son-in-law, a jagged pain knifed through the King's head, making him stumble to the wall and overturn the weapons stacked there.

David heard the noise and rose to greet the King. He saw the twisted expression on his face, saw him raise the javelin and dropping to the floor, heard it whoosh through the air and bury itself in the wall. Eyes wide with fear and confusion, David jumped up, pushed the King aside, fled to his own house, locking himself in with Michal.

"I don't believe it!" she said.

David, breathing hard and red-faced shook his head, yes.

"We are in open war now," she said. David dipped his head in agreement. "He has wanted to kill you for a long time, but the God of the Covenant has restrained him. Now, once again, Yahweh has full charge of him and he is ruled by fear and doubt."

David nodded. "What are we to do?"

"You must go and I will stay and do what I can." David looked a question at her; she shook her head, no. "No," she said. "He will not harm me." She leaned forward and kissed him fully on the mouth. "You know him well enough to know that."

"I thought I knew him until a moment ago, when he tried to kill me."

She kissed him again and he responded with even greater passion. "That is different, Husband; very different, and you know it." David dipped his head in agreement. "But clearly," she said, "you are no longer safe here." She looked through the casement and saw stealthy movement in the gathering darkness. "He will not attack the house.

He has sent men to murder you when you step outside in the morning. If you don't save your life tonight, tomorrow you will be a dead man. Let us wait a little longer," she stroked his cheek, "and when it is full dark, we will make your escape." Moving away from the window, she opened her arms to him and he stepped into them. Hugging and kissing, as if for the last time, they lay together then two hours later, in the full darkness, Michal lowered David from the window and watched him make his way safely passed her father's assassins.

No sooner had David disappeared into the shadows, than the captain in charge came to the door and demanded that David accompany him to the King. "A moment," Michal told him. Then to give David more time to escape, she took her teraph, the one Ahinoam had given her, from its niche, wrapped it in extra bedding, rolled it into an approximate human shape, covered it with a blanket and hoped anyone looking at it in the dark would think it her sleeping husband.

Still stalling, she sent word to the captain that David was sick and bedridden. Knowing the King's fierce desire to have David dead, the captain disbelieved the servant and insisted on entering the bedroom. In spite of Michal's protest and threats to report him to her father, he did so, saw the blanket covered bedding, apologized and went to the King to report. Two hours had passed; David was well away.

"Bring him to me, bed and all," King Saul ordered. "So that I may slay him myself!"

The soldiers returned to David's house, forced their way past Michal into the bedroom, and discovered the ruse. Another hour had passed and David was further away. Only Michal remained to face her father's wrath.

They were alone in the great throne room, the King on his throne, Michal stood on the first step of the dais. "Why have you tricked me, Daughter?" King Saul asked, voice trembling and body shaking with suppressed rage. "You have let my enemy, the enemy of our House, escape my justice."

Justice indeed, Michal thought, staring straight in her father's red, darting eyes; madness is closer to the truth. "He told me," she lied, "to help him escape or he would kill me."

Saul stood, stunned by the brazenness and tactical brilliance of his daughter's lie. Now the ball was in his court. Trembling, he raised his hand to strike her. Should she be punished or not? She had put him in a difficult, un-winning position. Slowly, glaring at her, he sat back down on his throne, and with a gesture, dismissed her. Michal bowed and went away happy, knowing she had given her husband enough time to get safely away.

But David was still in the palace compound. Instead of running away, he went to Jonathan's rooms and before awakening him, stared down at his beautiful, half-exposed body. The Crown Prince was in from the Negev to report to the King. Although normally, Dathan would have accompanied him, this night he slept alone.

As he stared down at the sleeping warrior prince, David felt the same deep stirring of lust and love he felt for Michal and his penis erected. Kneeling at Jonathan's side, David bent, moistened his lips and kissed Jonathan heavily on his cheek.

"Yes, Master," Jonathan mumbled, still asleep, "more please, Master."

Ah, David thought, what was this? Jonathan had a Master? Who could it be? Jonathan stirred, rolled to his side, grabbed his dagger and in one fluid motion, had his arm around David's chest and the dagger at his throat. "What," he exclaimed, blinking. "David? I almost killed you!"

As Jonathan lowered the dagger, David kissed him fully on the mouth. "Ah, David!" Jonathan moaned. "Can this really be?" David kissed him again; Jonathan opened his mouth wider to receive David's tongue and sucked on it, feeling his penis erect, and Dathan's words tumbled through his mind, "You will serve no other man but me." Yes, Master, Jonathan thought. I am not 'serving' him, Master, I am loving him.

Sounds of running feet, clanking armor and shouts of alarm echoed in the courtyard. "What's that noise?" Jonathan asked.

"They are after me. The King, your father, has finally tried to kill me, openly for all to see. Your sister helped me escape, but I had to talk with you before I went into hiding. Will you help me?"

Jonathan kissed one of David's erect nipples and touched the bulge beneath his robe. "Anything, whatever you ask!" he said, voice low and hoarse with passion. "I have waited so long to know your body." He kissed David's other nipple, and David stoked Jonathan's curly hair. The noise outside grew louder as the palace guard was called out. David sat up.

"I cannot believe my father tried to kill you," Jonathan said. "He does nothing neither great nor small but that he discloses it to me. Why should my father hide this thing from me? It is not so!"

"Your father knows well that I have found favor in your eyes, and he has said to himself: *Let not Jonathan know this*. But truly as the Lord lives, and as your soul lives, there is but a step between me and death."

Jonathan shuddered as the reality of his friend's words came home to him and he remembered hints and rumors of the King's displeasure with the son of Jesse. "What does your soul desire, that I should do it for you?"

David embraced him. "Thank you, chaver."

"Soon will be the feast of the new moon."

Jonathan nodded his agreement. "In a fortnight," he said.

"I have no wish to kill your father," David said, "but neither do I wish to die. I must leave here now, but if it is possible to resume my former place in the King's service, I would do so."

Jonathan listened attentively.

"Here is what I propose: Normally, I would be expected to be at the King's table during the three days of feasting. If the King acts *as if* he misses me, for this is all for public show and he will most certainly know in what vicinity I am, you will explain that I had asked permission to return to Bethlehem to participate in the ritual sacrifice with my own clan. If he flies into a rage, you will know he remains intent on killing me.

"On the mornings of the second day and the third day, I will await you well-hidden in the trees near the archery range. Take a servant to retrieve your arrows, go there and practice. If you call out to your servant that the arrows have fallen short, I will know the King has calmed and I may safely return. But if he still wishes to murder me, call out, 'Look, the arrows are beyond you,' and I shall be warned and depart."

Jonathan nodded vigorously. "It shall be as you say, chaver! Let us hope I may call that the arrows have fallen short." They embraced.

Suddenly, David shuddered, began trembling, broke away and stepped back, fear twisting his handsome face. "Keep faith with me!" he said, his voice shaking, his eyes searching Jonathan's. "Kill me yourself if I am guilty. But do not betray me! Why let me fall into your father's hands?"

"God forbid!" Jonathan cried, embracing him. "We are two halves of a single soul. I love you more than myself."

"And I, you," David said. They embraced once more and David started to leave.

"Wait!" Jonathan cried. "It is not possible to escape dressed as you are, they will surely recognize you." Jonathan stripped himself of the robe that was upon him, and gave it to David, and his garments, even to his girdle and took his sword and bow from their place against the wall and gave them to David, also. David in turn, gave Jonathan his girdle, robe and garments, and in exchanging clothes, re-enacted the ancient ritual that confirmed the binding together of their souls. David escaped and came to Samuel.

# Chapter Nineteen

The old prophet joyously embraced the young man he'd anointed as King in Saul's place, feeling no regret about what he'd done. But being mindful of his sons' potential for treachery, Samuel took David and fled from his estates in Zulph to Ramah and thence to nearby Naioth where the shepherds had their tents.

After complaining about all that Saul had done to him, David slept for two days. Upon awakening, mid-morning on the third day, David stepped from his tent and found that other, younger ascetics had gathered around Samuel. Twenty of them sat in a circle surrounding the old prophet, beneath the bright, cloudless sky, all talking at once of Yahweh, and the pure joy of serving Him. Occasionally, three or four of them would jump up, whirl and dance, sing loudly and speak in tongues, then sit down again and resume their chatter.

When David stepped among them and sat down far from Samuel, no one acknowledged him, not even the old prophet. David did not mind, but sat peacefully, enjoying the sky and fresh air, lulled by the gibberish he heard around him. Soon his eyes closed and he felt his heart thrill, his limbs twitched and tingled and a desire to whirl and dance suffused him. Oh, what joy, what ecstasy! He stood, as did the men on either side of him. Their lips were moving and his lips were moving, but nothing intelligible came forth. The three of them clasped hands above their heads and twisted and pranced to music only they could hear. Then they let go of one another and David went whirling and spinning off, to fall, hours later, exhausted.

As David slept where he fell, Abija, Samuel's middle son, left his place of concealment and made his way to Gibeah to tell King Saul of what he'd seen.

"I followed my father and David from Zulph to Ramah to Naioth," he told the King. "I have heard the rumors of my father's traitorous actions, Sire, as have my brothers, and we want no part of them. If you still wish to take the traitor David, I can lead you to him."

Ish-Boshet, who stood by his father's side, clapped his hands triumphantly. "Yes, Father," he said. "Let us take this traitor, now! We need wait no longer!"

Trying to keep the gleam of triumph from his eyes, King Saul looked down, composed his face and nodded to Abija. "I am grateful," he said. "Here," he reached for the purse at his belt and held it out to Abija. "Take this, as a token of your King's gratitude."

Abija demurred. "No, Sire; my brother's and I seek no reward, only that you remember us favorably when my father's estates are reckoned."

Smiling thinly, King Saul re-attached the purse to his belt. "Very well," he said, gesturing to Ish-Boshet and an officer of his royal guard, "I shall remember. Now take my son and this officer and his men to the place in Naioth."

In Naioth, on the next day, the power of the Lord was stronger than the day before. Without food or water David and the ascetics were half crazed with hunger and thirst, yet still the ecstasy swept through them, driving them to speak in tongues, whirl and dance unceasingly. Now, as the sun rose, they stripped off their clothes to be naked as an offering before their God. Some frothed at the mouth, others had broken bones, and all were bruised and bloody. The King's men found them thus, and watching from between the tents, one by one, they too, succumbed to the mystical frenzy, stripping off their armor and clothes and whirling into the dance, jabbering unintelligibly, so that the spirit of God was upon the messengers of Saul.

When these men failed to return, King Saul dispatched another, stronger patrol. By the time they arrived and had also succumbed to the ecstatic frenzy, the Spirit departed from David and he came to his senses and fled Naioth to await Jonathan at the royal archery range in Gibeah.

More deeply enraged than ever when his third patrol failed to return, King Saul went in search of Samuel and the son of Jesse, the anointing prophet and anointed harper, on his own, and without retinue, arms or armor. Leaving his nearly ridden-to-death horse at the military encampment in Ramah, the King, tottering on the edge of sanity, blundered along the unfamiliar roads from Ramah to Naioth, cursing his swept-away messengers, the fanatical Samuel, the mesmerized Jonathan who had given his clothes, and his brazen daughter who had lied and betrayed him.

Nearing the place aflame with the radiance of the Lord, King Saul first heard the howls and the gibberish, and then felt the shaking earth as his naked soldiers heaved and danced upon it. As he walked on, he saw Samuel standing calmly at the center of a human whirlwind of frenzied gyrating naked men, like a rock in a wind-swept sea. The smell of their sweat, bodily wastes, and musk assailed the King's nostrils. Holding his hand over his nose, Saul continued, into the clearing. When Samuel saw him, their eyes met, and sparks flew between them. Saul lowered his hand and inhaled deeply of the powerful stench.

Samuel raised his arms high above his head and the King felt the spirit of the Lord enter him. His heart thudded, his limbs twitched and tingled, and his eyes rolled back into his head. Stripping off his garments so that he too, was naked, King Saul danced ecstatically before his God, spoke in tongues and hours later, fell down twitching and rolled in the dust before Samuel.

When the King awoke, bruised, bloody, and aching, he was alone. Heaving himself up, Saul searched among the rags and scraps of cloth scattered in the dust until he found something to cover his nakedness. Then cold, hungry and thirsty, he made his way back to the military encampment at Ramah. So miserable and terrible did Saul appear that the young guard did not believe he was the King and would not let him enter. The officer in charge had to be called and then the King was admitted.

Joel was waiting for him. Worried from not having heard anything of Saul for nearly three days, the King's good friend had ridden to Ramah, Saul's last known destination. As he saw his beaten, bloody, nearly naked childhood friend led into the post commander's quarters, dazed and disoriented, he wept, and ran to embrace him. "Oh, Saul, Saul, what has become of you?"

The King looked unseeing into Joel's face and did not know him. "I am cold and hungry, will you cover me and feed me, please?" he said in a weak, shaking voice.

Joel gripped Saul tighter to him, the tears pouring from his eyes. "Yes, of course! Yes, chaver, here," he threw a blanket around his shoulders, walked him to the commander's chair and gave him a honey cake. That was a mistake; it was too, rich. No sooner had Saul devoured it than he vomited. "Water," Saul croaked, wiping away the vomit with the back of his hand. "Water, please."

Joel gave him water, bathed him and nursed him back to health. Three days later, the King was himself again, but had no memory of the events at Naioth. Two days after their return to Gibeah, the feast of the new moon began.

On the first day of the festival, King Saul said nothing about David's empty place at the table. Joel was there, beside the King, as was Abner, and Saul's entire family. Saul felt a chill from Michal and Jonathan, but otherwise, David's absence went un-remarked. On the second day, however, the King asked Jonathan why David had missed two days of feasting at his table. Jonathan gave the agreed story and his father exploded.

"You son of perverse rebellion!" King Saul cried out. "Do I not know that you have chosen the son of Jesse to your own shame and the shame of your mother?" The King pushed back his chair and stood pointing first to Jonathan, then to Michal. "You have allied yourselves with the man that seeks the crown your own father now wears, that you, Jonathan, would wear one day, if the son of Jesse does not take it from you. Now I see how it will be! As long as Jesse's son remains alive on earth, neither you nor your crown will be safe. Send at once and fetch him unto me. He deserves to die!"

"Deserves to die! Why?" Jonathan shouted. "What has he done?"

"Can you truly not know, my son?" Saul looked sadly at his son. "I do not believe you. He allowed himself to be crowned King of Israel while I live. That is treason. Do you support *treason*?"

Michal too, stood. "There is another way to look at it, father. It is not David against you. It was not David's will, but God's will."

Stunned, the King dropped into his chair. Both children were traitors, active co-conspirators with the man he feared at hated most! Sitting back, King Saul felt his spear leaning against the wall. He seized it, stood, and growling, brandished it first in Michal's direction then at Jonathan. Michal gasped and ran from the hall. Staring at his father until the King lowered his spear, Jonathan stood his ground then turned on his heel and walked from the hall.

Joel, who had tried to restrain the King when Saul had first seized the spear, now took it from him. The King buried his throbbing head in his hands. The guests sat in silent horror. "What have I done?" Saul asked, looking into his friend's face.

"More than you wanted to, Sire," Joel said. "But you were provoked."

"They will say it is an evil spirit from God," the King said, gesturing to the fidgeting guests.

"Some may, Sire," Joel said, "but I think most will say they witnessed a loving father betrayed and a watchful, intuitive ruler defending his crown." King Saul sighed, lowered his hands and looked into Joel's face. "After all, everyone knows what Michal and Jonathan have done and that you are correct to assert that they acted treacherously and betrayed the interests of their House."

"Thank you, chaver," the King said, standing to embrace his friend. "Please, everyone," he said, raising his cup of wine. "Before we go on with the feast, join me in a toast to the House of Saul." Raising their cups, everyone stood and said loudly in unison, "The House of Saul!"

The next morning as arranged, Jonathan met David on the archery range. He left his servant at home, feeling that after last night, there was no longer a need for elaborate pretense. "Look," Jonathan cried, "the arrows are beyond you!" Alerted that the King still wanted him dead and that he could never return to court, and realizing the grave danger in which he had placed his wife and best friend, David emerged from his hiding place, knelt before Jonathan, and bowed humbly three times.

Crying loudly, Jonathan raised up his soul mate, embraced and kissed him. David returned his fervor and they embraced and cried together, then stepped apart. "Go in peace," Jonathan said, through his tears. "We have pledged each other in the name of Yahweh who is witness forever between me and thee, and between my seed and thy seed forever." Embracing again, they parted, Jonathan to return to the Negev and David to the wilderness southwest of Jerusalem, neither knowing if they would ever embrace again.

The following day, before returning to the Negev, Jonathan apologized to his father. Torn by dreams of bitter conflict and murky betrayal, the Crown Prince had not slept the night before. He wondered who sent those tortured dreams, Yahweh or the God of the Covenant? As Jonathan arose distraught and shaking, he felt for the first time that he now had a hint of what his father experienced all the time, everyday. With that connection, Jonathan thought the God of the Covenant had sent the sleepless night to bring him this new appreciation of his father's life.

He didn't know as much about this God as he did about Yahweh, but he thought from things his grandmother and aunt had said, that compassion, love and forgiveness were what the God of the Covenant was all about. Although he still felt an inchoate attraction to David, Jonathan now understood that he could not allow that feeling to dominate his life. What he'd felt before David, honor and duty, his House, his family and his father, would again be the central focus of his life.

The King too, was full of remorse. Ahinoam, Abadantha, Joel, and Abner had all come to him after the feast, together and singly, to remind him that his family and his House were most important, and that he needed to restore Michal and Jonathan to his good graces.

Now, as Jonathan entered the throne room, followed by Dathan, King Saul rose from his throne. Most of the nobles, military leaders and courtiers were present, arrayed in their finest robes and jewels. Bright sunlight shone down through the open ceiling and glittered off the armor, weapons and jewels. The King opened his arms and Jonathan hurried into them, they embraced and stepped back.

"The House of Saul stands united as one," King Saul intoned, raising Jonathan's arm high. "We are the anointed of the Lord, dedicated to Him, His people and the land He promised us!"

Jonathan spoke as his father lowered his arm. "I have but one love and only one love! My duty and honor are pledged to it. That love is the word of God. Yahweh has anointed my father Saul, King, giving him dominion over this, our promised land. Nothing can come between God, my father and me!" The assembled dignitaries cheered. Jonathan again embraced his father, turned smartly on his heel and, followed by Dathan, left the throne room.

Michal had left the dais and was waiting for him. Waving Dathan out of earshot, Jonathan hugged her fiercely. "Always remember that you are royal princes of Israel! Though we both love David, we must put that below our love of God and Country."

"Yes, brother," Michal said, "I agree, but what we feel for David will always be a part of us."

Jonathan dipped his head in agreement. "I will follow his activities with great interest. And will pray, though our father continue to hunt him, that he remain unscathed, and that he not do anything that will force me or you to actively take up arms against him."

Michal moved her head in agreement, leaned forward, and kissed him on the mouth. "If you approve, I will send people into his camp that we may know what he does."

"Yes," Jonathan said, enthusiastically. "Good! I approve. Do that and write me about what you find."

"Writing may be misconstrued. I will send you messengers and come to the Negev more often to visit you. After all, now I am a widow of sorts, and have the time."

Jonathan smiled, kissed her on the cheek, beckoned to Dathan and departed.

# Chapter Twenty

Shivering and completely alone in the howling dark wilderness, David prayed. "Oh, Yahweh, hear Thy servant! Why hast Thou forsaken me? I freeze. I starve. I thirst. Was it not You Who caused me to be anointed? Was it not You who plucked me from my family? Did you not raise me up to be at the right hand of the King and to marry his daughter? Now You have made me a homeless fugitive without any resource. I bleed. I hurt. I dread. Guide me aright that my suffering ends, Your will be done, and I assume my rightful place. What would You have me do now, almighty Master?"

Silence. Wind-blown sand stung David's staring eyes. He stumbled and fell. He pulled sharp rocks from his bleeding knees and hands. An animal scurried in the scrub. His stomach ached with emptiness, his tongue thickened with thirst; silence filled the vast, dark wilderness. Far off, a tiny light flickered. David walked towards it. The flickering light disappeared as dawn broke, colder and blustier. He came to a footpath, then a road, and followed it all the next day seeing no one. Wretched, into the middle of that night, he continued, still without human contact until he reached the sacred city of Nob, the site of Yahweh's temple.

A simple two-story structure in the center of a ramshackle compound at the far edge of the small town, the temple compound housed Abimelech, the High Priest and served as the living and training center for Yahweh's priesthood. Half-mad with hunger and thirst, David entered the temple and finding its outer courts deserted, violated its sanctity, by going through the second court, and into the third court, the Holy of Holies. There in the dim, smoky light of the oil lamps mounted on the walls and swaying on chains suspended from the ceiling, he found Abimelech, kneeling in prayer.

Hearing footsteps behind him, the High Priest started. His eyes went wide with alarm. He turned, recognized David, took in his disheveled, beaten condition and asked, "Why art thou alone, and no man with thee?"

"I am under orders from the King," David lied. "I am to let no one know about the mission on which he sent me, nor what his orders are. When I took leave of my men, I told them to meet me in the wadi. Now we are in need; what have you? Give me water and five loaves or as many as you can find."

Eyes darting with trepidation, the High Priest said, "There is no common bread under my hand, but there is holy bread in the sanctuary, if only the young men have kept themselves from women." David shuddered. Eating the holy bread, loaves specially prepared each Sabbath and placed in the sanctuary, made of pure wheat flour, sprinkled with frankincense, would be a sin against Yahweh. Yet Yahweh placed him in this predicament, leaving him without a choice. David sighed. "Let Him strike me down, I will die anyway if I don't eat."

David would also be committing another sin if he ate the holy bread. Only consecrated priests could eat the old loaves, taken from the sanctuary after the Sabbath. That is what Abimelech meant when he said, "only if the young men have kept themselves from women." David knew, as did every Hebrew warrior, that this law came from the ancient military practice of maintaining ritual purity before battle. He also knew he had lain with Michal just three days ago, rendering him unclean by sexual contact with a woman. Thus, he would commit two further sins by eating the holy bread.

"Of truth," the son of Jesse lied to the priest, "women have been kept from us these three days. The young men's bodies have remained holy, and how much more will they be holy today." Though unconvinced, yet fearful for his life, Abimelech agreed to give David the loaves, and in so doing, joined in his sin.

After giving David the loaves, Abimelech left the sanctuary and returned with a large water skin. David drank thirstily and slipped it over his shoulder. "Have you a spear or a sword here at hand," David asked. "I have no weapon with me because the King's business was so urgent."

For the first time since David's intrusion into his prayers, the High Priest smiled. Shadows from the hanging oil lamps danced on the walls and reflected in his eyes. "I have had this here for years, David, with no understanding of why I kept it, until now." Abimelech stepped behind the ephod, one of the last of the great bejeweled, carved stone idols of Yahweh, more of a four-foot tall monolith than a human form, and came forth with a large sword wrapped in an altar cloth. "Behold!" he said, removing the cloth, "the sword of Goliath!"

David's eyes widened. He knew this sword, had used it to cut off his distant cousin's head. He stretched out his arms, hands opened, and the priest laid the sword into them. As he gripped the large sword's hilt with both hands and felt its heft, David searched his mind for when he'd last seen it, as the glory and depthless gratitude of that day nearly ten years ago, returned to him.

Covered in blood, he'd carried the Philistine's head and sword across the Valley of Elah, deaf to the cheers of his comrades. Though Abner stood before the King's tent, and tried to take the sword and head from him, David brushed past him and laid his trophies at the King's feet. Saul had embraced him. Now David sighed, wondering if he'd ever again feel the King's arms around him.

"Thank you, Abimelech," David said, holding the sword, gathering up the loaves, and drinking again from the water skin. "The King will more than repay you!"

As Abimelech nodded uneasily, Doeg, the Edomite, a fierce and venal man, well versed in the struggle between David and Saul, smiled. He'd seen David enter the compound, followed him and, lurking in the temple's second court, heard and saw all that transpired. Doeg remained in the second court not only to stay unobserved, but also to avoid sinning against Yahweh. Though not a Hebrew, Doeg had a healthy respect for the Hebrew God and His rituals. As David slipped away into the wind-blown gloom, making for Gath, Goliath's home, Doeg too, slipped away, towards Gibeah and the King's palace.

Doeg had difficulty being admitted to King Saul's presence. But once in the throne room, he saw how the open break with David had thrown the court into disarray. Many of the King's counselors and captains, although they were Benjaminites, wanted Saul to make peace with the hero David. Standing tall in his gleaming armor, spear at his side, the King appealed to their tribal loyalties. "Hear me, Benjaminites," he said, "will the son of Jesse, a man of Judah, give you fields and vineyards? He can give you nothing because he has nothing. He cannot be restored to my favor, nor should you wish it! He is no longer worthy and you must show your worth by joining me and hunting him down!"

The King staggered, fierce pain ripping through his head, and gripped his spear to remain upright. Abner and Joel moved to help him but were stopped by his loud, "No!" It hurt the King to be so in need of his clansmen's support, but it hurt more to think of how they seemed to betray him. Breathing deeply to allow the pain to dissipate, Saul's puffy red eyes looked angrily over the assemblage. "All of you have conspired against me," he said, pointing and slowly moving his arm from left to right across the room. "None of you disclosed to me that my son made league with the son of Jesse. None of you feel sorry, or disclosed to me that my son stirred up my servant against me."

"I am loyal to you, Sire," Doeg said, making his way through the crowd to stand before the King. "Though only an Edomite and not a Benjaminite, I know the King will recognize my loyalty and reward it. I have seen the son of Jesse and will take you to him."

Saul slumped into his throne, exhausted by the now dissipated pain. "Yes, by all means. What is your name?"

"Doeg," the Edomite said, proudly, standing before his King, big chest puffed out, hand on sword hilt, blue eyes sparkling in his beardless face.

"Good," King Saul gestured indolently, sitting more erectly. "Doeg the Edomite. Tell me what you have seen and I will tell you your reward."

"I saw the son of Jesse coming to Nob, go in to Abimelech in the sanctuary and I witnessed the High Priest giving him food, water and the sword of Goliath."

A shout of disbelief filled the air. The King stood. "*Now* who will go with me to inquire of Abimelech?" They roared their approval. "Thank you, Doeg," King Saul said. "Your reward shall be great and you shall receive it in Nob after we have spoken with the High Priest." Doeg bowed his head and stepped back.

Abadantha and Janina had been standing at the back, near the large double doors, and after everyone had left, went to Saul. He was again slumped on his throne, head in his hands. The scent of their bodies and soft rustling of their robes caused him to look up, and seeing them, his face brightened.

"Mother! Sister!" He exclaimed. "Daughters of the Covenant, how good of you and how gracious to come to me in my time of great need. I have felt so terribly alone. Your presence lightens my burdens and gladdens my heart, reminding me I have been too much with the God of the Scrolls." The harshness of the dry breeze blowing from the desert seemed to soften and Saul caught the scent of the nearby arbor.

Janina stroked his sweat dampened, thinning hair.

"Don't, Mother," he said. "My hair is damp with sweat."

Janina continued stroking. "You are my son; allow me to soothe you."

Saul sighed and leaned back. Janina was older, grayer, but still had the figure, bearing and sparkling eyes of a young woman with a full life ahead of her.

Dantha too, seemed younger and more vigorous than her years and Saul was still attracted to her. "This business with David is unbelievably difficult, brother," she said. "We have talked of it before." As Dantha shifted her body, the hem of her chaste white robe caught the grit at her feet.

He raised his eyes to hers and nodded.

"It is good you are aware of being too much with Yahweh."

Saul shuddered.

"The more you are aware that there is another source of support and guidance, the more likely you will be to choose it."

Saul smiled, ruefully. "Being aware and choosing, are two different things."

"Yes and no," Janina said, leaving off her stroking and coming to stand beside Dantha facing her son. "For in the moment of awareness, you can and do choose. Choose to be with the Covenant, my son. That has always been difficult for you I know, but difficult is not impossible. You are called to greatness, Saul, are great already and we are proud of you. Choose the Covenant, and no matter what action you take, all will be well." A fig blossom fluttered from the tree above them, danced a moment in the dry air then settled at their feet.

Abadantha smiled. "Remember, Brother, it is not *what* you choose to do, but *who* you choose to do it with."

"Michal and Jonathan hate me for my pursuit of their lover. But I must hunt him down."

"You are not responsible for your children's choices," his mother said, "only your own. Your choice seems to be: pursue with Yahweh or the Covenant."

Abner pushed open the big double doors and strode down the center aisle to the throne. Bowing deeply to the Queen Mother and her daughter, he said, "The troops are assembled and ready for the journey to Nob."

"Thank you, mother, sister," the King said, standing. "I pray to the Covenant that I choose aright." Saul adjusted the thin golden circlette crown he always wore. When would it ever seem comfortable and correct?

Six hours later, riding hard, King Saul, Abner, Doeg and seventy of Abner's hand-picked, battle hardened cavalry arrived at Nob.

As the heavily armed men galloped through the town, the people of Nob left their work and followed them. Someone saw the King at the head of the column and excited shouts of, "The King! The King!" filled the air and people began running, eager to see their King. The cavalry rode twice around the holy compound, leaving mounted men to form an evenly spaced perimeter on the second pass. The compound gates swung open and Saul, Abner, Doeg, and twenty troopers raced inside, kicking up clouds of dust. As the priests poured forth, eager as the townspeople to see their King, Saul and the others sat tall on their war horses, bright armor dulled with dust, sweat running down their dusty faces.

Angrier now than he had been when Doeg first told him of Abimelech's treachery, the King's eyes flashed and his hands clenched and unclenched on the reins as, leaning forward, he searched the crowd for Abimelech. At last! "Why have you conspired against me, priest, you and the son of Jesse?"

Stunned, the High Priest said, "Who among all thy servants is as trusted as David? Who is the King's son-in-law and the commander of thy bodyguard and is honored in thy house?"

Saul stared stonily down on him. Abimelech was shaken. Something was dangerously amiss.

"Be it far from me! Let not the King impute anything unto his servant, nor to all the house of my father, for thy servant knows nothing of all this!"

"Doeg," King Saul said, pointing to Abimelech, "is this the man you saw feed and arm and nurture the son of Jesse?"

"It is, Sire."

Still pointing, voice a growl, Saul said, "You shall die, priest, you and all of your father's house." A wail of doubt and disbelief arose from the confused and bewildered priests. But Abimelech was calm. He gazed sadly at his King and spoke softly to the one hundred and twenty priests gathered in the courtyard. "Fear not brothers! We are enfolded in the love of God; what can harm us?"

"Slay the priests of Yahweh!" King Saul commanded. No one moved. Had the King gone mad? Were the rumors true? "They must die for they too, are against us," Saul said, reasoning with his soldiers. "Their hand is also with David, and because they knew that he fled and did not disclose it to me."

Still no one moved; who could live after committing such a sin, spilling the blood of men who had consecrated their lives to the service of the living God? For a moment, Saul thought he felt Abadantha's hand on his shoulder and her soft voice encouraging him to choose again. But no, this was insolent insubordination. All of them had sided with David against him. Eyes glowing, almost flaming red, Saul turned to Doeg. The Edomite returned the King's stare, levelly.

"These men are nothing to you. You are not Hebrew, nor a worshipper of Yahweh. Slay them now and your reward shall be great."

Smiling, a strange and eerie smile, Doeg bowed his head, pulled his long, curved sword from its scabbard and fell upon the unresisting priests of Yahweh. The courtyard ran with blood, the stink of blood and gore, feces and urine floated around the immobile troopers; three of them vomited; one fell from his horse.

Covered with the thick evidence of death, Doeg had to continually wipe his eyes so he could see. He had to grip his sword with both hands to keep it from slipping away in the sticky ooze that drenched it. Abimelech knelt and led the priests in the Schma, and they continued chanting, eyes closed on their knees until the last of them was hacked to pieces.

Sitting erect in his saddle, Saul watched the slaughter with a dispassionate dispossessed demeanor. When, an hour after he began, Doeg finally let the sword slip from his grasp and stumbled across the severed heads and limbs to the King's side, arm up, hand open, Saul took a fat purse from his belt and dropped it down to him. Doeg caught it and panting, barely able to breathe, collapsed into a puddle of dust covered with carnage.

Looking from mounted man to mounted man, eyes radiating red ferocity, the King commanded, "Go now. Go now and smite Nob! Leave nothing alive! Kill men and women, children and sucklings, oxen and asses and sheep!" Standing in the stirrups, reaching his arms up to heaven, eyes spitting the red fires of Gahanna, he swung around, to his right then left touching each of them with his white-hot rage. "Go! Make an example of all who would betray Saul, King of Israel. Go now; leave nothing alive in Nob!"

Unsheathing their swords with a shout, the soldiers went, galloping from the bloody courtyard, trampling the human remains, and left nothing alive in Nob. Only the wild-eyed King and the crumpled Doeg remained in the unearthly stillness of the Temple courtyard.

Word of the atrocity at Nob spread swiftly and fear became the peoples' constant companion. It was not enough that they had the Philistines to contend with, now they became trapped in the escalating back and forth skirmishing between David and the King. Nob showed that they dare not openly support David, but without a legitimate base of support, David and his growing band of followers had to live off the land, and those that did not willingly support him, were forced to do so, or forfeit their lives or the lives of their families. Poor Israel! David had become a bandit, King Saul seemed to be insane and the Philistines raided at will.

King Saul, in hot pursuit of David, was using the ruins of Nob as a base. Abadantha made plans to go to what was left of the city and pray with her brother. But worried about both her son's and son-in-law's motivations, Janina convinced her daughter not to go. She, Dantha, and Michal used their fear and time to further develop their understanding of the Covenant.

In the Negev, Jonathan and Dathan discussed what their response should be. Though he loved David, it was completely clear to Jonathan that the son of Jesse was now in open revolt against the House of Saul and Jonathan's place was with his father.

Dathan agreed. "We are secure here, at the moment," he said. "You may want to take a reinforced cavalry company with you."

"Yes, we are strong here. However, the rumors don't suggest my father needs more troops. He needs moral support; legitimacy. The people need to see what happened at Nob was a momentary aberration; that their King is sane."

Dathan dipped his head in agreement. "When will you depart?"

"Tomorrow, at sunrise."

"Good." Dathan made a hypnotic pass across his slave's face and Jonathan's eyelids dropped shut. "Then you will have no objection to serving Me and Mistress Shasheesha until you leave."

Jonathan's eyes opened and he licked his lips sensuously. "No, Master, I would have no objection."

# Chapter Twenty-One

"Now the King has no access to God's counsel," Eliazer, the sole surviving priest of Nob said to David. "Having killed all the priests, Saul has no one to inquire of the Lord for him."

The son of Jesse smiled sadly and patted the priest on the shoulder. "You are right, Eliazer. I am most grateful to Yahweh for sparing you from the massacre at Nob, and mourn with you the death of your father, the High Priest." David stared into the younger man's face. "Will you be my priest now, Eliazer?" Abimelech's son smiled tentatively and nodded. "Good," David said, clapping both hands on his shoulders. "Let us inquire of Yahweh, then. I have set aside a tent for your use. Go now into that peaceful space and seek God's guidance. Ask, 'Is the son of Jesse still Your anointed one, and how shall we proceed now?' Eliazer dipped his head and went to meditate.

An hour later, the priest wandered through David's small encampment at the Oasis of Ziph and found David talking with Gareth, his chief lieutenant. Perhaps one hundred people were in the camp including David's mother Embet, his stepmother Nitzevet, and father, all his brothers and their families, as well as two civilian survivors of the Nob massacre. When Gareth finished talking and left David alone, the priest told David that he was indeed, still God's anointed, yet God wanted him to fend for himself.

David was disappointed. "No guidance on where to go to live, for food and water?" The priest shook his head, no. "No guidance on besting Saul?" The priest again shook his head, no. "So," David said, voice trembling with frustration and anger, "I have not massacred Yahweh's priests, nor desecrated His holy city, but the man who did those things goes free and prospers while I, His faithful servant, go without the guidance I so desperately need. What good is this God?"

"Be careful you do not blaspheme, son of Jesse!" Eliazer said.

"Yes, yes, of course," David said, catching himself.

"Perhaps," the priest said, "His silence is because of some earlier trespass."

David laughed. Some earlier trespass? What sin had he *not* committed? Yet wait, could Yahweh have turned his face from him for lying to the High Priest and eating of the holy bread; and what of the High Priest's own gruesome death? Could he, David, have lured the man to sin? But no, Abimelech's punishment was far in excess of the nature of his sin, wasn't it?

"Perhaps," David answered, and fitting an arrow to his bowstring, he thanked the priest and turned back to his target. "I miss Michal," he thought, taking aim. "She was a warrior, bright and strong, compassionate and loving, too. Her passion and sage advice would be most welcome now."

Every day, two or three people dissatisfied with their lives, mostly men, drifted into the encampment at Ziph. Soon, David knew, they'd have to move again, not only to elude Saul, but because there would not be food and water enough. That's what he'd been talking about with Gareth. The original plan was to go to Gath, but that was a Philistine city and to go there, would clearly mark him a traitor, not only to Saul, but also to David's own people. He'd go to Gath if he had to, but he and Gareth agreed it would be best to stay in Judah, in the hill country of the southern Shephelah, if possible.

The downside of that was they had to live off the land, raiding small farms, flocks, and larger estates for sustenance, becoming bandits in the process. Of course, whenever possible, they would raid Philistine villages and caravans, but if they did too much of that, they'd foreclose their Gath option. They could also defend the Judean villages from other bandit raiders. This worked for a while, but as David's band grew, ultimately numbering six hundred, their numbers became oppressive, even to liberated villages. Because the King had rarely troubled or taxed the Judeans in the southern Shephelah, there Saul had many allies in his search for the bandit David.

Gareth brought word that Keilah, a walled town ten miles northwest of Hebron, was continually under attack by the Philistines, who took the wheat, "right off the threshing room floors." This was the perfect opportunity for David! They could play the heroes, defending their kinsmen from the enemy, have a secure base to rest, and refresh themselves. Besides, David was growing tired of the nomadic life style and ready for the comforts of a city or even a village.

Gathering his fighters around him, David proposed they raid Keilah and drive the Philistines out. "Keilah is too deep in Philistine occupied territory," one of David's better warriors, said. "If we are not successful, we will have to fight our way out and may be badly mauled." There were *ahs* and *ayes* and other sounds of agreement.

"There is much wine, wheat, cattle, armor, and Philistine iron weapons. It would be worth the risk," Gareth said. There were more *ahs* and *ayes* in response to this.

Holding up his hands for silence, David gestured for his priest, Eliazer, to come forward. "If the priest inquires of Yahweh and we are blessed, will you go forth?" Sounds of agreement again issued from the warriors. "Can you inquire of God, here and now, Eliazer, or do you need solitude?" David asked.

"I can inquire here and now," the priest said, closing his eyes and gently swaying side to side. The nervous fighters fell silent and stood still. A few moments later, Eliazer, opened his eyes and smiling, declared, "the Lord is with us. Keilah will be ours. The Philistines will be defeated. So says Yahweh." A cheer arose and David and his fighters went to Keilah within the hour.

They had to. Hunted everywhere and safe nowhere, David needed a place with adequate food, water, and security. Keilah could be that place, although its elders, artisans, and prominent farmers were loyal to the King. Perhaps, he could bring Michal to Keilah… David smiled at the thought of her bravery and memory of her tender flesh, or even Jonathan! But no, Jonathan was with Saul right now, hunting him.

The Philistines had left a small squad of soldiers in the town. David captured them without a fight, early the next morning. One of them was Captain Hafiz. "You're David, son of Jesse," Hafiz said, rubbing the sleep from his eyes.

"Do I know you?' David asked.

"No, but I know you. I was present when Saul was anointed. He would give much for your head."

"Indeed," David said, smiling. "So, you have followed the progress of our royal family?"

Hafiz smiled back. "You Hebrews are barbarians! What do you know of 'royal families'? Come to Sidon or Gath if you want to see royalty!"

David slapped the man. "You are my prisoner! It's not wise to talk so disparagingly about my King!"

Rubbing his cheek, Hafiz glared at David. "You are nothing but a bandit and wanted man, while I am cousin to Achish, King of Gath. I know whereof I speak!"

David nodded. "Good, cousin to Achish, King of Gath," he said, "I have spared you and your men to take a message to your King, to show him I am not a barbarian." Hafiz continued glaring at him. "Tell your King that I need allies and there may come a time when I will accept his hospitality. Tell him I free you and your men as a token of my good will."

Hafiz dipped his head. "Very well," he said, "I shall tell him. Give me my horse and I shall go."

David laughed. "Your horse is mine, Philistine! You may walk back to Gath. Now take your men and go. My lieutenant, Gareth, will give you water skins and bread." David strode from the room to stand in the courtyard facing the rising sun, watching as Gareth led Captain Hafiz and his men away.

"I want to meet with the elders of Keilah, now," David said to Gareth when he returned. "Find them, wake them and bring them to me!"

"Wouldn't it be better to wait and let them have breakfast?" Gareth said. "This is not a good beginning if we wish to have good relations with these people."

David patted his sword in its sheath at his side. "This will guarantee our 'good relations' with the people of Keilah," he said. "Now do as I asked! Take a squad of men if you need them."

Forty minutes later, Gareth and his squad returned with nine groggy men still rubbing the sleep from their eyes. David saw that their robes were clean and well mended, their beards neatly trimmed. Well-to-do burghers, he thought sullenly as he stared at them, hands on hips, the kind of men that supported their King. He might need men like this someday, but now they reminded him of what he'd lost and how he suffered. "Who speaks for you?" David asked angrily, surveying them.

"I do," said a lean, clean-shaven man, not the oldest of them.

"Who are you?" David asked.

"Nehor, the scribe," the man said, eyes meeting David's.

"You are the leader of the elders?"

"I am."

"Well, Nehor, we have liberated Keilah from the Philistines. You are safe now and may resume your normal lives."

"Thank you, Lord David," Nehor said. "We are grateful. What can we do for you in return?"

"I will require food and shelter for my people. There are six hundred of us."

"Six hundred?" Nehor said, disbelievingly. David nodded. "You 'liberated' us from twenty Philistines and now you expect us to support six hundred?"

"But the Philistines raided your granaries and raped your women and we are Hebrew like you!" Gareth said.

"And you will not rape our women? And feeding six hundred, will that not 'raid' our granaries?" The other elders were nodding and grumbling.

David stepped forward and slapped Nehor. "Enough!" he said. "We are your liberators. I go to bring my people here. They are tired and hungry. Prepare to feed and welcome them within the hour!"

"Michal has sent a request to join us, Father," Jonathan said to the King as they rode south and west of Gath with a thousand men in search of David. The King smiled and Jonathan was encouraged.

"She shows her true heart, Father, her true dedication to our clan. She is sorry for deceiving you and begs your forgiveness." Saul nodded, noncommittally. "Remember how well she and I worked together at Michmash?"

Saul's face darkened. He had failed at Michmash and been saved by his children. Jonathan immediately saw his mistake.

"We are one family, Father, the royal family of Israel! Michal understands that as I do. We love David, but not more than you, Sire."

Saul smiled slyly. Perhaps he could use his daughter to bait a trap that would finally lure the elusive usurper and false king from hiding or, at the very least, coax him to stand and fight then be slaughtered by Saul's superior numbers. He nodded to Jonathan, "Yes," he said. "Alright. Tell my daughter she is welcome to join us if she is willing to fight."

"Thank you, Sire!" Jonathan said, turning his horse. "I shall tell her myself!" and he rode off through the scrub toward Gibeah.

"Of course I will fight!" Michal said the next evening when Jonathan arrived at his sister's sparse rooms in Gibeah. "I will fight *Him*!" They were in the empty throne room, sitting on the steps of the dais, their voices echoing despite the rich woven tapestries on the walls and floors.

"Please, Sister," Jonathan begged. "You cannot win. The best you can hope for is that he will die before he marries you off to someone else."

Michal considered this. They were in the empty throne room, sitting on the steps of the dais, their voices echoing despite the rich woven tapestries on the walls and floors.

"Look around you, Brother," she said, gesturing. "This luxury might be yours if our father kills my husband. How sad for me, for I love you both. David would have made a good king, as you will. But who would have succeeded our father?" Michal arose and paced. "You and David would surely have fought. Perhaps the way things are is for the best. I am torn, Brother, badly torn! I do not want either of you to die! Surely, one of you must. I will go with you, but I know not why." She paused, returned to Jonathan's side and stroked his face. He smiled up at her. "I go to escape boredom. I go to be close to the point of decision. I go because I can no longer stay."

"And you will not fight with the King?" Jonathan asked.

Michal shook her head, no. "Only if I am sorely provoked or am guided to do so. Come," she said, leading him from the throne room, "eat and rest so we can depart at first light."

Michal did not sleep well. Thoughts of her future mingled with concern for her people's future. The conversation she'd had with Janina and Abadantha five days ago, resulting in sending the summons to Jonathan, nagged at her. She'd had a very similar conversation with them before she married David.

Abadantha had smiled warmly at her. "I don't think the son of Jesse understands the Covenant as we do," she said. Aunt Abadantha had aged quite well, her skin was still smooth and barely wrinkled and her eyes shone with the enthusiasm of youth. Janina dipped her head in agreement. She too, showed few of the ill effects of aging.

"David is a warrior, Aunt," Michal replied. "You know that too, Grandmother!" she said looking from one to the other. Both of them nodded.

"My son, your father, became a warrior, too," Janina said; "and in the course of things forgot who he was and his promises to God, our God, and the God of the Covenant. He became a servant of Yahweh instead."

"The Covenant is matrilineal, Michal," Aunt Abadantha said. "You know that. We're counting on you to transmit its love and blessings to your husband. If you do not, it may be lost to our people forever."

Michal nodded solemnly. "You know I understand," she said, looking at them with warmly glowing eyes. "I already see David's commitment to Yahweh. I will do my best."

She had not been able to reach David. They simply had not had enough peaceful time together. As she thought about this, she felt it was a sad, personal failure. She worried she might never have a chance to reach him, and the light of the Covenant might be extinguished forever.

Dantha understood her niece's feelings. Reaching out to stroke the young woman's cheek she said, "It is not over, until it is over, Michal. You may yet have a chance to be with David again. It will be difficult and dangerous; you will be caught between his soldiers and

Saul's, yet you yourself are a warrior and know about difficulty and danger." Michal's face brightened.

"And it may be," Dantha continued. "If you do not succeed in the coming weeks, you may see him and influence him years from now; or bring the Covenant to a woman who *will* influence him. The path is wide open before you. Accept your place in God's will and glory in it! Use all the power, strength, wisdom and courage It has lavished upon you. Throw off your sorrow and self pity and go forth!"

"Yes, Aunt, I shall go forth! I will write my father today."

Michal tossed fitfully that night. She resolved to do what she could. Renewed connection to the Covenant focused and comforted her. She did not know how or if she would speak with David again, but she would deal with that when and if the opportunity arose. Knowing the God of the Covenant would guide and sustain her, Michal fell into a deep and restful sleep.

# Chapter Twenty-Two

With Jonathan riding with his father, Dathan returned to Negev to be with Shasheesha. They had built a small, private pleasure palace behind high, stout walls within the Hebrew enclave that dominated the oasis of Yeroham. The fortress and military encampment was at one end, their high-walled, private palace at the other. Shasheesha had mellowed with the years and although still attractive, deeply sensual, and sexually active, she was no longer as voracious as she'd been when she'd first enslaved Jonathan.

The King's son still served and worshipped her when he was able to. She hadn't found anyone as dedicated, adoring and sensual as Jonathan, but she made do with other slaves, preferring Moabites to Hebrews, finding that their idol-worshipping religious rituals made them easier to train, more sensual and erotic, less demanding, and more obedient.

During this visit, she and Dathan switched roles frequently, taking turns serving and worshipping one another, as they had before the Hebrews had captured them at Jabesh. Although Jonathan was now well trained, Shasheesha still preferred her husband to be a slave to her, and Dathan enjoyed it, too. She also enjoyed being a slave to him. His body was larger and more muscular than Jonathan's, as was his penis. She could give herself over to enjoying her husband's massive erection more readily than she could her real slaves penises, Moabite or Hebrew, though the circumcised Hebrews were cleaner.

There could be no exchange of roles with Jonathan. She never served or worshipped his penis. Shasheesha was always the Master and Priestess, he, always the slave and worshipper. Experience had shown her that that absolute distinction was essential to keep Jonathan at her feet. She had no such concerns with Dathan; it was a great pleasure to have her husband with her! They sometimes involved their real slaves in their games and rituals, but more often, preferred being alone.

The isolation and solitude of the Negev and of their high-walled pleasure palace, coupled with Dathan and Jonathan's infrequent visits, gave Shasheesha much empty time. To her credit, she spent a great deal of it in meditation and prayer, deepening her relationship with the great Goddess Astarte. Her devotion and single-mindedness opened her more deeply to the Goddess and she began having dreams that foretold the future. She'd dreamt of Saul's attempt on David's life with the javelin and saw Jonathan meet David. Because he was so deeply enslaved to her, Shasheesha's dreams of Jonathan were extremely vivid and clear, as were her dreams and visions concerning Dathan. She knew when Dathan was returning and where Jonathan was now. She'd had such dreams even as a child, but now, with her deepening connection to the Goddess, their frequency was greater and their vividness, and accuracy uncanny.

"I dreamt of our slave Jonathan last night," Shasheesha said, rolling over beside her Master. "He is in danger and will die horribly."

Dathan was shocked, but he knew the power of his priestess wife's visions. "Soon?" he asked. She nodded. "Is there anything I can do to prevent it?" he asked.

Shasheesha shook her head, no. "But you can make contact with David, so we are not left out in the cold when the time comes."

"Shall I tell David or anyone else what you have seen?"

She smiled sadly. "It would do no good, Beloved," she said, stroking his cheek. "I too, will miss our Hebrew slave prince. His father will die, too, as will all but one of his brothers. Soon the House of Saul will be no more. Go now, be with Jonathan and his father while you may, and attempt to make contact with David."

Dathan dipped his head. "I will take a small group of warriors under Uriah the Hittite and perhaps leave them with David so that we may be kept informed."

Shasheesha shook her head, no. "I don't know exactly when Saul and Jonathan will die. What you propose is traitorous as long as either of them lives. Take Uriah with you and introduce him to David. When the time is right, send him to be David's man."

Dathan smiled. What a blessing she was! "It shall be as you say, my Queen," he said, sniffing and kissing the smelly foot she thrust into his face as a reward.

"Oh," she said, lowering her foot. "I dreamt of Michal, too. She will be going to join Jonathan and Saul in search of David. She may have left already, but in case she has not, stop in Gibeah and perhaps you can escort her. Together you might have an even better chance of finding David."

Captain Hafiz rose from his knees in Achish's throne room and bowed to the King. The royal palace of Gath was one of the wonders of the Philistine Federation. The room was lined with columns finished in Thracian marble, with marble on the floors, and rich silk draperies from Cathay on the walls. The many courtiers scattered around the room were well fed and well dressed with beautiful jewels and precious metals gleaming on their persons.

"So," the King said to his Captain, "Do you think David will make a reliable ally?"

Captain Hafiz looked down, then back into the King's narrow brown eyes. "I think, Sire, that if he says he will fight for you, he will fight for you."

"Even against his own people?"

"David is above all, a practical man, Sire. If he cannot rule in his own land now, he will bide his time until he can."

"But I have heard that the Hebrew god, Yahweh, had their prophet Samuel anointed him." Hafiz nodded. "What of that, Hafiz?"

"That is the key, Sire," Hafiz said, looking into Achish's eyes feeling the King's understanding. "Because he is their anointed one, he cannot give up until he is King. He will be indebted to us if we support him when he needs our support."

"I disagree," said another soldier near the King. "And, I," said another. "And, I," said other courtiers. The King looked from Hafiz to the dissenters, then back to Hafiz. "What say you, Hafiz?"

"I, not they, have lived among the Hebrews. I, not they, have been near both David and Saul and the entire Hebrew royal family. I can only tell you what I experienced, Sire."

King Achish snorted and waved Captain Hafiz and the others back to their places. "We need not decide now. But I appreciate Captain Hafiz' advice."

Nehor the Scribe went into the temple in Keilah. It was not much, just a single story building made of clay bricks, lined with rough-hewn timber benches. The two torches burning at the front of the room cast eerie shadows over the eleven men already there. Nehor went to the front of the room and stood between the torches. "It has been nearly two weeks since David and his bandit gang 'liberated' us." Hisses and boos arose from the others. Nehor gestured for quiet. "We have been talking in ones and twos about what to do, and all agree we must take collective action before these locusts eat us out of all we have." Nods and yeas of agreement echoed the room. "As I see it, we have three possible courses of action. We can go to David as a group, and ask him to leave." Mutterings of disagreement echoed the room

"We can inform the Philistines of his presence here and 'invite' them to remove him." More negative mutterings. "Or we can send an emissary to King Saul." Nods and yeas of agreement.

"I will go to the King," said a young blacksmith's apprentice.

"Thank you! How soon can you leave?"

"Sunrise tomorrow."

"Excellent. If the King cannot bring his entire force with him, ask him to send a scouting party." The young man dipped his head.

"Good," Nehor said, gesturing for everyone to leave. As the men rose to depart, a shadow lingering at the entryway, slipped away. It was Gareth, David's lieutenant. He went straight away to David.

"It was as I warned you, Son of Jesse. You have been too harsh, and there are too many of us."

David scowled, and then shrugged. "When?" he asked.

"The blacksmith's apprentice sets out tomorrow at sunrise. My scouts say Saul is two day's ride from here. Allow a day for the apprentice to find him; that gives us three days to evacuate."

"I will burn this place!" David said, savagely.

"You will be King someday, Son of Jesse! Kings do not burn towns belonging to their own people."

"They do if those people have been traitors!"

"They are not traitors, neither are you king. They are being loyal to their true king, as they will be loyal to you when you are king."

David snarled, kicked the sheepskin he used as a bed. "Very well Gareth, prepare our people to leave. I want us out of here by sunset tomorrow!"

"Which direction?"

"To the hill Hareth first. It's only three miles from here. Then through Hebron to the wilderness of Ziph."

"To pass through Hebron will be dangerous, David," Gareth said.

David nodded. "We will do so at night. We must have supplies and there are many rich Calebite estates around Carmel. One in particular belonging to a man named Nabal, may be an especially juicy target." Gareth nodded and went to organize their departure from Keilah.

Jonathan and Michal made excellent time, nearly riding their horses into the ground after they encountered a royal messenger heading back to Gibeah to bring reinforcements for the King's siege of Keilah. Neither Jonathan nor Michal thought David obtuse enough to allow himself to be besieged. They wanted to be there in case it was so; obviously, Saul thought it was so.

The section of Judah they rode through normally leaned toward David, after all, he was a Judean. But because of his banditry, the people were against him, giving aid, information and comfort to the rightful king and withholding it from David and his six hundred followers. The road from Gibeah to Hebron, branching to Keilah, was a royal road, made of hard packed clay, with well stocked way stations, manned by Judean families eager to share what they had and what they heard with those who passed by and could pay. The drought made the road dustier than usual and the vegetation, groves, orchards, and fields stretching away from its sides were withered and dying.

Michal thought the brown devastation surrounding the road offered a fine metaphor for her relationship with David. So verdant, green, and filled with possibilities when it began, its potential to nourish and succor her seemed to wither as each new report of his banditry, arrogance, and willful marauding reached them as they rode to Keilah.

She also thought the brown devastation was a perfect metaphor for the present condition of the House of Saul. "Jonathan and I are like the dying vegetation and spiraling dust devils." She shook her head thinking about their father's mad pursuit of David in the oppressive and relentless heat. But sadder and more sobering was the possibility that the drying up and withering would be the future of her family and her House. "Not if I can help it!" she said loudly, spurring her horse to greater effort. Jonathan didn't hear her, but had no choice but to rush after her or be left behind, to eat her dust.

Michal allowed her tired horse to slow, letting its more gentle rhythm between her legs remind her of how it felt to be atop David. How she ached for him, lusted for him, in spite of her disappointment with his ethical lapses! The proud warrior princess of the House of Saul felt her dilemma keenly. Love of family, House and husband was tearing her apart. All her instincts demanded swift, decisive action. Now, finally, she hoped she was moving towards some kind of resolution, after having stewed and delayed for nearly a year. Yet what that resolution might be, she had no idea.

One thing was certain: she needed to talk with David for both their sakes and for the Covenant. Shifting her weight in the saddle, Michal squeezed her legs more tightly around the horse's flanks and sighed at the pleasant sensation, knowing that if she allowed herself, she could easily reach orgasm. Lust and love, love and lust, and God, the God of the Covenant. Surely, that God wanted her and David to be together, to extend the House of Saul with their children.

But then, what of Brother Jonathan? Wouldn't he, not she, be the one to take the throne after Saul's death? Yes, yes, it was difficult and she'd thought of it ceaselessly, many times before and always arrived back to this place, with no answers, no real plan and no clear resolution. It frustrated her warrior nature. But that wasn't so, not now. True, she had no definite answers about who would succeed her father. In spite of his being an outlaw bandit, Michal knew she still wanted to bear David's children. She also knew the Covenant was vital and had to be preserved and extended, that she loved her brother, and loved her father least of the three of them.

The gentler rhythm of the horse brought sexual memories to Jonathan also. But he was the horse, the slave stead, and Shasheesha, his Mistress, ruler and owner, the rider. It was he who lay beneath Her, She in the superior position, he in the inferior, as befitted his place in Her world. She was so magnificent, sexy, arrogant, and dominant! He had no choice, and wanted none, but to submit to Her and be Her slave. Jonathan squeezed his legs more tightly against the horse's flanks, feeling his erection grow. From the first moment he saw Her all those years ago, aloof and beautiful, although in chains, standing beside Her husband, his Master, Dathan, he was drawn to Her.

It was She who introduced Jonathan to the worship of Astarte and taught him how to really please and serve a woman. Until he met Shasheesha, he had thought sex was a ten-minute activity, pleasant, even necessary, but nothing special. But as Shasheesha enslaved him and became his Mistress and Owner, he learned to put Her needs above his own and how to spend hours in mindless erotic bliss worshipping Her body with his mouth, tongue, face, and hands. Ah, God, there was nothing, nothing, not even the excitement of combat that could match the thrill of serving Her! She teased and humiliated him, praised and punished, filled every moment with Her whims and selfish desires, and he loved it.

Sex, prayer, and worship belong together, She taught him. That was Astarte's will for Her slaves and worshippers and Jonathan submitted himself completely to the Goddess's will, surrendering his body, heart, and mind to the enchanting seductive Shasheesha, the Goddess on earth. He felt guilty at times, worried that his sexual servitude, adoration and worship of Shasheesha/Astarte blasphemed, and he feared Yahweh's vengeance. As time passed and his Mistress/Goddess led him to ever more blissful states of submission and arousal, he forgot about Yahweh's vengeance. When he did think about Yahweh, he remembered his grandmother's distinction between the fearsomeness of Yahweh, and the gentleness of the God of the Covenant.

Jonathan came to understand that since what he and Shasheesha did harmed no one and made him a better person, soldier, and prince, then it must be of the God of the Covenant, even though it broke every one of Yahweh's laws. Sex, prayer, and worship belong together Shasheesha/Astarte taught him and now, and each time he was in danger or confused or unsure, when he prayed, thinking of Her and his worship of Her and his sexual servitude to Her, Jonathan knew that was true.

Yet he still had a nagging and deepening sense of foreboding. His thoughts and feelings about serving and worshipping Shasheesha, especially in trying times, were growing less and less satisfying. Something deeper and more transcendent was being called forth. What was going on around him with his father and David, demanded more, and he feared he didn't know what that 'more' was and how to give it. Jonathan's head hurt when he thought about it.

He brought his horse nearer and just ahead of Michal's and looked into her face. How intense she was! It took her a few seconds before she realized he was looking at her. She smiled at him. Jonathan pointed to a distant plume of smoke on the horizon. "That would be our father's encampment," he shouted. Michal nodded. "We should be there in three or four hours, just before sunset." Michal nodded again then urged her horse to a faster pace. Jonathan rushed after her.

Saul was eager to see his children. When his outriders reported they were near, the King rode out to meet them alone. Michal and Jonathan reined in as they saw the lone rider approaching. "It is Father," Jonathan said, smiling.

"Yes," Michal replied, her smile more tentative than her brother's.

"He has forgiven you, Sister," Jonathan said, noticing her look of concern. "I know he has!"

I wonder, Michal thought. But as the King rode up to them, the tears glistening in the corners of his eyes and running down his cheeks told her Jonathan had been right. They dismounted and ran to embrace one another, all three of them crying.

"It is good to see you, my children," Saul said through his sobs, wiping his eyes with the back of his hand. "So good! Thank you for coming all this way."

"We are of the House of Saul, too, Father," Michal said, also drying her tears.

"Yes," the King said, "yes, indeed you are." He turned to Jonathan. "How are things in the Negev?"

"Good, Sire," Jonathan said.

"Did you see the reinforcements I sent for?" Saul asked.

"They are a day behind us," Michal replied.

The King scowled. "They will not be necessary. I'll send them back after they've rested."

"Why is that, Sire?" Jonathan asked.

"David has left Keilah," Saul said. "The scouts think they fled to the hill Hareth, about three miles to the east, and thence through Hebron to Ziph." Michal's face fell. Saul looked at her with a wry expression. "You are no more disappointed than I, Daughter, believe me!"

Her father's tone and expression put Michal more at ease and she smiled at him. "I was hoping to see him," she said, "to bring him home, to stop his marauding."

Saul nodded, sadly. "Would that were possible, Michal. He's a traitor, you know."

"But Father, he is my husband and your son-in-law and a hero of the people."

"Not anymore! He may be your husband, but he is no longer a hero of the people. It was the people of Keilah, who summoned me and wanted him out." The King shook his head sadly. "He must be stopped. It is our duty to protect the people, even from him, especially from him."

Michal bowed her head, heart heavy, near to breaking with the weight of understanding. "I still love him, Father," she said simply, realizing she'd never said anything like that—anything so personal—to him before.

Saul sighed, how terrible and painful. His duty was clear. Putting his hand on Michal's shoulder and looking mournfully into her face he said, "He must be stopped. You understand that; and if it comes to it, I will kill him, Jonathan will kill him, or one of our soldiers will kill him. It's us or him."

"I understand you, Father." Michal's voice shook as she turned from him to her brother. "But I see it differently. Please, let me talk with him, just once more."

"If you can find him," Saul said, wearily, "talk with him. I will give you two days, and then I will hunt him down. Take Jonathan with you."

# Chapter Twenty-Three

The next day, early in the morning, Dathan and Uriah the Hittite arrived in the King's encampment. Jonathan, walking alone in the early morning dew, saw them ride in. When the two men dismounted, Jonathan greeted his Master warmly with a hug. Dathan introduced Uriah, then gave Uriah the reins and told him to take the animals to the encampment and await him there. Uriah bowed and obeyed. Seeing this and hearing Dathan's commanding tone, Jonathan felt his deep, servile desire arise in his chest and stir his penis. Dathan was so strong and manly, it was natural that he, Jonathan, although a prince, should bow down before him and be his slave.

As if reading Jonathan's thoughts, Dathan put his hands on his hips and smiled calmly and confidently into his slave's eyes. Jonathan could not help himself, feeling his Master's power and will wash over him, heedless of who might see him, he once again became Dathan's lowly slave and bowed himself down before his Master's face in the dust at his feet, and raised his Master's foot and placed it on his neck in the classic gesture of devotion and fealty.

Dathan grunted, pressing his foot down on his slave's neck. "Good slave boy," he said, glancing about him to be sure they were unseen. "Now, lick the dust from My feet, slave," he commanded, placing both sandal shot feet squarely before his slave's mouth. Eagerly, slave Jonathan served his Master's feet, cleaning them, tasting the dust and salt and inhaling the odor of leather and foot sweat. The slave licked until told to stop.

"Kneel up, slave," Dathan commanded. Jonathan obeyed. Dathan looked into his slave's eyes with a strange blend of arrogance and compassion. "You have been a good slave to Me, Jonathan."

"Thank You, Master." Jonathan thrilled to the praise. "Serving You has brought me joy and deep satisfaction."

"I know, slave, your devotion shines through all you do for Me."

"I have been made better by my submission to You, my Lord. Being Your slave has been one of the most fulfilling and satisfying things in my life."

Pleased and wanting to reward his slave, Dathan raised his dusty sandal to Jonathan's face. "Sniff, then kiss, then lick, My good slave boy." Jonathan hastened to obey. "Enough," Dathan said. "It's getting light; we might be seen. Arise and treat Me normally."

"Yes, Master."

As they walked side by side to the corral, Dathan said, "You said being My slave was one of the most satisfying things in your life. I know your love of combat was one of those. Is your enslavement to My wife, your Mistress Shasheesha, another?"

"Oh yes, Ma... , eh, Dathan," Jonathan said, pausing and looking deeply into Dathan's handsome weatherworn face.

Dathan put an arm round Jonathan's shoulders and resumed walking. "I must tell you out of the love I bear you, your father and your House, that Shasheesha, always able to see the future, but now more able than before, has sent me here to tell you she has foreseen a grizzly death for you, your father, and the demise of your House."

Jonathan froze; so his vague feelings of doubt were more than mere vague feelings, they were presentiments of the future! "Is there anything that will prevent that?" He asked, eyes searching Dathan's face. Dathan shook his head no.

"Does Shasheesha see when this will occur?" Again, Dathan shook his head no. Jonathan became incensed. "Then why tell me, Dathan? If there's nothing we can do, and don't know when?"

"Because, Jonathan," Dathan said, taking the younger man's hand in his, "as long as we are alive, there is hope. I tell you this so that you will live more fully while you may. Be more careful and do not put yourself into the thick of combat as you love to do."

Jonathan looked away and sighed. "You were right to tell me, Dathan," he said, looking back at him. "You have been a good friend as well as a good Master." Jonathan brought Dathan's hand to his lips and kissed it.

Entering the camp, they took the salutes of the guards and saluted back. "I was to go with Michal to find David tomorrow," Jonathan said.

Perfect, Dathan thought, just the opportunity he sought! "Perhaps it would be best if I accompanied Michal and you remained here." Jonathan thought a moment then agreed. They saw Uriah the Hittite coming toward them. "I will take Uriah as well. Perhaps David will find a use for him and he can keep us informed as well."

Jonathan smiled. "Excellent suggestion, Dathan. Come," he said gesturing to Uriah, "let's introduce you to the King."

Michal and Uriah waited on the hillock, just inside the trees, watching, their horses munching the scruffy grass. "There," Uriah said, pointing. "David and Dathan approach!" Michal didn't see them at first. When she did, her heart raced in anticipation. What would he say to her she wondered? Would he tell her how he missed her and loved her? Would he dismount and rush to her?

David did none of those things. Wary and suspicious, despite agreeing to meet his wife, he still feared a trap. Uriah and Michal rode into the open to meet him to allay his fears. David reined in his horse to await them. He sat erect and immobile. Taking in his body language, Michal's hopes fluttered in her belly. Her throat tightened, and her heart twisted. Uriah dropped back, Dathan joined him, and Michal was alone with David at the top of the hill.

David nodded to her as she rode up to him, a slight smile of greeting on his lips. She dipped her head in recognition. "How are you, my husband?" she asked, noticing new scars on his bare arms and legs and a small one on his left cheek, near his eye. For a moment, her heart fluttered with empathy, then she quickly composed herself.

"As you can see," he said coolly, "I am well. You too, seem well." No terms of endearment, no real concern just a distant, formal interest.

"Yes," she said. "I too, am well. I hoped to encourage you to return to Gibeah and take your place in the royal household."

David smiled wryly. "The royal household is here, on my horse's back and in my tent."

"Oh, David! How could you! My father... you're a traitor and a bandit!"

"Your father," David's voice reeked with anger. "Your father tried to kill me and would kill me now, if he could."

Michal looked down. "True. But what about *us*? Have you no love for me?"

For the first time, David's eyes looked at her with compassion. "I did love you, Michal; and still do love you, in a way. But things are different now. Everything is different now. We will never be together again. Your father used you to keep me at bay. He will use you again to make another political alliance. That is the way for a princess of the royal house."

Anger flashed in Michal's eyes, though she knew he spoke the truth. She stared back levelly at him. Unrequited passion for him, for his strength and his body, burned but she refused to acknowledge it. "So be it, Son of Jesse," she said, using Saul's name for him; and, gripping the reins more tightly, wheeled her horse and galloped back toward the King's encampment.

Uriah the Hittite urged his horse after her, but Dathan grabbed the reins and restrained him. "No," he said. "You go with David. Remember," Dathan looked over his shoulder at the son of Jesse sitting calmly on his horse, "he wants you with him; needs you, and will richly reward you for your service to him."

Uriah nodded. "I remember, sir," he said. "And I am ready to go with him. But I am concerned about my wife, Bathsheba. I do not want to leave her alone for long."

"I understand fully, Uriah," Dathan said, patting the younger man's shoulder. "Bathsheba will be fine. If you would like," he stared into Uriah's eyes, "I will ask Shasheesha to go and stay with her." He smiled inwardly. And make her, her slave.

"Would you, sir?" Uriah was grateful. "I know how much Shasheesha values her privacy. Would she make such a sacrifice for me?"

"I believe she would, Uriah. Go now. David grows impatient. Keep me informed!" Dathan slapped Uriah's horse on the rump and watched as Uriah the Hittite galloped off to David. Then, immediately spurring his own steed, he raced to catch up with Michal, now a small figure on the horizon.

Michal drove her horse at a gallop the entire way back to her father's encampment with Dathan beside her. Two hours later, horses covered in lather, they arrived. Notified of their approach, Saul waited outside his tent, and held the reins of Michal's horse as she dismounted. Surprised by this gesture of gracious service and seeing the look of concern in her father's eyes, Michal threw herself into his arms. Dathan dismounted, took the reins of both horses and led them away as father and daughter embraced warmly.

"He is not the same, Father," Michal said, crying, then stepping back. She let Saul hold her shoulders at arm's length and gaze compassionately into her eyes. "He doesn't love me anymore."

"It was always a marriage of convenience, Michal," the King said, softly.

"No!" Michal's voice was loud and adamant. "No. I know he loved me as I loved him."

Saul nodded solicitously. "Perhaps he did, but a marriage to a princess of the royal house was quite useful to him. Now, that usefulness is past." Burning with anger, Michal's eyes blinked back her tears. "Show him how wrong he was about you, my daughter," Saul said. "Show him what a prize he let slip through his fingers, Michal, what a warrior princess does in the face of scurrilous rejection." Michal wiped her tears away and looked a question at her father.

"There is a Hebrew lord in Gath," Saul said, "Paltiel, who is aligned with our House. At some point it is almost certain the son of Jesse will take refuge in Gath. Should you marry Paltiel, and should David go there, your marriage will be a constant reminder of our power, your power as a beautiful warrior princes and the power of our House."

Pushing the King's hands from her shoulders, Michal stepped back and stared into her father's face. Will it never end, she wondered? Oh, how terribly right David was! Must I always be a prize, a spoil of dynastic bargaining? Is there no place for love and honor? Michal knew the answer even as she thought the question. No, there was no place for love for a royal princess. Yes, she would always be a prize, a spoil of dynastic struggle. There could be honor for a warrior princess. She had never met, nor heard of this Paltiel of Gath, but marrying him would preserve her honor and the honor of her House, and perhaps, might even bring some sort of peace, if not love.

"Yes, Father," she said, stepping back into Saul's embrace. "Yes, all right, arrange it, and soon."

"I will, Daughter," the King said, smiling down upon her. "Spoken like a true princess of the House of Saul!"

# Chapter Twenty-Four

David's movements through the villages of the Judean wilderness towards Carmel were a constant concern to the people. The few who might have helped him, did not, fearing to do so would make them traitors in the King's eyes and who, after his horrendous massacre of the priests at Nob, was feared as much as David. A few of the most prosperous shepherds and estate owners formed an informal network of mercenary soldiers to protect themselves and their estates. Most of these prosperous men realized their few mercenaries would be no match for David's hardened veterans in a pitched battle, but hoped the mercenaries would deter random raids.

As the shearing season approached with its festivals and feasts, a time when the landed gentry would be more vulnerable and in need of more disciplined protection, not less, the mercenaries were drawn into the feasting and became lax. Nabal, the Carmelite, one of the richest among them, with three thousand sheep, was well aware of the danger.

Nabal thought of himself as a reasonable man, willing to share his wealth, but not submit to blackmail and intimidation. He honored Yahweh in both spirit and deed and even tolerated his wife Abigail's dalliance with the Sisterhood of the Covenant.

As they walked in the late afternoon sunlight among the blossoming fig and pomegranate trees, Abigail said, "I have been giving this matter of David some thought, Husband." She stood still and looked into his face. "Should he come to us, I know you will show him the common courtesy due any guest or visitor."

"Indeed, I shall," Nabal responded, admiring the fine-boned features of his wife's face, her soft skin like cream, her shimmering, long brown hair. "But only for David himself, not his six hundred followers. And I shall not be threatened! The man's reputation precedes him, Abigail." She smiled and squeezed her legs together as she nodded. Indeed it did, she thought, lasciviously.

Seeing his young beautiful wife's sensual movements, Nabal scowled. "If I am not mistaken," he said. "The Covenant agrees with Yahweh about a wife's duty to her husband."

"I have never dishonored you, Husband," Abigail said, touching Nabal's bearded cheek. "Nor shall I. I am younger than you and life bubbles up in me. I would be misleading you if I said I was not aroused by what they say about David ben Jesse. Besides, my judgment is not clouded by vain concepts of manly honor." She walked closer to him, looked deeply into his eyes and lowered her hand from his cheek. "For a woman, the survival of the family is preferable to a death with honor. The Covenant would have no one be so overwhelmed by pride and honor that they would sacrifice life and limb, home and hearth."

Nabal grunted, turned away, and then looked back into Abigail's big beautiful eyes. "As a woman protected by a man's pride and honor you may say that," he said. "But where would you be without a man's honor? What would protect you from other men, men without honor?"

Abigail dipped her head. "You are right, Husband. A man must have his honor to protect his wife and family. I respect that. But a foolish honor that endangers family, home and hearth may not be tolerated. As a woman, I must not acquiesce to such a foolish honor, but take whatever actions I believe necessary to prevent such 'honor' from endangering me and mine."

The captain of Nabal's small troop of mercenaries, a tall Sheban, entered the garden and bowed to them. "What news, Captain?" Nabal asked, seating himself next to his wife on a stone bench.

"Ten of David's young warriors, heavily armed, approached the flocks in the north grazing ground. I was there and spoke with them." Nabal nodded. "Their leader, a man with reddish-blonde hair, possibly one of David's brothers, told me that David and his followers had come upon our 'vast' flocks as they grazed but had taken none of them, although they were in sore need, nor had they done any harm to those who tended them." Nabal nodded. "The leader asked that the owner of these flocks show his gratitude for what was not done to the sheep and shepherds."

Nabal flung himself to his feet, face flushed with anger. "Gratitude? For what was *not* done? Did he actually say that?" The Sheban nodded. "And how am I to express my 'gratitude?'"

"He did not say, sir."

"By all that's holy!" Nabal said. "Return to that man and say in Yahweh's name I offer David ben Jesse and only David ben Jesse the hospitality of my house."

"Is that all, sir?"

"Yes. Go now and deliver that invitation." The captain saluted and left.

"Don't you think that will provoke David?" Abigail asked.

"I will not submit to intimidation and blackmail. Gratitude for what he did *not* do," Nabal sputtered. "Even the Philistines do not deal thusly. The man must think me a fool."

"Not a fool, husband," Abigail said. "But rather a wise man. It is no shame to submit to one with superior arms. I hope your reply does not enrage him overly much."

Nabal clutched his heart as pain shot through him, then, as it subsided, steadied himself on a lemon tree. "You are concerned more for him than me?" he asked, pain-filled eyes staring unbelievingly into his wife's face.

"No, Husband," Abigail said. "I fear for *us*. I only want to soothe you and especially David so he will not attack and destroy us. I know he is quite capable of that."

Nabal sat down, his breathing easier. "You are a good woman, Abigail. But I beg you do nothing rash."

Abigail stood, smiling down on her husband, and said, "Surely David ben Jesse is a reasonable man. He is the King's son in law, married to the King's daughter."

"He *was* that, but is no longer," Nabal said. "He is a bandit now. You cannot reason with a bandit."

"But the divine spark animates him as it does you and me. If we meet him and seek the divine spark in him, he will find it in us."

Nabal reached up for her hand and held it. "You have no experience with men like this, Abigail. They are fierce, mean, and nasty. They have a raw power that can charm, even overwhelm, but the only thing that will satisfy them is complete submission, and I will not do that."

"Fear not, husband. Let us reason with him first, then if that fails, perhaps my feminine charms," she ran her hands up her body, "and a few cartloads of food will win the day."

"I forbid it!" Nabal said, trying to rise but clutched at his heart again and panted.

Abigail looked down at him sadly. "Rest yourself, Husband. I will only do what must be done. Everyone expects a woman to be submissive. If reason fails I will be submissive." Nabal opened his mouth to speak; she placed a hand over his lips to gently silence him. "We shall be blessed and forgiven for giving into superior force. David will respond to me, no one need be hurt or die." She bent and reached to stroke his damp cheek. "Please, Nabal, I beg you, rest easy. You will save David the trouble and kill yourself if you continue as you are. The God of the Covenant is with us. I feel It, here," she touched her chest. "All will be well if you allow it to unfold. I am confident, prepared and willing. Please, allow me to serve in the way that is being revealed to me."

"I fear for you, my wife. You have no idea of that man's raw power and what it might do to you; or of how you might be seduced and changed by it."

"All will be well, Husband. We must trust in the power that is in us and even in David."

Although clearly not convinced, Nabal dipped his head in agreement, rose unsteadily, and allowed his wife to support him as they returned to the estate house.

Early the next morning, as Nabal and Abigail were eating a breakfast of dates, honey cakes, and goat's milk, their mercenary captain came to them.

"I spoke to David ben Jesse last night and would not disturb your meal, but the news is not good."

"Please," Abigail said, gesturing to the empty chair at the table, "sit and tell us."

The captain looked to his Master. "By all means, Captain, please, sit, eat."

"Thank you, Sir," the captain said, seating himself and taking a plump, shiny date.

After the captain chewed most of his date, Nabal said, "David did not respond well, to my invitation?"

"Not at all, Sir. It provoked him to great rage."

"I feared so," Abigail said.

"And what did he say, Captain?" Nabal asked quietly, ignoring Abigail.

"He left the tent, shouting, 'Let every man strap on his sword! That landowner, Nabal, is an ungrateful wretch! We should have taken the flocks and herds when we first had the chance. God do the same to me and more if I leave alive a single one who pisses against the wall!'"

"Ah," Abigail said, blanching, "this is the death and destruction I so feared."

Nabal stood and looked sharply at her. "Not yet, wife; it is not over yet." He turned to the mercenary. "Captain, how many men can you muster?"

"Perhaps fifty, Sir. David is coming with four hundred and they are angry and hungry."

"Does this sound like a 'reasonable man' to you, wife?"

Abigail swallowed and looked down. "Captain, rally the fifty and any others you can muster and I will join you at the front gate in thirty minutes." Dipping his head, the captain began to withdraw.

"Wait," Nabal said. "How far distant is the bandit?"

"He will be here by mid-day, Sir." Nabal waved the Sheban away, rose and went to strap on his sword and armor. Abigail followed him.

"Please, Nabal, there is still time for reason, let me go to him and beg him to spare us."

Nabal reached up to slap her, but restrained himself. "Do you not understand woman. Only force will do now. I... I..." Nabal grabbed his chest, staggered and fell to the rough-hewn wooden floor. Abigail bent to tend him. He was unconscious but his breathing was steady, his color slightly red but otherwise good. She stood and called for her maid. The woman came quickly. "Put him in bed and tend to him! I must go; there is a great disaster to be averted."

Rushing to the storehouse, Abigail supervised the preparation of a 'gift offering' to David, hoping to deter his murderous wrath and make amends for any unintended offense. The offering consisted of two hundred loaves, two skins of wine, five sheep slaughtered and dressed, five measures of parched corn, a hundred clusters of raisins, and two hundred cakes of figs. As it was all being loaded onto carts so David's people could just take it and go away, Abigail dismissed all but five of the mercenaries and made known her decision to accompany the offering. She was a part of it, after all, had known that to be true earlier, even as she dressed, taking great care with her hair, skin and eye shadow and donning her finest robes. Now, flushed with anticipation, she looked more radiant and beautiful than ever. With the Sheban captain at her side, she mounted her youthful donkey and rode at the head of their column of carts.

An hour from the estate, the gift caravan encountered David's mounted scouts. The men rode around and around the column, whooping and hollering, kicking up dust, then tiring of their sport, took station beside the carts and escorted them to meet the rest of David's advancing column. Filled with anxiety and anticipation, Abigail's heart beat rapidly and her breathing became labored and shallow.

Surely, David would be reasonable, even if these men were not. But what if he wasn't? What if Nabal was right and David's arrogance, selfishness and power overwhelmed her? Soon she would know. Then he appeared. Resplendent in a metal breastplate, helmet and greaves gleaming in the sun, David galloped up to her, sword in hand, eyes blazing and reined in.

"What have we here?" he said, devouring Abigail with his blue eyes. "Who are you?" She stared right back, unflinchingly. He was close enough for her to smell his sweat, his leather and his horse's sweat. She wrinkled her nose. "Does my smell offend you?"

"I am Abigail, wife of Nabal. I come in the name of friendship to offer you the hospitality of our estate." She gestured to the carts. "And, yes, your sweat offends me."

David came closer, the scent of him nearly overpowering her. "Are you included in this so-called hospitality?" he asked.

"No. I am not. I am a daughter of the Covenant; I am like a sister to you, David ben Jesse." God, he was magnificent! Everything they said about him was true: virile, young, tall, brawny and ruddy, bare, hairy legs and arms burnished by the sun, muscles rippling. She inhaled deeply, filling herself with the odor of his sweat, feeling light-headed and unexpectedly warm and moist between her legs.

"No," he said, voice low and guttural, eyes burning into hers, dominating her. "No, you are not like a sister to me. You are a prize, a spoil of war, a mere thing." She shuddered. No one had ever spoken to her this way. It made the hair on her arms stand on end. He licked his full lips. "I swore an oath to Yahweh, to revenge myself, His anointed, for the unseemly treatment your husband meted out to me. I swore death to all the males on Nabal's estates. But you," he sneered at her, "are a female, a prize, a mere thing, a spoil of war for me to dispose of as I will."

Shuddering with fear and arousal, Abigail steadied herself and tried to retain her dignity. A mere thing, *his* thing, to do with as he pleased? His eyes glowed into hers and now she *was* feeling like a prize, a thing, an object to be possessed by him, by this powerful man. She rallied and made one more attempt to reason with him. "David ben Jesse, you are a hero of our people, wronged by our King and now by my husband. I beg you live from your heart, from that place of grace in which the Covenant resides. Look what I have brought you! You need not kill for this, we give it freely to honor you and make amends."

Unmoved, David sat aloofly on his horse, arms folded, staring unrelentingly into her eyes. "The Lord God Yahweh is with me, Woman, I need nothing else. You are mine, my prize, my property my thing. Submit. Give yourself to me now. You must submit, *want* to submit. Yahweh must be placated, as you submit to me, you submit to Him."

Submit. Her loins burned. Yes, abase herself before Him; grovel; give in to his masculine power. Submit; that would be so much easier. Submit to this powerful man and submit to God. Cease resisting. It was all coming together for her—David's power, the odor of his sweat, the masterful way he sat upon his horse, the hot dampness in her groin, his strength and beauty—she had to submit to him, *wanted* to submit to him.

He gestured arrogantly to the ground beside his horse. Abigail slid from her donkey, crawled to the place he pointed to, knelt and bowed her head in the dust. Oh, sweet submission! Her body shuddered as she orgasmed multiple times.

David smiled down upon her. He allowed her passion to subside. "Kneel up!" he commanded. She obeyed, eyes looking submissively into his. "Now are you like my sister."

"Thank you, my Lord," she said, meekly. "Please accept the offering of thy handmaiden. I, Abigail, am your handmaiden, my Lord."

"No longer the wife of Nabal come to reason with the bandit?"

Abigail's eyes closed and she shivered. "Peace be to Thee, my Master. Nabal's wife, Abigail, is also your handmaiden, Abigail. Please, accept all that I bring Thee including myself and spare the estates and lives of my people."

"Yes. I shall spare the estates and lives of my handmaiden's people for my own sake, so that all may know that I am a pious, good and generous man, the anointed of Yahweh."

"Thank you, my Lord and Master!" Abigail said, prostrating herself again.

"Enough, Woman. Enough! I have accepted you as my handmaiden and your offering finds favor in my eyes. Rise up and go now, return to your house. The time will come soon for you to serve me."

"Yes, Master." David's new handmaiden bowed down again before him. "Thank you, Master. It will be as you command. I will hold myself in readiness for you."

After David turned his horse, Abigail arose, hot and lightheaded, to return with her small retinue to her husband's estate. She found him little improved from the way she left him. For the next ten days, she tended Nabal, torn by the peaks and valleys of guilt and sexual arousal, thankfulness and trepidation, telling him nothing of her meeting with David and admonishing the servants not to tell him. On the evening of the tenth day, Nabal died, never becoming fully lucid. Two days later, a proposal of marriage arrived from David.

"Our Master has sent us to take you to be his wife," the messengers said.

Instantly caught up in reliving the raptures of submission, Abigail arose, bowed down with her face to the earth and said, "Behold thy handmaid is a servant to wash the feet of the servants of my lord." Then, saying nothing else, she rose, went with her Master's messengers to his camp, where they were promptly wed.

During the ceremony, Abigail felt the convert's deep reverence for Yahweh. Grateful to the powerful God of her new Lord and Master for bringing them together, Abigail prayed with great reverence and passion. "Oh, mighty One, I, your handmaiden am so grateful to have found favor in Your eyes, and beg Your forgiveness for having dallied with the false God of the Covenant."

Even her husband, who had lately been frustrated with Yahweh, felt his faith renewed by his new wife's passion. "Thank you, my great Lord and Master," he prayed, "for delivering this woman and all her estates unto me."

After consummating the marriage, David and Abigail returned to their estates to have a brief funeral for Nabal then departed in haste leaving a small contingent of David's people to hold and maintain the estate until the difficulty with Saul was at an end and David could live there if he chose. Haste was necessary, because the incident with Nabal further inflamed the local people against David and he could not linger. He moved on to Ziph, a remote stretch of hill country in Judah, but there, too, the locals were uncomfortable and petitioned the King to rid the land of him and his band of locusts.

Hearing of the death of Nabal and the wedding of Abigail to David, Saul, enraged, prayed to Yahweh with great fervor. "Oh, Master of the Universe, Lord of Justice and Righteousness, grant me, Thy most obedient servant, divine justice and allow me to put an end to this bandit pretender to the throne, this son of Jesse of Bethlehem! Grant me the strength to find him and kill him, in your name and for your glory."

With unusual precision, the delegation from Ziph described to the King the bandit's exact location on the hill of Hachilah on the south of Jeshimon. "Oh King, come down," pleaded the men of Ziph, "and our part shall be to deliver him up into your hand." Saul, wary of treachery and wanting to husband his resources, sent the delegation and his own men for fresh intelligence. They returned and told him that David and the remaining four hundred of his followers slipped out of Ziph and had gone to the wilderness of Maon.

Saul thanked Yahweh with a special sacrifice and, satisfied he could isolate David and trap him in this mountainous region, he handpicked three thousand soldiers and set off. Approaching from the side opposite David's encampment, the King divided his army into two parts, sending them around both sides of the mountain in a classic pincer movement. Before he was able to close the circle and cut off any opportunity for escape, a courier arrived from the royal headquarters with an alarming message: the Philistines had raided near Gibeah. Saul was forced to turn his army around and face the Philistines. Was this last minute save the hand of Yahweh, Saul wondered, or part of a pact between the bandit and Achish, King of Gath?

Thanking Yahweh for his narrow escape, David moved on. By the time Saul was able to resume the hunt, David's enemies among his own people had once again betrayed his whereabouts to the King. "He is En-gedi," they told the King, "with fewer than one hundred followers." Again, with a handpicked contingent of only three hundred, King Saul set out for the spring-fed pools of the oasis on the western shore of the Dead Sea. Surrounding the area, Saul's soldiers carefully tightened the perimeter, picking off and capturing many of David's men.

Needing to defecate and wanting to do so in private, the King entered a cave. Sighing in the cool air, he inhaled the damp moldy, but comforting earthy odor, letting the tension drain from him. Deeper in the cave, David and his men watched as, silhouetted in the bright sunlight from the cave mouth, the King of Israel squatted on the floor and relieved himself.

It would have been so easy for David to come up behind his arch enemy and slay him once and for all. But he heard Saul praying as he squatted. "Dear God, most merciful God, grant me peace, release me from this endless trial of murderous pursuit. You who have made a covenant with us, I beseech you. Give me respite from wrath of Yahweh. Show me that what I know in my heart, that both David and I are your children whom you love, is true."

At first, David was amused by the act of praying while squatting. However, realizing that he too, had prayed thus, taking advantage of the rare moments of solitude and reflection defecation sometimes provided, he felt a tingling in the cool, damp air, as if from a premonition, and allowed himself to be moved by Saul's words, feeling them resonate in his own heart. What to do? Sneaking up behind Saul, David drew his dagger, sliced off a piece of Saul's robe and climbed to a ledge overlooking the cave entrance to await the King's exit. The bright sunlight, blue of the sky, and windswept clouds felt good after the damp twilight of the cave.

When Saul emerged, David called to him. "My lord the King. Why do you harken to the ones who say: 'David seeks to hurt you'?"

Eyes wide with amazement, Saul looked up and instinctively drew his sword. Holding up the strip of cloth he'd just cut from the King's robes, David said, "Behold, this day your eyes have seen how Yahweh delivered you into my hand in the cave. As I heard you praying, I felt a deep kinship with you, as I did on the days when first we met. Some bade me kill you, but the kinship I felt ran deep and I said, 'I will not put forth my hand against my lord, for he is Yahweh's anointed.'" David waved the strip of cloth. "My Father, see the skirt of your robe in my hand. Moments ago, when I cut this off, I could have killed you!"

Saul looked at his cut robe and knew David's words were true, just as he knew his prayer, offered in the spirit of the Covenant, had been answered. Now he could let the pursuit, vengeance and hatred go. Sheathing his sword and sobbing, King Saul said, "Is this the voice of my son David? You are more righteous than I, for you have rendered me a good whereas I have rendered you evil." David jumped down from his perch and the two men embraced.

"Now I know you will surely be King," Saul said, looking deeply into David's eyes. "Only promise me you will honor my House and family."

David agreed. "But you are King now, my Father," he said, "and must remain King. When the time is right, Yahweh will pass the crown to me."

David's men, Uriah the Hittite, and Gareth in the vanguard emerged from the cave.

Having overheard the conversation, Gareth urged David to claim the crown now. "Saul may change his mind, Sire. Do not let this moment pass. Claim the crown; take it now! You also are Yahweh's anointed."

Led by Dathan, a cohort of the King's soldiers, that had been seeking their leader, came and stood behind Saul, swords drawn. "What say you, Gareth?" Dathan demanded, menace in his voice. "Claim the crown? Take it now? Not on your life!"

Saul extended his arms, staying Dathan's forward motion. "Hold, Dathan! Hold your men! David has done me a service and spared my life. I want an end to this strife."

"How so, Sire?" Dathan asked, unbelieving. "Are you in your right mind, my Lord?"

"Show them the strip you cut from my robe, David." David held up the piece of cloth. "Look, Dathan," the King said, showing the place on his robe from which the strip was cut. "You know I went into this cave to defecate in peace. As I squatted, David crept up behind me and instead of killing me, cut a piece of my robe. Sheath your swords now!" They obeyed reluctantly.

"Are you really going to give him the crown, Sire?" Dathan asked. "After all he has done, abandoning your daughter, raising an army against you, and pillaging our settlements? You cannot do that, oh King. To do so would destroy your authority. The son of Jesse is an evil doer and must be punished."

Saul listened, nodding. It was true. He himself, his House and all he'd built would be threatened by rewarding the son of Jesse for his crimes. He looked around. His force outnumbered David's three to one. He could end it now, right now! David's eyes found his. "The son of Jesse has done me a service," the King said. "We will not punish him and his people, but allow them to depart in peace." A moan went up from the throats of the King's soldiers.

"You will only have to find and subdue him in the days and weeks ahead, my King," Dathan said.

Saul nodded, looking deeply into David's eyes. "I will only have to find and subdue him if he returns to banditry. Will you refrain from preying upon our people, David?"

A sly smile slid across David's face. "Will you feed me and my people, my Father? If not, you leave me little choice."

"I cannot feed you, David." Saul pulled himself more erect and put his hand on his sword. "Refrain from banditry or face the consequences!"

David dipped his head. "Then we are free to go?"

The King nodded, and David and his men departed.

"Where shall we go, Sire?" Gareth asked when they rendezvoused with their now diminished group of two hundred. Before David could answer, Abigail threw herself into his arms.

"This behavior is unseemly, Wife," David said, lifting her into the air and swinging around with her. "Ah, but you do gladden my heart, Abigail."

"Thank you, Sire," she said, prettily, "pleasing you is all I live for!"

"There is no doubt of that!" Gareth said, annoyed that this foolishness intruded on their vital business.

Abigail kissed David fully on the mouth and he returned the kiss and set her down, scowling at Gareth. "Jealous, Gareth? Your woman waits there," he said, pointing. "Go, attend to her, we will talk in an hour."

Uriah the Hittite patted the disappointed lieutenant on the back to soothe him. "Consider the bright spot, Gareth," he said. "You at least have your woman here. My Bathsheba is far, far away." Gareth hugged him and they walked off.

"You are so different from Michal, Abigail," David said, caressing her fine, soft hair.

"Thank you, my Lord. I meant what I said about living only to please you."

"Yes, but you also please me in how you have taken the management of our supplies and settling of the petty disputes into your own hands. Those things, and the other tasks you do, were sapping my strength!"

"I know, David," she said, kissing him. "It is a pleasure to be useful. Nabal wanted me only for show and was not good at love making."

"It is good I found you and that he is dead," David said. Abigail shuddered in his arms.

"You can be harsh and cruel, my Lord."

"Yes, I can be. But never with you, Beloved." She felt the truth of his words as he gazed into her eyes. "Although what I must ask you to do now may seem harsh and cruel, please know that I don't intend it to be so." She dipped her head and he told her of the recent events with Saul. "I feel certain the grudge between the King and me is settled. We can no longer live off the land and be known as bandits. I must return you to your estates, for a time. I don't want to give the King an excuse to resume our conflict. Returning to your estates with the women and children will allow me to take the fighters with me to Gath."

"You would ally yourself with King Achish?" David nodded. "Would you fight against your own people?" David looked steadily into her eyes, but said nothing. "You would be a traitor?"

"Have I not been fighting against my own people all this time?"

Abigail nodded. "But if you fight from Gath under King Achish's banner, you are truly a traitor."

"What choice have I, Wife? I will try to avoid fighting our own people, of course." His tone was angry and anguished. "We are down to 75 able-bodied fighters. We cannot run from the King forever. He will kill them and me in the next battle. Ceasing the so-called 'banditry' and living in Philistine territory will remove one of the causes the King has for attacking me. I sincerely believe we resolved his desire for revenge at En-gedi."

Abigail stroked his cheek. "Yes, Master. I agree. All will be well with me, and the others on my estates. I will miss you mightily and be sad." She looked deeply into his eyes. "But you *are* the anointed of God and shall be King! We have only to keep body and soul together until that happens."

# Chapter Twenty-Five

David saw Hafiz from a great distance. At first, he thought the company of riders a mirage. Alone and too far ahead of the column for his own safety, David needed the solitude. "Oh, Yahweh, what has become of all my dreams?" The air was oppressively heavy. He'd been riding since dawn. It had been invigorating at first, but now was the time of day when the sun weighed down the world, drying up the breezes, silencing the birds, bringing introspection and mirages. "Are my dreams only a mirage, too, Lord?"

As if in answer, David saw what was coming toward him was no mirage but four or five men riding hard. He smiled. "Thank you, Abba. Perhaps my dreams are real, too." A moment later, David recognized Hafiz. As Hafiz and his men came clear, Gareth, Uriah the Hittite, and five soldiers rode up to him.

Uriah had become indispensable to David in the few months since Dathan assigned the Hittite to him. Quiet, calm, and an able leader with a good sense of tactics and strategy, David thought Uriah would make an excellent commander in his future army of Israel, a dream that still might come true. After all, he was only twenty-eight now, with ample time ahead of him to conquer Jerusalem and drive the Philistines into their seaside fortresses. But here came Hafiz and before driving the Philistines out, he'd have to ally with them. David swallowed hard. He did not want to be a traitor, would try not to be an active one, but knew that if he crossed over into Gath, he was one.

"King Achish is not sure he wants you in his territory," the Philistine Captain said, stopping his horse a few feet from David's. "I see no harm in it and only benefits to Gath. But many of the King's advisors feel you cannot be trusted."

David dipped his head in acknowledgement. "I understand. But may I still meet with the King?"

Hafiz nodded. "You may bring these two," he gestured to Uriah and Gareth, but the others will have to go back."

Again, David dipped his head. He was in no position to argue. He *had* to have a rest and stop running, not only for himself, but also for those who followed him. He was willing to be labeled a traitor for it, and was willing to beg for it, too. Somehow, he didn't think that would be necessary. Somehow— just as the mirage turned out to be real, so too would his dreams— manifest. Hafiz wheeled his horse and the three Hebrews followed.

In David's eyes, Gath was magnificent. A shepherd boy and desert warrior, he'd lived most of his life in the open or in a tent. Even Saul's palace and the improvements the King had made to Gibeah, would fit into a small part of the resplendent Philistine city. From a distance, as they approached, they saw five massive structures that rose four and five stories into the air. Hafiz, now riding beside him, told David that the tallest one in the center was the King's palace, the two on either side were the Temple of Baal and the Temple of Astarte and the two nearest them were towers guarding the huge city gates.

The buildings were made not of mud brick covered with stucco as Saul's palace, but of white granite blocks that gleamed in the sun. The walls protecting the city, bristling with heavily armed soldiers, were substantial. Three stories tall, they had space on top for three men to walk abreast. The traffic grew thick as they neared the walls and they could no longer gallop, but had to thread their way carefully between carts of all sizes, empty ones leaving, as well as fully laden ones bearing fruit, grain, vegetables going in. The foot traffic was also heavy with shepherds driving their flocks, children and men tending geese, donkeys bearing riders, sacks and baskets.

People in the robes and styles of many nations near and far, some folks with black and yellow skins that David had never seen before flowed around them. The noise of so many different tongues, animal sounds, and the creaking of carts, leather and the clanking of metal, made it difficult to hear; and the dust, rising in a cloud around them, made it necessary to keep one's mouth closed and eyes narrowed.

Shacks and shanties, some of stucco, others of wood and palm fronds, clung to the walls and the edges of the roadway. And wonder of wonders, as they passed through the colossal gates, the hard packed mud of the road gave way to cobbles. The streets of Gath were actually paved! Paving the floors of King Saul's palace was considered a great innovation, and here the wealth and power was such that they paved the streets!

The sound of his horse's hooves on the stones was strange in David's ears. The broad road they were on, a thoroughfare really, led straight to the royal palace, a half a mile away. Radiating off this splendid road, were many streets. Looking down them as they rode by, David noticed occasional small plazas and oases with wells and palm trees. The houses, what he could see of them behind their walls and shops, grew more luxurious and spacious as they rode toward the palace and temples.

Not far from the wall, down a street to their left, was the slave market. David glimpsed naked and semi-naked men, women, and children on raised wooden platforms with potential buyers inspecting the merchandise. David shuddered. Yahweh allowed his people to own slaves but they treated them as human beings, not cattle. The smells of the hot heavy air were full of roasting meat, frying grain cakes, and baking bread, mingled with animal dung, and human waste.

Slaves were using water from the nearby sea to wash away and scoop up this effluent. Public baths, one for men, the other for women, were located near the temples, so that the faithful might wash before worshipping. The shops lining the great public square in front of the palace and temples had stalls in front with colorful cloth and canvas awnings of red, yellow, and blue, shielding their displays of papyrus books, meat and fowl, leather goods, metalwork, fruits, vegetables and flowers. David was in awe of the abundance.

"When I am King," he thought, "this is what my capitol, poor isolated, land-locked Jerusalem, shall be. It might take years; I might never live to see it done. It might be for my sons to accomplish, but Jerusalem, the soul of my Judean heartland, shall be as proud and grand as this, perhaps grander."

"You and your men must bathe and change before being admitted to the King's audience chamber," Hafiz said, interrupting David's vision.

A bath, imagine that! "Do you always bathe before attending the King?" David asked.

"We do if we smell as bad as you do and are covered with the filth of the road," Hafiz said wrinkling his nose. "In fact after the bath, I think we will have to burn your robes."

Eyes wide with disbelief, David looked at the Philistine, who nodded. "You're not in the hinterlands now, David ben Jesse," Hafiz said, smiling. "Robes such as yours are easily come by and easily discarded. The King will be happy to give you and your men even better robes to wear. But now," the Captain said, gesturing to the bathhouse immediately on their right and only a short walk from the palace, "a groom shall take care of your horses, while you bathe and change."

As the clean, freshly robed bandit leader walked the short distance to King Achish's palace with Hafiz, following a few yards behind by Gareth and Uriah the Hittite, the Captain chided him. "Only a few months ago you forced me and my men to walk here from Keilah. Do you remember that, David?" David grunted and kept his eyes on the ground. Hafiz patted the Hebrew's shoulder. "Fear not, oh, bandit chief who would be King. I do not hold that against you. In fact," Hafiz stopped walking and waited for David to look him in the eyes. "I am grateful you did not kill us," David said, smiling thinly.

As they neared the palace, the street noise diminished. Dry heat floated up from the cobbles. They began walking again. "You have nothing to fear from me, David. It is those around the King, you must be concerned with. I have put what you did to me in a remote place in my mind. That will not be a problem. But there are those here that remember how you behaved when you were here some time ago." David blanched, choked and stopped walking. "You... Do people...

?" "Yes," Hafiz said. "People still talk about the 'mad David, King of the Hebrews'."

"But Hafiz," David said, embarrassed, but urgently. "This—what I and my people are trying to do here—will not work if powerful people in Achish's Court still think me mad."

"Mad?" Gareth asked as he and Uriah caught up with them.

"It is nothing, Gareth," David said.

"Madness in a great leader is not nothing," Uriah observed.

"Indeed," Hafiz agreed.

"And why," Gareth said, standing still and staring at Hafiz, "would this Philistine know about this 'madness' and I do not?"

David put a hand on his lieutenant's shoulders. "Hopefully it will be as nothing and not interfere with our present plans."

Gareth was not mollified. "Say more, David, please," he said, searching his leader's eyes. "We have risked everything for you and have a right to know, so that we may advise you better."

"Do you remember the time, perhaps two years ago, when we had many fewer followers and more options, and I disappeared for two weeks?"

Gareth nodded, gravely. "We were all worried about you."

David patted Gareth's shoulder. "Yes, thank you. I knew you were, but I had to proceed."

"Proceed?" Gareth asked.

"I went to King Achish's Court to investigate the possibility of taking up residence here in Gath."

Uriah, who'd been quiet, but listening intently, gasped. "How different things would have been, my lord, if you'd been able to stay here then."

David dipped his head in agreement. "I would still have been a traitor," he said, sadly.

"Yes," Gareth said. "But with good cause."

"A traitor is a traitor," Hafiz said. "We had best be going."

"A minute, Captain," Gareth said, looking hard into David's eyes. "Why didn't you stay then, and what is this 'madness' you were speaking of when we caught up with you a moment ago?"

"I became conflicted and guilty, Gareth," David said, softening his eyes as he gazed into his lieutenant's worried face. "I didn't think I could live here without Michal, without Hebrew friends, as an exiled traitor in a foreign culture." Gareth nodded. "Besides, the King and his courtiers distrusted me and wanted to keep me locked up. I feigned madness to show them they had nothing to fear and could be let go."

"It is different now, isn't it?" Hafiz observed.

"Yes," David said, looking levelly at the Philistine Captain. "Quite different. Now, I have two wives, six children and 400 seasoned warriors and their families with me, nearly a thousand souls."

"And still a traitor," Hafiz said, acidly.

"And still a traitor," David repeated. "And I hope King Achish will remember that, along with my 400 seasoned warriors, and distrust me, for a traitor to one King may easily betray another. And not wanting me too close, lest I turn on him, give me and mine a small town or village to call our own under his protection, of course, with the understanding that we will fight for him if need be."

"Even against your own people?" Hafiz asked. Not waiting for an answer, he turned and began leading them to the palace.

Achish's palace and throne room seemed even more elaborate than David remembered. The same courtiers and military leaders who were against him and wanted to lock him up on his first visit hadn't changed their minds. Now as then, Captain Hafiz was a good advocate for the Hebrew bandit chief; and now as then, the King favored Hafiz's position over those of his nobles.

"I will give you and your people the town Ziklag in the southwest," Achish said. "I expect you to be a just judge and ruler over the Philistines that live there, not to interfere with my own or other Philistine commerce, and in fact, to protect that commerce from bandits of the type you yourself used to be. And if Gath goes to war, fight alongside me, even if it means against your own people." David dipped his head in agreement. "Very good," Achish said. "Then kneel and swear allegiance to me and become my vassal." David knelt. "Do you, David ben Jesse, swear by your God and all that you hold sacred, to honor the terms just stated, to be obedient to me and to serve as my vassal?"

"I do, my lord King Achish. I so swear. I am now your most obedient vassal and will see to it that my people are also loyal to Gath and the House of Achish."

Achish touched his sword to David's head. "Arise, then, David ben Jesse, go to Ziklag with all your people and serve me well there." David arose and backed out, bowing from the throne room. Two days later, Hafiz and a small squadron of Philistine soldiers accompanied David and his people to Ziklag, a two-day march from the capitol.

"It was painful to see you kneel and swear allegiance to that fat Philistine," Gareth said as they rode south.

"For me, too, my friend," David said. "But this will work out well for us. Ziklag is close to the borders of Judah, my tribe, and from there we will not only be able to protect my people from bandits such as we were, but in so doing, we will also build an alliance with the Judeans that will become the foundation for my dominion over all of Israel."

"It is a good plan, David, and I believe it will succeed. But swearing as you did leaves little doubt that you are now, officially a traitor to Saul, King of Israel."

David smiled at Gareth. "Well said, Gareth. That is what I want our people to remember. I am now indeed a traitor to Saul, King of Israel, but not to Israel itself or the Hebrew people."

Uriah the Hittite, who was riding on David's other side said, "Only if we win, will it be remembered as you have said, my lord. If we lose, it will be remembered differently."

Abigail was walking in the same garden she had last walked with her dead husband, Nabal, but this time she had Michal by her side. "Oh," Abigail said, "that the Covenant would take hold in your father and my husband at the same time!"

Michal smiled at the irony. "Indeed," she said. "They do seem to alternate. When Saul is with Spirit, David seems not to be and when David is, Saul is not." The air was dry and sweet, not too hot, filled with bird song and the scent of pomegranates. "It is pleasant here, Abigail. You are so lucky!"

"Thank you, my sister! I am surprised, given your reputation as a fierce competitor and warrior that we are getting along so well."

Michal looked down and away. "I can't say I'm not jealous. But I know David and now I know you." Michal raised her eyes to Abigail's. "I can see that the relationship you have with him was not entirely of your making. After all, we are sisters in the Covenant and want to allow spirit to work through us."

"Thank you," Abigail said, embracing Michal.

"Have you heard about the earlier incident of the Covenant not being with them at the same time?" Michal asked.

"No."

"As you know, I'm just back from being with my father, and though he himself did not tell me this story, many in his camp shared it with me, trying to persuade me to encourage the King to stop the chase."

"Tell me," Abigail said, nodding.

"It was before their encounter in the cave at En-gedi. David and Gareth, his lieutenant, snuck into my father's camp well after midnight and walked right up to him."

"Where were the King's guards?" Abigail asked.

"No one seems to know. In a repeat of the incident in the cave where David cut off a piece of my father's robe while he was relieving himself, David picked up Saul's spear and water jar and walked away."

Abigail smiled broadly and nodded. "That's my David!"

"*Our* David," Michal added, patting Abigail's shoulder. "But here's the best part. One of the guards, who had been sleeping, awoke and reported that Gareth begged David to kill his father-in-law. The guard reported that David said, 'No one can lay hands on the Lord's anointed with impunity.' "

"Ah," Abigail said. "David was thinking ahead to when he himself will wear the crown and someone might want to kill him!"

"Yes," Michal agreed. "Very likely. Then, full of himself and safe on a nearby hill, David taunted Abner, the King's general, for not guarding his King. Saul heard David's voice and called out to him: 'Come to me, my son David. May you be blessed!'

'Thank you, my King and my father. Let us have peace!'

'Come to me, my son. You shall achieve, and you shall prevail.' That is the benediction of a father to his heir.

Michal continued, "Impressed, but knowing how unstable Saul is, David refused the King's invitation, sent Gareth to bring back the spear and water jar. They parted friends, but the Covenant was not with David enough to risk embracing his father-in-law"

Abigail nodded vigorously. "I doubt I would have done differently than David," she said. "But now," Abigail looked down. "David is really a traitor, living in Ziklag in Gath, serving the Philistine King Achish as Achish prepares to attack your father."

Michal also looked down. "And my father is badly outnumbered and likely to lose that battle; perhaps even die in it."

# Chapter Twenty-Six

"Would that we had David and his men with us in this coming fight with Achish," Jonathan said to his father.

"What do you expect from such a traitor?" Saul said, bitterly, pushing through the tent flap and stepping into the wind-whipped darkening sky. The moon was just beginning to show and from time to time, blown by the gusting wind, large, nasty looking cumulus clouds hid its face. The night was eerie, filled with ghostly menace.

"Father?" Jonathan called.

"Stay there, my son, I must have a few moments alone." I must *know,* Saul thought, shivering. Is this my time; will this be my last battle? There is one who can tell me. "Guard!" he called. "Bring my horse!"

As the King rode, his long ago conversation with Samuel on the eve of his coronation drifted back to him. Although the night was warm, Saul shuddered. I have honored neither Yahweh and the Scrolls nor the God of the Covenant, he thought.

"I have seen such dark and terrible things for our people in the future," Samuel had said, looking up, into the sky with hazy eyes. "It is a distant future, perhaps thousands of years hence, but the pain and fear, and the sheer horror of it, surpasses anything we can conceive of now."

"I have seen such things, too, Samuel."

The old prophet had looked into Saul's eyes again. "If I believed that anything I did now, today, could change that future, I'd be obligated to do it. But how can I know which things to do and which not? I'd go out of my mind thinking about it. All I can do is trust in the Covenant, the belief that doingness itself, that sense of urgency and the need for certainty, a sense of absolute right and wrong, is the problem.

"Uncertainty is part of living, Saul, but we are loath to accept it. We can't know, but *want* to know, *insist* on knowing. We rely too much on prophecy and necromancy. 'Thou shalt not suffer a witch to live,' Yahweh decreed to Moses on Mount Sinai. All the black arts were condemned as an 'abomination to the Lord.' Biblical law says, 'There shall not be found among you one that uses divination, a soothsayer, or an enchanter, or a sorcerer, or a charmer, or one that consults a ghost or a familiar spirit or necromancer.' Dutifully enforce these ancient laws, Saul."

Although his mind drifted, the King did not slacken his pace, but spurred his horse to greater effort.

"I did that, Samuel, "he said to himself. "You know I did. I outlawed necromancy and witchcraft in Yahweh's name and banished from the land all who trafficked with ghosts and spirits. Still, people have a need to know the future, to feel certain. Now, I myself feel such a need, and strongly, too! You used to re-assure me of the outcome of our greatest battles. Now I have no one… "

"The only thing we can truly know is our identity as spiritual beings," the prophet continued. "I have to believe that when I trust in the Covenant and relax into my identity as Spirit and allow It's joy and peace to guide me, that when I do have to do something, I will do it from that place and whatever I do will be for the best."

Saul snorted.

"I no longer do even that," Samuel said after a few moments of silence. "But I am torn, Saul. Always there is a sense of urgency; always Yahweh commands me to act." He'd bowed his head and massaged his temples.

"Yes," Saul thought, "my head aches with doubt and the need to be sure, too, Samuel. Oh, Samuel, Samuel! Who can I turn to now? We did not part friends but you cared for me once. We sought for the Covenant together, even as we were slaves to Yahweh. Will you advise me once more, or will what I am about to do doom me forever?"

As was his habit, the King had sought Yahweh's help first, trying to inquire of Him. But since he'd murdered Yahweh's priests at Nob, Saul's shame and guilt prevented him from being truly open to Him and receptive to His word.

He'd sat with Abadantha and meditated on the Covenant, but nothing, no peace nor insight, came to him. Unable to repair the breach with God, he felt desperate for help, yet certain supernatural guidance was there for him, and Saul sought a third way, magical guidance from the dead Samuel. Even though necromancy was clearly and strictly against Yahweh's ancient law, a law the King himself had vigorously enforced, so desperate was Saul, and so out of touch with both his head and his heart, that he felt he had no choice but to find a spirit medium and inquire of Samuel about his future and the future of his house. That this might cut him off from *all* divine succors and support forever was no longer a concern for him.

Two months earlier, Saul had overheard a few of his courtiers saying that one of the banished witches had returned to area around Endor. In the midst of hunting David and organizing for the Philistine invasion, the King had not gone after her. Now he was glad he hadn't. Now he thought that perhaps this was the opening, the sign he'd been seeking, the invitation to learn what he wanted to know.

Saul had heard the common rumors and myths about witches worshipping Astarte or being incarnations of Astarte, and although that made the King more eager to hunt them down, it also gave him pause. Something his mother, Janina, had told him long ago, when he was a child, about Astarte and the Covenant softened him and made him want to leave the women alone, as did the common name Janina and the people used for witches, the ghostwife.

Nearing Endor, Saul again hesitated as the full magnitude of what he was about to do dawned upon him. This seeking out of witches was deeply forbidden even by Moses. The Scrolls held that not only was the occult sinful, it was utterly false and useless. As a leader in the war against the belief in the underworld, against demons and spirits of the dead, against soothsaying and necromancy, Saul knew how bitter the battle was. Yet, he persisted.

He was tiring now and the night had turned colder. The moon

shone eerily through the vast sky, its light reflecting dully off the desert sand and scrub. His nostrils twitched with the smell of wood smoke. Where was it? He wondered. I should have found it by now. That looks familiar. Have I been this way before, an hour ago?

Then, in the distance, he thought he saw a decrepit wooden shack shimmering in the moonlight; shimmering as if it was dissolving and reforming then dissolving again. Rubbing his tired burning eyes and brushing the desert grit from his dry eyelids, the King rode hard toward the shimmering hovel. The closer he came to it, the cooler it got. He shivered by the time he got near enough to see it clearly. Still, it seemed to recede even as he rode closer. He saw the flickering light of a fire, through the shack where the walls should have been. He realized it was only a lean-to, not a shack. The wind was moaning, even as it dissipated into a dead, lifeless chill.

Sweating with fear, even as he shivered with cold, Saul circled the structure twice, saw no one inside and dismounted. After tying his exhausted horse to a nearby acacia tree, the King moved closer to the fire. As he came nearer, he saw the hunched over figure of a woman sitting with her back to him. Again, he rubbed his burning, tired eyes. She hadn't been there a moment ago! The figure flickered in the fire's glow like a vapor of fine dust. She grew more solid as he approached, then as he ducked under the roof of the lean-to, he spoke to her. "I have need of your services, witch," he said.

Her voice was soft, almost melodious and strangely seductive. "Do you wish to lay with me, sir?" she asked.

"Turn and let me see you, witch!" Saul commanded. The woman turned and Saul gasped! She was young and comely, like his daughter Michal, not at all what he'd expected. "Are you a witch?" he asked.

"The King has banished witches from this land, sir."

"Who do you serve, woman?"

"I serve the Goddess."

"You blaspheme! You are a witch! Tell me you are a witch!"

"Yes, I am a witch. Does the gentleman wish to consult me as a witch or as a handmaiden of the great Goddess?"

"As a witch!"

"The King has made witchcraft and consulting witches a crime punishable by death, sir."

Saul smiled. "I can assure you, witch, that you have nothing to fear from the King." Freeing a full leather purse from his belt, Saul threw it to the ground in front of the woman.

She picked it up and hefted it, her face shimmering in the flickering firelight. "Very well, sir," she said, turning to fully face him. "How may I serve you?"

Saul shuddered, gasped, and grabbing his chest, tried to still his wildly throbbing heart that threatened to burst from his chest. This was impossible! What he was seeing could not be! It was not possible! Yet it was happening, horrific and awful, the woman's face was shifting grotesquely, rapidly sliding from one face to another: Janina's, Abadantha, David, Michal, Samuel, Jonathan, all distorted with fear and terror.

The King cried out and hid his face in his hands. "Enough! Stop! Enough!"

The witch laughed, a phlegmy guttural sound, low in her throat. "You," she said, pointing a skeletal white finger at Saul. "You have conjured these! Not I. They are yours! I know nothing of them."

"Yes, yes," Saul said, voice shaking, as lowering his hands, he forced himself to look upon the horror where the witch's face should have been. "They are mine. God help me!"

As he said, "God help me!" the faces stopped flashing across the woman's head and her own returned, shimmering there.

"Whom would you consult?"

"Samuel," Saul answered. "The prophet Samuel."

"Ah, ahhhh," the witch said, looking up into the King's face. "Indeed. And you are?"

"Never mind who I am, witch! Conjure Samuel for me! I will talk with Samuel!"

"I dare not!" The witch said. "So great a person cannot be disturbed. Let the dead rest in peace!"

"I also am so great a person, witch! Obey me! Conjure me Samuel!"

"I dare not! Who are you?"

"I am Saul, King of Israel. Now obey me, witch! Conjure me Samuel!"

The witch snarled, screeched and raised her arms to the sky, hands clawing at the moon. "How have I displeased You, Goddess, oh mighty One?" she screamed. "Pity me! I am trapped! Doomed by Yahweh if I raise His prophet, and hung by the King's Law if I do!"

"You may be doomed by Yahweh, witch, but I promise you, you will not be hung by the King's Law if you do raise Samuel, only if you don't!"

The witch lowered her arms, took a step forward, tilted her head and looked up into the King's angry face. Then, nodding, she said, "It is you who are doomed, King! It is you who violate both the law of God and man!"

"Proceed, witch!" Saul snapped. "You have been paid. Conjure me Samuel!"

"As you wish, King... " The frightened, terrified faces again began their shimmering dance across the woman's head. Saul stepped back, agog at the spectacle. In a moment Samuel's face, less frightened than the others, but deeper in pain, fixed itself on the witch's head.

"No! Oh, no!" It was indeed Samuel's voice, but trembling, as if the vocal chords were disintegrating. "What have you done, Saul?" The prophet's face on the witch's head stared out at the King, seeing him, but also seeing through him. "Now has Yahweh cursed you once and for all!"

"But Samuel, it is I, Saul," the King said, voice shaking. "Did we not once, together, seek the Covenant with God? In the name of the Covenant; please, Samuel I beg of you... "

"Yes, Saul," the prophet said. "The Covenant. But you do not believe in it. You never really did. It had no true place in your life. Perhaps if it had, the troubling situation would not have come to this. You are now a dead man walking! You and your house will be no more! Yahweh, the Lord God of Israel, has cursed you and yours! You shall die tomorrow, as will your son, Jonathan, and shortly thereafter your family will be cast down and your crown will pass to David."

"Can this be so, Samuel?" Saul tore at his hair, beard and robes as one in mourning.

The witch shook her head, "Yes." Her own face returned to replace Samuel's.

"Aiyeeeee!" Saul screamed, dropping to his knees and reaching out to the woman, who leaned back away from his grasping hands. "Aiyeeeee! No, no, please; this cannot be so!" Tears streamed down Saul's cheeks. His eyes burned fiercely and as he watched, the woman began fading. "Please, please," he begged. "Dear God, no! In the name of all that is holy! Do not abandon me this way, my Father! Love me! Am I not Your child as we are all Your children? Please, please, mercy, I beg You!"

Shuddering, the King fell on his side and lay still. When the sun of the new day woke him, Saul was alone, but for his horse still tied to the acacia tree. No shack, no remains of a fire could be found, just the sure knowledge, deep in his heart that he would die that day in the coming battle.

Yet was he King and he had a nation to defend and a battle to fight. Never before had the Philistines penetrated so far into the country. No longer just on the coast, they had reached the area of the major trade route— the King's Highway—which led through Mount Gilboa, up to Beit She'an and then up to Damascus. Strategically, they had the Israelites in a vice between the great highway in the west and the sea in the east.

Having heard the worst, Saul wasted no more time wondering and worrying. Before going in search of the witch, Saul had deployed most of his ill-equipped and ill-trained force in the Jezreel valley facing the better-equipped and trained Philistines.

In the frantic scrambling after David, the King had used a small cadre of his best troops, the people who would normally have officered and trained the bulk of the Army. Without this cadre, the King's once formidable fighting force had degenerated. Discipline was poor, morale low and weapons rusted and in disrepair. The Israelites were outnumbered four to one and even with a well-equipped and trained force, Saul would have had a tough fight on his hands.

As he galloped towards the Israelite encampment, he tried to review the terrain in his mind and formulate a viable strategy. It would have been better to occupy the high ground of Mt Gilboa, and he and

Jonathan had agreed to put a small force there. That was intended as a fallback position, only. They had no real strategy for either attack or defense.

Saul allowed the horse to slow. It's one thing for me to commit suicide in this battle, he thought, but to take the whole Army, or what's left of it with me, is another matter. Please, Abba, do not turn your back on your people for my transgressions!"

Then the King was swept by a wave of bliss. The horse had stopped walking and Saul let the reins slide through his fingers. He was tingling all over! A benign warmth spread from his belly up to his head and out to his arms and legs. He sighed and knew a peace he hadn't known since he'd been a child learning about the Covenant with his mother.

In an instant, the bliss was gone and he was back to normal, but the King now knew what he would do. Arriving in camp as the sun brightened and the soldiers prepared the morning meal, he gathered his sons and his General, Abner, around him.

They stood just inside the flap of the King's tent, with the noise, bustle, and good smell of meat and porridge cooking enfolded them. Saul's sons: Avinadav, Malkishua, Jonathan, and Ish-Boshet, were fully armed—as was Abner—their metal breastplates, chain mail, and helmets gleaming in the sun. An aide was waiting and caught the reins of the King's horse when Saul tossed them to him as he dismounted. Beaming, the King hugged each of them in turn. "We will lose this fight," he said, still smiling but more somberly.

"How can you smile and say that, Father?" Avinadav asked, while the others nodded their agreement.

"I am only facing facts," Saul said, looking slowly into each of their faces. "You know I am right, do you not?" Slowly, each of them nodded. "Then it is good that we acknowledge what we know and do what can be done to mitigate our losses."

"But isn't that a self-fulfilling prophecy, Father?" Avinadav asked.

"Yes," Malkishua agreed.

The King smiled sadly. "Yes, it is. The facts support it. And," Saul looked away, out of the tent, away from his sons, "I fear this will also be end of the House of Saul." The silence was heavy.

"Why is that, Father?" Jonathan asked.

"Because, my son," he turned and looked at them all, still smiling sadly, "if we take the leadership battle positions we normally take, in the thick of the fighting, we shall all be killed." The royal princes let their eyes fall to the ground. "You do want to take those positions, do you not my sons?" One by one, each of them raised his eyes and nodded. "Good!" the King said, tears streaming down his cheeks. "Good! You do us proud! The spirit of the Lord will be with us!" Saul opened his arms. His sons stepped into them and they embraced, tears mingling.

Abner, who had been watching, tears also running down his cheeks, coughed. The King and his sons stepped apart. "Earlier, you said something about mitigating our losses, Sire. What do you have in mind?"

"Yes," the King said, clearing his throat and wiping his eyes. "Indeed." He gestured to his tent and the map table. "Look here," he said. And so they made their deployments.

# Chapter Twenty-Seven

The slaughter of the Israelites was much worse than Abner, the King, and his sons had anticipated. Their strategy and tactics were based on hand-to-hand combat, which, although they were outnumbered, at least gave them the advantage of the motivation that arises from fighting for one's own homeland. What happened was that the Assyrians had schooled the Philistines and for the first time in Israelite experience, used chariots and arrows in a particularly deadly combination.

The Philistine archers were able to stand at 30 cubits, without risking life or limb, and rain a deadly hail of arrows down upon the massed Israelites. Half the Israelite troops were dead or wounded within the first thirty minutes. The remaining half, including Saul's sons Avinadav, Malkishua, and Jonathan, stood their ground and were trampled beneath the horses' hooves and chariot wheels.

Abner, Saul, Ish-Boshet, and perhaps 260 soldiers retreated to the slopes of Mt. Gilboa, where they joined the 300 men who had been positioned there as a ready reserve. As the arrows once again began to rain down upon them, the King sent Abner, his son, Ish-Boshet, and 400 of the 560 soldiers around the mountain, with orders to establish themselves on the east bank of the Jordan. After a brief argument, Abner and Ish-Boshet obeyed. The King remained to fight a rear guard action. Once again, the arrows took their deadly toll and soon King Saul and his weapons-bearer were the only ones left alive.

All about them was horror and carnage. The mountainside, the field below them, and the clearing in which they stood, were strewn with blood and gore, grotesque, broken, and crushed bodies, hacked off limbs, arrows protruding from heads, eyes, and torsos. The moaning, crying, and weeping of the wounded and dying assailed their ears and hearts. The stench of feces and urine, vomit and blood clogged their noses and made it difficult to breathe.

Wounded in two places, his left shoulder from an arrow and his left thigh from a chariot scythe, King Saul knelt on one knee, leaning on his iron broadsword. His weapons-bearer knelt beside him, lifting and lowering the King's great shield to ward off the falling arrows. Several arrows, the ones with steel tips, were stuck in the shield, shafts and feathers protruding.

"You have been my good and loyal guardian, Ariel," the King said. "Now it is time to end this struggle." Pulling his dagger from its sheath, King Saul gave it to the young weapons-bearer. "Please, Ariel," he said. "Take this and plunge it home!" Before he could respond, a flight of many arrows, launched from very near, pierced both the shield and Ariel's armor. He died instantly. As the Philistines approached, bows lowered and swords drawn, King Saul ran screaming to the nearest of them and impaled himself on the man's sword, dying almost immediately.

The man upon whose sword King Saul killed himself, was an Amalekite mercenary named Nestor. When, two days after Saul was killed and beheaded, Nestor, the Amalekite, made his way to Ziklag, to tell the bandit-traitor, David, of Saul's demise, hoping for a substantial reward, Nestor showed David the King's armband and crown to prove Saul was indeed dead. David wept, ripped his robes, tore his beard and ordered Dathan, who, through Uriah's good offices had become one of David's aides, to kill the Amalekite on the spot.

Dathan obeyed instantly. Drawing his dagger, he plunged it into the unsuspecting Amalekite's heart. As the hot crimson blood spurted forth and the Amalekite's body slid to the ground, Dathan bent, took King Saul's crown and armband from the dead man's hands, and offered them to David, saying, "Now these are yours, Sire."

Mechanically, David took the objects from Dathan's hands. Staring numbly at the royal crown and bracelet, he shuddered, feeling a sense of his own mortality. Even kings can die badly. Oh how the mighty are fallen! "Remove this body," he said, voice raspy with emotion.

Dathan gestured to Uriah the Hittite and together they carried the Amalekite's body from the tent to the disposal trench. When they returned, Captain Hafiz was talking with David. Hafiz was the official Philistine liaison to David and had not fought against King Saul.

"You are King in Israel now, Sire," the captain said. "Put on the crown you hold in your hands. It is yours by right!"

David slowly shook his head no, still staring at the dead king's royal objects. Would this be done with my things, when I am king and dead? He wondered.

"You *were* anointed, Sire," Dathan said. "King Saul is dead. He died a hero's death. You are our rightful king now!" Still, David stared.

"Because you are our ally," Hafiz said, "I think King Achish will support your claim, Sire."

David blinked and came out of his trance. Abner and Ish-Boshet, and an unknown number of Saul's soldiers were still active, he thought. Plus, many among our people are still loyal to Saul and think me a traitor. Also, the Philistines now control the bulk of my territory. Yes, it would be useful to seem to remain an ally of Achish.

David smiled into the Captain's face. "Thank you, Hafiz," he said. Putting the crown and armband on a nearby table, he reached out and gripped the Philistine on both shoulders. "I appreciate your counsel. The situation *is* very uncertain just now and your help and support would be most valuable."

"Will you not place the crown on your head, Sire?" Hafiz asked.

David looked at the Philistine with narrowed eyes. "Were I to do that, Hafiz, I would have to kill you. I would be King and would have to defend my country against the Philistine invaders." Hafiz gulped, the color drained from his face and he gripped his sword in its scabbard more tightly. "But fear not, friend Hafiz. I shall not put on the crown... yet. Go now," David said, dropping his arms from the frightened man's shoulders. "Speak to King Achish. Then return to me with his words. In the meantime, let us continue as allies."

The Philistine bowed, left the tent, mounted his horse and rode toward Achish's encampment in the Jezreel.

"Well played, Sire!" Dathan said with deep admiration in his voice.

"Thank you, Dathan!" David smiled and patted his aide on the shoulder. "It is good to have men about me who fully understand our strategic position. In a way, nothing and everything has changed. We still have only our 400 fighters, against however many Abner and Ish-Boshet can muster. I am still viewed as a traitor by most of my countrymen and as Saul's son and a Prince of Israel, Ish-Boshet is the rightful heir and next King. It lacks only his anointing to make him King, while my anointing was in secret with the anointer, Samuel, long dead. In addition, we have the country overrun by Philistine invaders." David sighed. "No. Now is not a good time to claim the throne."

"The people would rally round you, Sire," Dathan said. "If for no other reason than to rid the country of the invaders. The people are frightened, without food and homes; many are being murdered and enslaved."

"True, Dathan. Once the question of the succession and the positions of Ish-Boshet and Abner are settled, then the people will rally round. Not until then will the time be right to wear the crown."

King Saul had ordered his most loyal friend and lieutenant, Joel the Danite, to go to safety with General Abner and Ish-Boshet. As was his way, Joel had hung back to help if he could and saw his friend's death and mutilation. Howling like a jackal and tearing at his clothes and beard, Joel threw himself to the dusty ground and wept. When he gained control of himself and looked up, Joel saw a soldier standing near Saul's body holding the King's severed head by the hair. They had cut the King's head off! As Joel watched, struck dumb with horror, Philistines warriors lined up to plunge their swords into Saul's mutilated torso and spit in his face. It was too much! Overwhelmed by what he was seeing and exhausted by the fighting, Joel passed out.

The last rays of the sun streaked the sky blood red, as Joel rose to his knees, dizzy and aching, his consciousness slowly returning. The stench of death and mutilation filled the air, choking him. He coughed then vomited. Looking around, he saw he was alone and the King's body was gone. He knew they would take the King, and Jonathan, and the bodies of Saul's other sons to be displayed on the walls of Beit She'an. A King's body is a great trophy to his enemies. Such a sacrilege was intolerable! It must be retrieved and buried with respect!

The battleground was not far from Jabesh-Gilead, the city Saul had saved in his first battle as King, Joel realized as his head cleared. Songs of King Saul's clever triumph against the Ammonite King Nahash's greater strength as he surrounded Jabesh were still sung everywhere in Israel. The people of Jabesh had appealed to King Saul. The situation was desperate, for the only way the Ammonite King would accept surrender was if every man in Jabesh allowed Nahash to gouge out his right eye.

"Perhaps," Joel thought, "if I can get there, I can rally the people of Jabesh and they will help me rescue the King's body and those of his sons."

Joel met the men of Jabesh on the road to Beit She'an. "We heard about the battle at Gilboa," their leader said. "Were you there?"

"Yes. I am Joel the Danite, King Saul's friend."

"I am Joseph. We have heard of you, Joel. Welcome. Join us! We go to retrieve the King's body."

"Thank you, Joseph. You do a great service to our people." Joseph nodded. "I see you have no weapons."

"We are not fighters, Joel. Our plan is to approach Beit She'an at night, take the bodies of Saul and his sons, and return to Jabesh. As you see we have slings, ropes and ladders."

Joel nodded. "A good plan; and you are well prepared. It will be an honor to join you. I ask but one thing, Joseph." Joseph inclined his head attentively. "Send one of your men to Gibeah for Janina and Abadantha, the King's mother and sister that they may join us in Jabesh for a proper funeral when we return."

"Yes!" Joseph said. "A proper funeral with the King's mother and sister in attendance."

The two men nearest Joseph and Joel stepped forward. "We will go, Joseph."

"Good!" Joseph said. "Thank you! We will see you in Jabesh in three days."

The two men from Jabesh found Janina and Abadantha sitting quietly in the palace gardens. The initial horror and shock of Saul's death and mutilation had dissipated, but the marks of deep emotional suffering were evident on their faces.

"My ladies," one of the men said. "We have come to take you to Jabesh-Gilead for King Saul's funeral." The woman stared mutely, unbelievingly at the men. "We know it is difficult to believe. Jabesh owes the King a debt that can never be repaid. Twenty of our men along with Joel... "

"Joel?" Janina interrupted. "Joel lives?"

"Yes, my lady. By now he and our men will have taken the bodies of your son and grandsons from the walls of Beit She'an and are on the way back to Jabesh."

"Is that possible?" Dantha asked. "Can God be so good? We have been praying and praying... "

"It is possible, my lady. I do not know for certain, but I know my brothers and they will not fail. Come now and we shall be in Jabesh in time for their arrival."

As they walked, a few paces behind the men from Jabesh, Janina and Dantha cried and reminisced. "Do you remember as we sat peacefully in Devorah's oasis and spoke of the Covenant and your brother had no time nor desire for it and all he wanted was to be a soldier?"

Dantha nodded. "I never thought then that I would outlive him or that he would be the first King of Israel." Janina shook her head as tears poured from her eyes. Dantha dabbed at her mother's tears with a bit of cloth and kissed her on the cheek. "Do you think things would have ended differently if your brother had found the Covenant more useful?"

"No, Mother. I don't." Tears gathered in her own eyes. "I think, perhaps Saul would have suffered less, felt the at-one-ment and known greater peace. But he was always more outer directed than inner directed. His accomplishments, and they were substantial, came from his sense of God as a power outside himself."

Janina nodded, her eyes dry now. "Samuel and God's Law written in the Scrolls always held the greater significance for Saul. Guidance from those sources was clear, objective, and tangible. Saul could never trust his own inner knowing. He just wasn't built that way."

Janina stopped walking, faced her daughter, looked deeply into her eyes, smiled, and then hugged her. "You make me so proud, Daughter," Janina said, stepping back from the hug. "The Covenant lives in you!"

Dantha bowed her head. "Thank you, Mother. Perhaps it lives in David, too. God knows it has no lodging in Ish-Boshet."

# What People Are Saying About
# Devorah:
## Book One Of The Convenant And The Scrolls

I finished reading this edgy novel – perhaps even ground breaking. I've never read a novel like this before. M guess is that in some ways this novel is without precedence.

In the first chapter, I was captivated by Devorah. Steve Liebowitz uses his abundant creative imagination to develop fully the character and story of the Holy Bible's Deborah. He audaciously reframes the more conventional perceptions of God. His rich writing style uses sensory language such that people, situations, and landscapes are vividly depicted. Without once mentioning Jungian psychology or using jargon, he weaves a fascinating tale that subtly suggest connections between the conscious, unconscious, the shadow, and the dark side. Steve uses appropriate graphic violence and sexual situations to provide necessary and fertile context. King David of Israel is Deborah's direct descendant. Anyone interested in ancient history and the evolution of religion will want to read this fascinating and provocative book.

—Richard Allbritton, BS, MS, MPA, Miami,

"This treatment of the life of Deborah evokes the spirit of the biblical age, bringing new life to old tales."

—Rabbi Edwin Goldberg, D.H.L. Temple Judea

"In this work Dr. Liebowitz challenges us to engage with the question of what constitutes a personal "walk with God" and helps us realize that humans have grappled with this issue for millennia. A must read for anyone seeking to live a life "in spirit."

—Roselyn Smith, Ph.D., Clinical Psychology, Florida Licensed Psychologist, author and voice over of "5 Minutes to a Stress Free You," at i-tunes and Amazon.com.

"I enjoyed this very much. Everything…worked for me. The site, characters, central conflict. Devorah, the sensuality in the surrounding cultures. My husband read your chapter as well and loved it, particularly "all the naked women running around." There's a solid hook.

—Sandy Nathan, Vilasa Press, Rancho Vilasa, 2835 Long Valley Road, Santa Ynez, CA 93460, http://www.sandynathan.com

"Masterful use of words and imagery, fleshing out the lives of Biblical characters. A must read for anyone interested in Old Testament history! Good for you, for doing this. You have my admiration."

—Beth Gaudio - "I have no claim to fame but my 4 children and 4 grandchildren. Just a pastor's wife, Realtor, and church administrator."

"Finally took the time to read this material. It's wonderful! Steve uses the historical context and the characters, such as Devorah, to impart deep spiritual ideas in a very palatable way. He quickly sets up the dichotomy we humans face in knowing "God," with the questions of whether there is one God, or many, and whether we are one with God, or we are separate. His characters are highly believable and leap off the page in the reader's mind. Compelling—I want to read to the end without putting it down!

> —Ilene L. Dillon, M.S.W., Coach, Parent Educator,
> Radio Host, *Full Power Living,* www.emotionalpro.
> com, www.raiseincrediblekids.com

# Excerpt from:
# David The Usurper,
## Book Three of The Covenant and The Scrolls

The last rays of the sun streaked the sky blood red, as Ish-Boshet watched Joel rise to his knees in a pool of blood. Joel coughed, the stench of death and mutilation filled the air, choking him. Then he vomited. Looking around, Joel saw he was alone and Saul's body was gone. They will have taken him and Jonathan and Saul's other sons to be displayed on the walls of Beit She'an. A King's body is a great trophy. Such sacrilege was intolerable! The bodies had to be retrieved and buried properly.

Now at the walls of Beit She'an, Ish-Boshet saw, hanging thirty feet above him, impaled on black iron spikes that ran from groin through neck, the four headless bodies of his father and brothers. Paralyzed by the horror, Ish-Boshet could not look away from the brutal mutilation oozing pinkish gore. A stinking slime of pink, yellow and green dribbled from countless wounds—sword cuts, javelin gashes, spear wounds. Most terrible was the congealed putrification around the place where their heads had been; torn jagged flesh, shards of bone and the spiky pitted whiteness of what had been a human spine. Rotten slime that had once been human flesh, blood and organs stained the wall and puddled on the ground.

Ah, too much, too horrible; Ish-Boshet turned away.

Further along the wall, just over the city gates, were the heads.

Ish-Boshet stared and stared, screaming, crying out, sobbing, moaning, trying to know which was his father's, Jonathan's, Abinadab's, and Malchishua's. But he could not know. The birds had pecked out their eyes and even now, rats swarmed along the battlements, chewing the soft flesh that had been their lips.

Ish-Boshet moaned and trembled, tossed and turned.

Creeping slimy worms slithered around the rats running in and out of the gruesome shredded holes where their penises had been. Ish-Boshet shuddered. Rats, worms and birds ravaged any semblance of humanity in the horrors impaled on iron spikes above him. Agonized cries of sorrow and wails of grief hung in the air. Ish-Boshet raised his hands to his ears. It was too much, too terrible, too horrible! Tossing and turning, he sat up in mid scream.

"Ish-Boshet! Ish-Boshet!" the woman called as she shook him awake. It was Amelia, his wife. "Ish-Boshet. You were dreaming again! Wake up!"

Body wracked with sobs, Ish-Boshet clung to Amelia as if he were an infant and she life itself. "There, there," Amelia soothed cradling him and tilting his head back so he could see her face. His sobs eased as he gazed into her calm, reassuring eyes. "They are with the Most High now, husband, one with All That Is. They suffer not nor do they bleed." Ish-Boshet nodded, sighed and sat up.

"Oh, Amelia," he said, voice shaking. "It is too terrible… "

# Also by Steve Liebowitz

**Available Soon from Harmony-Quest Publications *HQPubs.com***

*Twelve people meeting each week at Miami International University to interpret their dreams encounter the ancient Aztec goddess Coatlicue and are thrust into a secret struggle between Good and Evil.*

**The Dream Group Trilogy**

How-to books on dreams, spirituality and sexuality fill shelves in libraries and bookstores. Support groups meet in homes, churches and universities. **Gateways** is the first book of **The Dream Group Trilogy** *a series of novels about one such group.*

"People join our Group to learn how to interpret their dreams, then stay to make them come true," said Dr. Joshua Wilbeth, founder of the Miami International University Dream Group. "We in the Dream Group are the torch bearers of the ancient, mystical traditions

      -- Hindu Tantra, Christian Gnosticism and Jewish Kabala.

"For thousands of years, these traditions have empowered humankind by helping us experience sex and dreams as sacred parts of a sacred universe – the sacred marriage of spirit and flesh. The 12 people in my Group have reconnected with those ancient truths. The three books in this trilogy are the fictionalized accounts of our true-life encounters with the Goddess and the liberating power of sacred sex and lucid dreaming, and point to y*our* divinity and the sacredness of y*our* sexuality."

As _Gateways_ begins, the 56 year old professor is planning another trip to Mexico City to complete twenty years of research into a form of energy he believes transmits thought through dreams. With this trip Josh hopes to confirm what he's long suspected, that the worship rituals for the Goddess Coatlicue enabled the ancient Aztecs to tame that energy.

Dr. Wilbeth asks his graduate assistant Paul Holcomb to take over while he's away. After reluctantly agreeing, Paul is badly shaken when he realizes he's acted-out an erotic dream. Afraid and frustrated, unable to recall the dream's details, he realizes it's recall or be doomed to an endless cycle of compulsion.

Another member of the Group, Angela Saunders, would be more than happy to use Paul's unresolved compulsion to enslave him. Angela, 44, a sexually dominant, black real estate broker wants to take Paul from his girl friend Magdalena Renaldo, 20.

Fighting for insights, Paul recalls the dream. He is naked, kneeling in an ancient temple, flesh gleaming with sacred oil. Fully aroused, he bows down before a voluptuous young woman dressed as an ancient

Aztec Goddess. He pours out his devotion, wanting only to adore Her, but She ignores him. Angela will not.

The Angela-Paul-Magda triangle is one of the genres driving the action. There's mystery and suspense as the multi-generational, ensemble cast becomes enmeshed in the conflict between the sacred and profane - the Azules and Rojas, two secret international cults vying for sacred ancient Aztec religious artifacts. There's history and adventure in the midst of Cortez' conquest of Mexico. And eroticism, as ancient pagan rituals are re-enacted in Miami and Mexico City. But, like the *Celestine Prophesy*, the books in the *Dream Group Trilogy* are, above all, tales of spiritual rebirth and personal renewal.

# About The Author

**Steve Liebowitz** is still married to his first wife, Tanya, (they wed in 1969) and lives in Miami, FL, with two dogs.

His interest in non-traditional ways of understanding Life and the Bible began under fire during the first TET Offensive in Vietnam in 1968. In The Covenant and The Scrolls series, he shares the idea that the power we call 'God' is much more than most of us think It is.

This awareness sustained Steve in the defense of his doctoral dissertation in 1990, and continues to support him in his Business Coaching and Management Consulting practice today. In addition to his PH.D, Dr. Liebowitz holds two Masters Degrees. Not only has Steve researched these ideas, he's *lived* them and continues to live them.

www.ingramcontent.com/pod-product-compliance
Lightning Source LLC
LaVergne TN
LVHW051543070426
835507LV00021B/2381